BORDERS, BOUNDARIES, AND FRAMES

Since 1944, the English Institute has presented work by distinguished scholars in English and American literatures, foreign literatures, and related fields. A volume of papers selected from the meeting is published annually.

Also available in the series from Routledge:

COMPARATIVE AMERICAN IDENTITIES

Race, Sex, and Nationality in the Modern Text

EDITED BY HORTENSE J. SPILLERS

ENGLISH INSIDE AND OUT

The Places of Literary Criticism

EDITED BY SUSAN GUBAR AND JONATHAN KAMHOLTZ

Borders, Boundaries, and Frames

ESSAYS IN CULTURAL CRITICISM AND CULTURAL STUDIES

EDITED WITH AN INTRODUCTION BY
MAE G. HENDERSON

ESSAYS FROM THE ENGLISH INSTITUTE

ROUTLEDGE   NEW YORK AND LONDON

Published in 1995 by

Routledge
29 West 35th Street
New York City, NY 10001

Published in Great Britain by

Routledge
11 New Fetter Lane
London EC4P 4EE

Printed in the United States of America

Library of Congress Cataloging-in-Publication Data

Borders, boundaries and frameworks / edited, with an introduction by Mae Henderson.
     p.   cm.—(Essays from the English Institute)
    Includes bibliographical references.
    ISBN 0-415-90929-5 (HB) : —ISBN 0-415-90930-9 (PB)
    1. Exiles in literature. 2. Outsiders in literature. 3. Criticism. 4. Auto-
biography. 5. Popular culture—United States. 6. Multiculturalism.
I. Henderson, Mae. II. Series.
PN56.5.E96B67 1995
809'.93353—dc20   93-42245
                                                      CIP

Contents

Introduction: Borders, Boundaries, and Frame(work)s

MAE G. HENDERSON

For Keneth Kinnamon

Borders are set up to define the places that are safe and unsafe. . . . A border is a dividing line, a narrow strip along a steep edge. A borderland is a vague and undetermined place created by the emotional residue of an unnatural boundary. It is in a constant state of transition. The prohibited and forbidden are its inhabitants. *Los Atravesados* live there . . . those who cross over, pass over, or go through the confines of the "normal."

—Gloria Anzaldúa[1]

Working right at the limits of several categories and approaches means that one is neither entirely inside or outside. One has to push one's work as far as one can go: to the borderlines, where one never stops walking on the edges, incurring constantly the risk of falling off one side or the other side of the limit while undoing, redoing, modifying this limit.

—Trinh T. Minh-ha[2]

A book's "borders"—its packaging, format, and the contexts in which it is read and published— are inseparable from its more apparent content. Not only [is] an author . . . part of the text . . . but so [are] its editors and readers. . . . every book, every reading, is laced and surrounded with circumstances worth considering, border crossings within the text as well as at its edges.

—Diane P. Freedman[3]

Forever on the periphery of the possible, the border, the boundary, and the frame are always at issue—and their location and status inevitably raise the problematic of inside and outside and how to distinguish one from the other. The relation of inside and outside is the question informing Jacques Derrida's speculations in *The Truth in Painting* (*La Vérité en peinture*), which contains essays that examine the *parergon*—a space that is neither essence nor ornamentation: "neither work (*ergon*) nor outside the work (*hors d'oeuvre*)." Examining the spatial limits of the outside border (external edge) of the painting and the inside border (internal edge) of the frame, Derrida "disconcerts any opposition" between "the outside and the inside, between the external and the internal edge-line, the framer and the framed" in his attempt to deconstruct the self-presence of the visual image.[4] In a well-known earlier piece, "Living On: Border Lines" ("Survivre: Journal de bord"), Derrida also takes up the problem of translation and its institutional resistances in his challenge to the notion that a text is defined by determinable borders and limits marking its structure, unity, and referentiality. Constructing two parallel and simultaneous essays demarcated by a horizontal dividing line, he demonstrates the "necessity of such an overrun, such a *debordement.*"[5] Derrida's destabilization of endings and beginnings, boundaries and divisions, invites us to question a multiplicity of borders: between outside and inside, self and other, public and private, subject and object.

The essays in this volume take up the challenge of working out—or reworking—the problematics of the borders, the boundaries, and the frame(-work)s that structure our various and multiple notions of identity—textual, personal, collective, generic, and disciplinary identities. The contributors to this volume write about subjects (and are often themselves subjects) who "refuse to occupy a single territory"—who cross geographical borders, cultural borders, national borders, linguistic borders, generic borders, specular borders, and disciplinary borders.

This volume or "text" (a strategic designation recognizing that the content cannot be fully contained within its borders), like the above epigraphs by Gloria Anzaldúa and Trinh Minh-ha, approaches the space of the border by "worrying the lines" between native and foreign, original and translation, personal and theoretical, public and private, self and other, inside and outside, margin and center, framer and framed. Anzaldúa can serve to remind us that while intellectual border crossings may not entail the same kinds of perils as those confronted by *los atravesados,* there are nonetheless professional risks incurred when one lives and works "on the borders"—even in an intellectual community itself defined by marginalization to the academic mainstream.

"Each work generates its own constraints and limits," writes Minh-ha at one point, and at another, "walking [or writing] on the edges" can be hazardous.[6] In raising the issue of what is at stake in boundary crossing or working "on the edges" in literary and cultural studies—in particular the investment in being "safe" and "unsafe"—we are also reminded that borderland inhabitants are always considered transgressors and aliens. For, although "to transgress" literally translates as "to step across," it also carries with it legal and moral connotations—as in "trespass"—which are essentially negative.[7] Therefore breaking down structures of resistance not only speaks to breaching the ramparts that bolster the systems of containment and categorization, as Derrida insists; it also concerns the modifying of limits in order to transform the unknown or forbidden (metaphorical borderlands) into inhabitable, productive spaces for living and writing.

But to follow Minh-ha's lead—"to push one's work as far as one can go: to the borderlines" means transgressing those limits that ensure safety, acceptance, and even friendship. Such transgressive moves speak to the incumbency, indeed the necessity, of the intellectual who is located on the cusp of two or more domains (whether of geography, gender, culture, genre, or discipline). Expanding on Abdul JanMohamed's notion of the "border intellectual" as one who stands at the border of two cultures, we use the term to designate an authorial subject position that occupies the interstitial space of the crossroads as a site of potential transgression—interrogation and production—in a contested living and working domain.[8]

Often, for the border intellectual, the contested existence of borders (both internal and external) creates the desire, or even responsibility, to transgress. (It is well to remember that without the notion of the boundary, there can be no transgression, and without the possibility of transgression, there would be no boundary.) Such a subject position carries with it the intellectual obligation, as George Steiner says, of "pressing the unpleasant questions, the questions which are in bad taste, the embarrassing questions, the taboo questions." Because daring to trespass, to "step on someone else's toes," may well put at risk professional security and cultural authority, surely the border intellectual must share Steiner's belief that if it is safety and legitimation that matter most, "then the intellectual is in the wrong business." [9] Indeed, as Stuart Hall, black British cultural studies analyst, tells us, ". . . dangers are not places you run away from but places you go towards."[10]

In a sense that differs from and overlaps with Emily Hicks' description of "the multidimensional text," I would like to utilize here several terms which she introduces—"border writing," "border texts," "border subjects," and "border culture"—to designate the common concerns of much of the writing in this volume.[11] In her illuminating work on border writing in the context of Latin American culture, Hicks asserts that "border writing emphasizes the differences in reference codes between two or more cultures [approaching] the experience of border crossers, those who live in bilingual, bicultural, biconceptual reality."[12] Defining the border crosser as "both 'self' and 'other,' " Hicks' concept of border writing collapses the distinction between "a clearly defined 'subjective' or 'objective' meaning."[13] And although I use the term to describe an approach rather than a body of work that "rides the borders of a variety of literary, cultural, and ideological realms," Paula Gunn Allen's idea of "border studies" affirms a form of critical practice that reaches and registers a new area of experience and critical inquiry.[14]

Thus, the common feature distinguishing this collection of essays on cultural criticism and cultural studies is precisely its preoccupation with the notion of borders—and the problematics of border crossings. Divided into three sections, the contributions to this volume include Part I, "Crossing

Borders: Exile and Language"; Part II, "Blurring Boundaries: Autobiography and Criticism"; and Part III, "Breaking Frame(work)s: Popular Culture and Cultural Studies." Together, these essays challenge the divides of language and geography, merge literary genres, subvert cinematic and perceptual frames, and transgress (inter)disciplinary boundaries. Moreover, they seek to demonstrate some of the visual and critical mediations that resist or enable academic or professional trespass.

In *An Alchemy of Genres,* her study of American feminist cross-genre writing, Diane Freedman calls attention to the "many forces behind a published text." Although it is not my concern here to speak to the precise circumstances bordering the production of this text, it is to call attention to the "border crossings within [this] text as well as at its edges"; that is, to call attention to the relationship between methods of study and new and diverse subjects and objects of study. The collapse of borders in scholarship reflects and parallels the collapse of borders in the postindustrial world. Our conceptions of rigid geographical and cultural borders have given way to globalism, multiculturalism, and transnationalism, while generic boundaries have collapsed into "blurred" or "mixed" genres. And if our traditional expectations of the cinematic frame have been challenged by an awareness of positions and positionalities overdetermining the perceptual frame, our notions of disciplinarity have also yielded to interdisciplinary studies, and crosshatched fields of reference that can be neither contained nor limited, but must constantly refer to something outside, inside, or beyond themselves.

I. CROSSING BORDERS: EXILE AND LANGUAGE

In a secular and contingent world, homes are always provisional. Borders and barriers which enclose us within the safety of familiar territory, can also become prisons, and are often defended beyond reason or necessity. Exiles cross borders, break barriers of thought and experience.

—Edward Said[15]

In his essay "Mind of Winter" Edward Said constructs a relationship of oppositional co-dependency between the notions of "exile" and "home." As Said suggests, the associations between these two concepts can often be ironically reversed, with home becoming a place of endangerment and exile, a place of sanctuary. At the same time, living outside the borders of the "homeland" and inside the borders of "another country" often entails a border journey into the memory and imagination that negotiates between old and new, past and present, self and other, safety and danger.

The four essays by Jane Marcus, Kathryn Hellerstein, Anita Goldman, and Scott Malcomson push in several directions, with the common object of exploring, in a variety of registers, the semiotics of exile and the problem of its representation in the lives and writings of individual artists and intellectuals. Each deals with the border subject's positioning between cultures; together, they demonstrate the multiple ways artists, intellectuals, and activists traverse borders. What JanMohamed describes as the interstitial space occupied by his border subject is what anthropologist Victor Turner, drawing on his study of tribal ritual and Arnold Van Gennep's *Rites of Passage*, calls a space of "liminality" (from the Latin term "limen," meaning "threshold").

Turner's model of social drama and "liminality" provides a handy conceptual model for the study of exile—or border crossing "betwixt and between" countries and/or cultures—as a processual rite. Although in Turner's model the rite of transition which he describes as "liminal" normally refers to "the passage from one social status to another," it is "often accompanied by a parallel passage in space, a geographical movement from one place to another." This passage, writes Turner, involves the "literal crossing of a threshold which separates two distinct areas [read: "borders"], one associated with the subject's pre-ritual or preliminal status, and the other with his postritual or postliminal status."[16] Liminality, then, describes a processual state or border zone mediating between cultures, races, or nations—a zone sometimes characterized by what Turner describes as the "blurring and merging of distinctions."[17] In this site of cultural limbo, Turner argues, the ritual (border) subject may pass through a place or period in which one experiences freedom from the constraints of normative or oppressive social structures.[18] Liminality represents "the possibility . . . of standing aside not only from one's own social position but from all social positions and of formulating a potentially unlimited series of alternative social arrangements."[19] What is most interesting for our purposes, then, is how this "ritualized move into liminality" that we are calling border crossing becomes a site in which the border subject often discovers the cultural creativity and cultural authority to formulate "new models, symbols, and paradigms."[20] In examining the lives and productions of these exiles, émigrés, refugees, and expatriates, the essays in Part I of this volume are, in many ways, centrally guided by JanMohamed's questions concerning how these individuals "cross borders; what are their intentions and goals in crossing borders, and how do these in turn affect the kinds of barriers they are inclined to break [in their creative and intellectual work]?"[21]

In each of these four essays, we see that there is something creative as well as destructive—something potentially damaging as well as enabling—about the condition of exile in its various existential, psychological, spatial, and temporal dimensions. For Nancy Cunard, exile is a productive and exultant condition; for Kadya Molodowsky, exile becomes an occasion for self-expression; for W. E. B. Du Bois and Frantz Fanon, exile is either a compulsory or a liberating condition that exhibits a particular relationship to existing political institutions and available discourses on identity. For Ahmet and his fellow Bulgarian Turks, exile is both an experience of temporal displacement and one of unbounded identity.

Each vision of exile, moreover, presents possibilities of radical opposition to or reconciliation with the dominant culture. In Jane Marcus' essay, Cunard's aesthetics and politics of exile are demonstrably in opposition to traditional norms; in Kathryn Hellerstein's rendering, Molodowsky turns away from these oppositional, political meanings for exile and seeks instead to integrate and contribute to the mainstream culture; and for Anita Goldman, Fanon's and Du Bois' expressive strategies of assimilation register and contribute to the work of resistance, whether these political enunciations of protest ultimately involve civil disobedience or acts of retaliatory violence. Finally, by Scott Malcomson's account, identification with Europe figures a future of hope and exile for the Bulgarian Turks.

Jane Marcus' essay, "Bonding and Bondage: Nancy Cunard and the Making of the *Negro* Anthology," opens this collection by exploring the boundaries of culture, class, race, and sexuality that women traverse in the context of modern and self-imposed exile. Her study of Cunard demonstrates how the politics of exile may be mapped onto terrain where the question of identity itself has been disclosed as problematic. As one who "never settled down, never made a home," Cunard's exile as a British subject in Paris in the 1930s can be described as a kind permanent liminality defined by her transgression of family, class, national, and racial boundaries.

Recognizing the relationship between her own marginalized position in the academy and the expatriation of women in cultural and literary history, Marcus has elsewhere written that "feminism is a natural medium and method for the examination of exile, for, in its explicit articulation of otherness, it places the critic in the position of exile, aware of her own estrangement from the center of her discipline . . . negotiating dangerous identifications with her subjects, edgily balancing on boundaries and testing limits."[22] Writing from the position of the feminist critic in exile, then, Marcus examines the sexual and political radicalism of an exiled historical subject who also "negotiated dangerous identifications with her subjects." It is precisely the complex relation between gender, sexuality, and race, Marcus suggests, that explains how Cunard's gender and unorthodox sexual practices account for her exile from studies of Modernism, African and African-American culture, and left-wing politics.

In her renunciation of family, class, country, and culture, Cunard chose to locate herself intellectually and politically in another place, another country that, for her, more nearly represented "home." Marcus figures a woman willingly and willfully exiled from race and nation—and who has, in turn, been exiled from a literary and cultural tradition. Cunard's chosen condition of exile is an ironic figuration because, as Marcus tells us, "a woman exile is an uncanny figure, for her very body means home and hearth; it signifies the womb/home of humankind." Yet, for Cunard, exile was not an agonistic, but an exultant, condition.

Clearly, it was her own exiled status that prompted Cunard's identification with other marginalized and subjected peoples and led to her political, artistic, and intellectual activities on behalf of Africans and African-Americans, themselves exiled from homeland and historical past by slavery and colonialism. Fleeing the elitism of upper-class British society to a black lover in avant-garde Paris, Cunard's exile is staged as a series of border crossings, defined in part by her rejection of mother and motherland—her mother figuring, for the "undutiful daughter," England's colonialist past, as well as its nationalist and imperialist racism.

This project of emancipation is also, by Marcus' account, one that entails Cunard's fetishization of her body in the service of challenging the conventions of modernist primitivism. "Constructing her own path to liberation as a White Negress," Cunard photographically stages her body in a series of scenes which move "beyond the borders of modernist primitivism a la Picasso." Crossing not only racial codings of black and white, but sexual codings of femininity and masculinity, Cunard's performance of gender is as ambivalently fraught as is her performance of race.

Cunard, then, both *images* and *imagines* herself through the Other, materializing in the medium of photographic representation her personal and political identifications. In her effort to dissolve the boundaries between Self and Other, Cunard's exile and photographic self-staging positions her at the intersection of cultures and races, classes and genders: black and white, England and the Continent, civilized and savage, colonizer and colonized; male and female.

Surely contemporary readers will be tempted to compare Cunard—styled by Marcus as a "princess of primitivism" and "signifier of 'Black is Beautiful' "—with contemporary white women entertainers like Madonna or Sandra Bernhard who, as bell hooks writes, "publicly name their interest in, and appropriation of black culture as yet another sign of their radical chic."[23] And while it is also important to recognize the historical and social context which distinguishes the modernism of the 1920s from the postmodernism of the '80s and '90s, we should bear in mind Marianna Torgovnick's admonition that "with regard to views of the primitive, more similarities exist [between past and present historical moments] than we are used to acknowledging."[24]

Like Madonna, Cunard was able, in her appropriation of blackness, to "create a cultural space" in which she could "invent and reinvent herself"— yet clearly, in Cunard's case, without benefit of "public affirmation and material reward."[25] One might ask, however, was it a mark of her class and race entitlement that Cunard was able to discover in blackness a means of opposing and subverting the privilege and provincialism—as well as the classism and racism—of her own family background? Further, the contemporary critic may pose the question of whether or not Cunard's "transgressions" are subversive or complicit with the dominant culture. Does she replicate or reproduce the colonization her actions and commitment are surely meant to repudiate? What, finally, are the implications of Marcus' own critical act of recuperation?

Another issue raised by Marcus' provocative and controversial piece involves the political and ethical question of what it means to assume the cultural and critical authority to write "across gender, class, race, or ethnic lines."[26] Clearly, Marcus claims her subject's ethnographic authority, a claim that is bound to be questioned by contemporary scholars. The question implicitly raised here is how the symbolic appropriation of the Other relates to the question of self-exile. In other words, does the appropriation of and identification with the Other represent an exile from the self—an exile which can only and finally return self to self?

But Marcus' essay on Nancy Cunard not only raises the difficult question of identity and identification; it also continues to revise our reading of Modernism, and forces us to rethink the Harlem Renaissance as a movement and period. Marcus demonstrates that as a poet and publisher of the Hours Press (in which appeared the works of Beckett, Pound, and other modernists) and as editor of *Negro*—"an inaugurating effort in claiming Afro-American culture" and "the monumental internationalist forerunner of all our current work in cultural studies"—Cunard has earned "recognition as a major intellectual and political figure of the Twentieth Century." Marcus' project thus signals a new departure in that it promises to reclaim Cunard—to rescue and find an historical home for this fascinating figure, suppressed in one tradition and falsified in another.

In an earlier piece on exile and women, Marcus writes that the "self-conscious woman writer has no country and wants no country, opting for the whole world as her country, equating exile by gender with the internationalism usually equated with Jews."[27] Kathryn Hellerstein, in her essay "Exile in the Mother Tongue: Yiddish and the Woman Poet" makes this connection between woman, writing, exile, and Jewish cultural practices.

The term "diaspora" is taken from the Greek word for "dispersion." As a term, it is most frequently associated with the voluntary dispersion which configures the Jewish Diaspora. But there is another term in Hebrew—namely, *galut*—which is associated with, but distinguished from, the term "diaspora." If the first refers to the voluntary dispersion of the Jewish people, the second refers to their forced dispersion, or what one might more commonly call "exile." For the border subject, the boundaries separating desire from compulsion as a motivation for exile are often blurred and complexly imbricated.

Kathryn Hellerstein examines the dialogics of linguistic, cultural, and gender identity in the contexts of personal and historical diasporic disloca-tion. Linguistically, she maps the progressive displacement of the Polish woman poet Kadya Molodowsky (who migrated to the United States in 1935) through the migrations of Yiddish—"that language in perpetual ex-ile"—in which she wrote and published. Yiddish, the vernacular and "mother tongue," for Hellerstein, comes to constitute "the cultural paradigm of [Jewish] historical exile, a language that migrated with the Jews . . . from Western to Eastern Europe, in the late Middle Ages, and then to America, in the late nineteenth century." Complicating the linguistic exile for the woman writing in Yiddish, however, was her exclusion from the *loshn-koydsh*, or the Sacred Tongue, figured by the languages of the Bible and the Talmud (Hebrew and Aramaic), as performed in liturgical ceremony. Molodowsky's dilemma, however, was defined not only by her exclusion from "the inner culture of traditional Judaism," but her continued marginali-zation from the "mainstream" of Yiddish literary culture, even when she sought to "transpose the language of women's private prayers into the poetry of modern Yiddish literature."

Curiously, Molodowsky evades any discusson of what Hellerstein specu-lates to be the complex motivations behind her exile—located somewhere between involuntary compulsion and voluntary desire. Nonetheless, Hell-erstein suggests that both Molodowsky's Zionist politics and modernist aesthetics embody her struggle to address, if not resolve, the issues bound up with internal and external exile. Hellerstein, finally, constructs a complex cultural portrait inscribing the predicament of a woman who crosses borders of language, community, and geography, only to be beset by the discovery of borders within, which structure a semiotics of exile in her life and writing.

On both the material and symbolic levels, then, Molodowsky's exile becomes a manifestation of border crossing that exposes the relationship between language, gender, and community. However, translation constitutes another dimension of Hellerstein's project, one that complicates the notion of border crossing by implicitly addressing the ways in which the translator, like the exile, figures as a kind of trespasser—someone who both crosses and crosses out boundaries of language and community. For Hellerstein, the archetypal image of the exile must be complemented by the figure of the translator. Indeed, if the translator's task is to cross the divide of linguistic borders, the status of the translation itself is defined by its suspension be-tween two cultures, two languages, and two texts.[28] Nevertheless, Minh-ha speaks to the appropriativeness inherent in the act of translation—an act she describes as "a politics of constructing meaning":

Whether you translate one language into another language, whether you narrate in your own words what you have understood from the other person, or whether you use this person . . . to serve the direction of your [work], you are dealing with cultural translation.[29]

Hellerstein's project, then, can serve to remind us that in the broadest sense of the term we, as critics, are all translators and transgressors—who risk the perils of border crossings, as well as perhaps the occupational hazard of appropriation when we translate "what people say according to the logic and habits of [our] own language or mode of speaking."[30]

If Hellerstein's essay foregrounds the *literal* crossing of geographical borders (by the border subject) and the *literary* crossing of linguistic borders (by the author-translator), the other essays in this section deal with the literal and metaphorical crossing of racial, social, national, and temporal borders.

Contemporary conceptions of exile are predicated on the geopolitical notions of the nation-state, imperialism, and the ideologies of (post)colonial "national" cultures. The category of nationality—along with those of race and gender—have emerged as crucial anchors to modern ideas about the self. In the sixties, spokespersons such as Stokley Carmichael and Larry Neal invoked Frantz Fanon in their figuration of the status of African-Americans in the United States as subject to processes of "internal colonization." Some form of this analogizing also continues in the current debates on postcolonial cultural studies, in which African-American history and expression have been enlisted in framing the experience of colonial oppression, whether internal or external. In response to this trend toward globalization of the local and particular, there has also been an increased awareness of overlaps and gaps in the need to map out these distinctive "political locations" and cultural domains.[31]

In an analysis positioned on the border between African-American and postcolonial studies, Anita Goldman's "Comparative Identities: Exile in the Writings of Frantz Fanon and W. E. B. Du Bois" explores the relationship between the problematics of nationalism and the problematics of black male identity by comparing the writings of W. E. B. Du Bois and Frantz Fanon, two intellectuals in exile—"border subjects" defined within distinctive "border cultures." She argues that for each of these writers, the burden of representation configures their distinctive relation to existing political institutions into an equivocal drama of rootedness and estrangement.

Disrupting the concept of a unified nationalism, Goldman demonstrates how the exile's strategic border crossings—the transgression of a frontier separating the dominant culture from what Edward Said has called "the perilous territory of not-belonging"—give rise to recognizable differences or oppositional identities within culture.[32] In their respective renderings of exile, Fanon and Du Bois both claim that the articulation of challenges to racism and imperialist encroachment requires a volitional, creative act of self-representation. In Du Bois' *Souls of Black Folk*, this exilic act of self-invention is accomplished by means of his invocation and critique of the discourse of civil rights. Du Bois' self-contradictory assertion of rights and race as essentialist and competing discourses constitutes, for Goldman, a critique that points up the necessity and insufficiency of each to represent the self. This critique is registered in Du Bois' model of black identity that emerges from his conceptualization of African-American exile, a condition which he names "double-consciousness." For Goldman, the notion of double-consciousness "is one that allows [Du Bois] to profit from the oppositional possibilities of liberalism and racialism without being enslaved to these identitarian categories as artifacts of white Western culture."

Whereas Du Bois defines African-American exile as the deprivation of civil rights—and thereby depicts the political stance of the exile as being similar to that of the civil disobedient—Goldman argues that Fanon's conceptualization of exile and identity exhibits his engagement with an entirely different tradition in political thought. Liberal ideas of government and the sanctity of rights are transformed when theory travels east from Du Bois' political and cultural domain and crosses the borders of Fanon's Algeria. Fanon's distrust of democratic language as "language which has forever lost its referential capacities by having been put to bad use" leads to his outright rejection of rights rhetoric. Instead, he emphasizes the importance of existential knowledge—an inner transformation that precedes any engagement with existing political institutions—and prescribes a vision of exile as the free and willed manipulation of the white mask of colonial discourse as a means of struggle. This central difference explored in Goldman's comparative analysis serves as a compelling reminder, as Said puts it, of "the extent to which theory is a response to a specific social and historical situation of which an intellectual occasion is only a part."[33]

Scott Malcomson crosses the border between the theme of exile and the modality of narrative, creating an essentially autobiographical moment structured in the experience of exile. What Malcomson's essay "Disco Dancing in Bulgaria" demonstrates—and what recent critical trends have focused on—is the way in which the personal narrative can not only subserve the ends of theory, but can serve as a modality of theory itself. And yet it is also an act of trespass upon the boundaries of academic discourse *tout court*: a reminder that the attempt to demarcate a line between inside and outside must fail not only with respect to disciplines, but to the larger institution that the disciplines inhabit. Such are the vagaries of postmodern knowledge and reflection.

Playing with, and turning the tables on, popular genres of travelogue, Malcomson takes up the issue of identity after empire—specifically concerning the putative remnants of the Ottoman Empire in contemporary Bulgaria—through what Toni Morrison, in another context, calls an act of "literary archeology." Within a narrative of cultural introjection, Malcomson presents a story of projected displacement. Malcomson's essay calls into question the identity of the modern nation-state, as well as the notion of authenticity and nationhood on which such cultural/political fictions depend. Analogous to the narrative intent underlying this autobiography in exile, the author's destablization of the boundaries between self and other is grammatically represented in the displacement of the first person narrative "I" by the second person narrative "you." Not inappropriately, this decentered, fragmented, postmodern narrative is itself linked to the liminal fluidity of a community that, for Malcomson, can "no longer really occupy the ground [it] stand[s] on."

Exploring the dialogics of subjectivity and the politics of (dis)location, Malcomson's narrative, then, not only interrogates the shifting relationship between author and subject, but also that between "ethnic" and "national" identities, cultural assimilation and segregation, Europe and its mythic alterity, Bulgarian and Turk. Alert to the oft-remarked fact that the so-called forging of a nation is, indeed, a matter of forgery, Malcomson directs our attention to the brutal symbolics of name-changing, the legacy of so many campaigns of "authenticity" around the world. If the province of identity is the homogeneity of the self-identical, marks of minatory difference are to be eradicated: Muhammad must become Hristo.

In the name of enlightenment, a process of cultural homogeneity or *priobshtavane* is pursued—the same logic, of course, that has had such tragic results in the former Yugoslavia, but of which no nation is wholly innocent. And yet, as Malcomson shows, the elisions of identity will not submit to such "purifying" strictures. Here are Bulgarian Turks who are, in some sense, neither Bulgarian nor Turkish, their supposed "Turkishness" evidently having been textualized only in the mid-nineteenth century. Here are "Easterners" who would compete on a metric of Europeanness and who experience exile in temporal terms. It is less place than history and time that mark the Bulgarian Turks—and, one suspects Malcomson as well—as exiles. As an estrangement from time, exile, in the context of the Turks in Bulgaria, acknowledges that the future itself must, for them, become a territorial possession of Europe.

What Malcomson juxtaposes to this eerie temporalization of exile is the prospect of a sheerly kineasthetic reclamation: the topos of "the Disco," a liminal space that is neither indigenous nor foreign, but rather a kind of incorporated space in which another dance of identities can be enframed. Yet this is not an altogether hopeful vision. The historicity of displacement that freights Malcomson's deceptively artless narrative will not let us forget the human cost of resistance. The dance of identity, we know, too often proves a *danse macabre*.

II. BLURRING BOUNDARIES: AUTOBIOGRAPHY
AND CRITICISM

Because systems of classification in literature begin with a notion of certain canonical forms
and then work outward to account for even the most unruly texts, they can never be precise
enough. All literary taxonomies tend to lose clarity at the edges and relegate certain borderline
phenomena to anomaly. Since the classification of rebellious texts can in this way easily turn
into repression, literary taxonomy should be looked upon warily by the feminist or otherwise
politically committed critics.

—Amy K. Kaminsky[34]

While every act of criticism is based on boundaries and exclusions that
delimit certain conceptual categories, literary criticism, in particular, has
historically privileged certain orders of genre. Autobiographical criticism,
as represented in the essays by Nancy Miller and Sara Suleri, displaces more
genre-specific notions of literature and criticism, and in so doing, serves to
enlarge our conventional notions of what constitutes literature in general
and criticism in particular. As autobiographical criticism, these essays not
only challenge the traditional genre criticism that has served to limit the
literary canon through its assumption of fixed genre, but also point to the
dangers of framing/bounding/containing by challenging the ways in which
identities are categorized.

Autobiographical criticism challenges what Amy Kaminsky regards as
the "contemporary orthodoxy in literary theory"—namely, the assumption
of an objective and impersonal critical stance. Subjective, engaged, personal,
anecdotal, testimonial, narrative, mixed genre—these are but some of the
terms used to designate a form of writing at the crossroads of autobiography
and criticism, a form that works against the premise of more putatively
objective, impersonal, legalistic, abstract kinds of critical practice. Constructing a fundamentally dialogic relationship between author, text, and
reader, Mary Ann Caws argues that "personal criticism . . . has to do with
a willing, knowledgeable, outspoken involvement on the part of the critic
with the subject matter." Personal criticism is, moreover, "an invitation
extended to the potential reader," she writes, "to participate in the interweaving and construction of the ongoing conversation this criticism can be."[35]
What her observations suggest is that the conjunction of autobiography and
criticism creates not only a personal and engaged criticism, but also a dialogic, polyphonic genre that has the potential to subvert any effort to stratify
these two forms.

Because of its association with women (and, most especially, women of
color who, I would claim, were among the first serious practitioners of
this contemporary form of criticism), autobiographical criticism has been
theorized from a gendered perspective.[36] Among others, Diane Freedman,

Jane Tompkins, Nancy Miller, and Thomas Farrell have linked personal and autobiographical criticism with women critics. In his discussion of the "male" and "female" modes of writing, Farrell writes that the female mode tends "to obfuscate the boundary between the self of the author and the subject of discourse, as well as between the self and the audience, whereas the male tends to accentuate such boundaries."[37] Freedman even links the permeability of generic border crossings between autobiography and criticism with what Judith Kegan Gardiner and Nancy Chodorow theorize as the permeability of ego boundaries in the formation of women's identity.[38]

And although Sara Suleri, as we shall see, wishes to dissociate autobiographical criticism from the "confessional," it is indeed a mode that—for better or worse—has been linked with this form, as evidenced by Diane Freedman's "critical confessions," a term focusing on "personal and professional silencing and repression" that articulates "the intricate tie between the personal and professional, the personal and theoretical."[39] Further, by privileging the impersonal at the expense of the personal, Jane Tompkins argues that Western epistemology facilitates an overlap between the "conventions defining legitimate sources of knowledge [and] the conventions defining appropriate gender behavior."[40] Summarizing this position, Barbara Johnson writes, "Not only has female personal experience tended to be excluded from the discourse of knowledge, but the realm of the personal itself has been coded as female and devalued for that reason."[41]

The critique of essentialism so central to the postmodern project has not only challenged our notions of personal identity, but also genre identity, thus putting into question notions of "generic purity" and the traditional distinctions that have obtained between personal and critical writing. Both Miller and Suleri practice autobiographical criticism in which the boundary lines between subject and subject matter are not always clearly demarcated; nor are they always constant. In their emphases on the ways in which the critical act inscribes personal identity, and vice versa, both critics demonstrate how the premise of autobiographical criticism disputes our assumptions that either the writing subject or written subject of criticism can fully contain its meaning. To explicitly acknowledge the ways in which we either enframe or are enframed by the textual object provides further evidence for the complexity and overruns of this relationship by calling into question the limits, distinctions, and divisions between outside and inside, self and other, autobiography and theory.

In her important work *Getting Personal* Nancy Miller has argued that what she calls "personal criticism" is a form that "entails an explicitly autobiographical performance within the act of criticism." "Getting personal in criticism," writes Miller, "typically involves a deliberate move toward self-figuration." As she construes it, personal criticism raises "the question of whether theory can be personalized and the personal theorized."[42] In the present essay, "Our Classes, Ourselves: Maternal Legacies and Cultural Authority," Miller examines contemporaneous accounts of a mother's death in Carolyn Steedman's *Landscape for a Good Woman* and Annie Ernaux's *A Woman's Story*, formulating a post-Chodorowian problematic of how to account for what one might call the "*non*-reproduction of mothering."

Although her immediate aim is to show "[how] the representation of the maternal body . . . records a culture's life and death stories," Miller's real interest in these two texts is animated by the issue of cultural authority and how it is constructed. These narratives constructing the daughter's autobiography and the mother's biography perform ambivalent dramas of maternal and class allegiance and betrayal, an engagement by which the daughter negotiates cultural authority. For Miller, these autobiographical memoirs not only mark the violence of the maternal engagement, but the daughter's "emergence out of her class culture." At the same time, these stories "supply powerful allegories for contemporary writing by women who wish to perform a cultural analysis."

Informing her analysis of how cultural criticism emerges from "an auto-biographical space" are the assumptions that "identity is a process" and that "autobiographical writing [is] a performance embedded in the social." Reflecting on the representation of "highly located [i.e., female, class-based] identities," Miller marks her own social location of middle-class privilege in relation to Steedman's work: As a "daughter of the . . . New York Jewish professional middle class [and a] middle-aged feminist intellectual," Miller sees herself interpellated as "the center from which, against which the bor-ders are defined"—that is, one who is "by definition . . . assigned to a position of cultural centrality and domination." Yet, as an autobiographical reader, she faces the dilemma of how or whether to "read across the divide" of class boundaries while, at the same time, reading "as a woman."

If her reading of Steedman suggests that the gender experience overwrites class experience, Miller's reading of Ernaux, in contrast, demonstrates the performativity and processuality of class experience, while again reaffirming the body and its link to class. The class differences emerging between Ernaux and her mother as a consequence of education result in a "social disidentifi-cation" that structures the mother/daughter relation within the family. While acknowledging that the body is located in distinctions of class, Miller never-theless seems to conclude that the violence of the mother/daughter relation-ship "crosses class identities." Miller finally calls into question what Stuart Hall, in another context, describes as "the great collectivites" that give meaning to identity: class and gender.[43] If "our classes, ourselves" serves as the conjunctural premise of Miller's essay, then "are our bodies ourselves?" remains the locus of an interrogation in which autobiographical criticism and its gender markings define a provocative moment that once again calls into question the relation of sexual difference to ontological difference.

Challenging the radical disengagement between autobiography and cultural criticism, Miller's treatment affirms what Freedman and others describe as "the intimate critique." These autobiographies become, not only for their authors but for Miller as well, vehicles for recounting personal experience as cultural criticism. Miller reads the text of her own gender role and class experience through women's autobiography and, in turn, reads autobiography though the text of her own experience. In creating an encounter described by Paul de Man as "the autobiographical moment in the process of reading," Miller demonstrates how personal history gets reread and rewritten in the reading process. Thus, by making the text a site of dialogic encounter, Miller—as critic and autobiographer—interrogates these texts from the perspective of her own experience, while, at the same time, allowing them to interrogate her experience.

Like Miller, Suleri establishes that autobiographical discourse represents a critique of culture, and positions this form of writing at the crossroads of history and culture. Considering the "very status of genre as a complicity of strategies," Suleri suggests that autobiographical criticism becomes a rubric that "sets up neither category as an integrity opposed to all other integrities." If Miller's "personal criticism" challenges the depersonalization of conventional theory, then Suleri's "unsequestered writing" serves to interrogate the essentialism of autobiography. If Miller's "reimbodied" text serves to refamiliarize the critic with the object of her criticism through the act of personalizing theory, Suleri's "disembodied" text would seem to defamiliarize that relationship through the act of "publicizing" the personal.

Suggesting that we rethink criticism in terms of its alterity, Suleri positions critical writing "at a discursive border that insists on the congruence between critical language and the idiom of its putative [autobiographical] other." Her own project in the present essay is to "identify . . . a possible border upon which the needs of both discursive practices would appear to coalesce." The location of such a border employs a new form of autobiographical criticism—"unsequestered critical writing"—that distinguishes itself from what Suleri describes as "a more pervasive contemporary intellectual discourse that seeks to interpolate its theoretical practices with reference to lived experience." Rejecting a style of criticism that asserts "radical subjectivity," a style incorporating "a confessional mode . . . predicated on a belief that there are . . . secrets to be told or to be withheld," Suleri proposes a kind of critical practice that "takes autobiography as a strategy of dismantlement that dispenses with such dichotomies as public and private or inside and outside in order to position itself at the borders of outsidedness."

Opening with an examination of Coleridge's *Biographia Literaria* ("an exemplary text of borderlines"), Suleri establishes "the vital publicity of an autobiographic voice." Reading Coleridge through Bakhtin, she deconstructs "the fiction of privacy" of the individual, including the "myths of either self-fashioning or of self-discovery," and concludes, along with Bakhtin, that "the individual is open on all sides, he is all surface." Examining essays by Wayne Koestenbaum, D. A. Miller, and Kwame Anthony Appiah, she demonstrates how each "turns the critical moment into an engagement with the autobiographical surface of reality." Like Koestenbaum's and D. A. Miller's, Appiah's work "twists autobiography into a cultural history that is inevitably engaged in mapping the outsidedness of insidedness."

Both Miller and Suleri take as their subtext rituals of death and loss in the context of cultural criticism. If Miller's concern is with contemporary narratives recounting the death of working-class mothers, Suleri's is with the loss of a father, a critic, and (through abandonment) a lover. Yet if Miller's discourse actually foregrounds the centrality of grief and the work of mourning to her project, Suleri, by way of contrast, pursues a discourse of understatment on "the fidelity of loss." If Miller challenges the critic to compensate for an insufficiency or absence in theorizing the personal, then Suleri, though clearly committed, disrupts the prolepsis of theory, displacing it with recurrent literary allusions. Perhaps most interesting, especially in light of the previous section, Miller's work *insists* on a condition of exile as characteristic of the daughter abandoned by the death or refusal of the mother, while Suleri *assumes* communality as the grounding for "shared secrets" (that, therefore, have no need to be actually spoken). But the most striking contrast between these two essays involves the nature and function of autobiographical criticism: the work of Miller's essay is to create a space and justify personal disclosure, while the work of Suleri's is to show that no disclosure is necessary. In fact, if Miller's theoretical posture is revelatory, Suleri's seems to be one of concealing what she calls "a necessary theoretical embarrassment." Her project, which critiques "traditional" forms of auto-biographical criticism, at the same time proposes what is perhaps a rhetorical alternative that she designates as "sequestered criticism."

Arguably, autobiographical criticism has the effect of once again reinstat-ing the fragmented postmodern subject by asserting the author-critic in a gesture of narcissistic self-embodiment. Even so, it strategically locates the writing subject in relation to the written subject. Viewed more broadly, the autobiographical assertion of cultural authority—what Adrienne Rich describes as "the politics of location"—is a double-edged sword. On the one hand, this authorial location solicits what Miller calls counter-identifica-tion as a confirmation of shared or authenticating experience. On the other hand, the author-critic's authority may be challenged or otherwise compro-mised by readers who claim their differences in location; in this situation, the occupier of a particular position may become the subject of critique.[44] Clearly, such a positioning renders theoretical practice a potentially "dangerous place."[45] Yet, as Suleri's "sequestered criticism" reminds us, such a critical stance draws its energy from a critical praxis in which the fixed boundaries of the self are "publicized."[46]

III. BREAKING FRAME(WORK)S: POPULAR CULTURE AND CULTURAL STUDIES

[A history of popular culture] must also be a history of intellectuals—in particular, those experts in culture whose traditional business is to define what is popular and legitimate taste, who supervise the passports, the temporary visas, the cultural identities, the threatening "alien" elements, and the deportation of orders, and who occasionally make their own adventurist forays across the border.

—Andrew Ross[47]

The historical relationship between intellectuals and popular culture—in particular, the antagonism of intellectuals associated with the Frankfurt School toward popular or "mass" culture—provides an illuminating backdrop to the current, central role of media studies within the larger project of cultural studies. As Andrew Ross observes, the critique of mass culture was "first advanced on the left as an explanation for the failure of socialist movements, and the growing successes of fascism."[48] The "traditionally mandarin prejudices of high German culture," harbored by these German intellectuals in exile, suggests Ross, led them to articulate a critique of capitalism that entailed a critique of mass culture. Consequently, he argues, mass culture was constructed as a "profitable opiate, synthetically prepared for consumption for a society of automatons" and became, during the postwar period, "a primary conceptual object of intellectual attention."[49]

With the advent of cultural studies as an academic discipline, popular culture has continued as a privileged object of study, but the relation between the intellectual and media culture in particular seems to have shifted from the days in which Theodor Adorno could challenge the ability of popular (unlike avant-garde) culture to negate the dominant ideology.[50] As Dana Polan observes, culture is no longer considered "an imperial and imperialist takeover of mind," but rather "as a complicated negotiation of inside and outside, of internal and external—a battle of meaning, a battle within meanings."[51] Popular culture, as George Lipsitz argues, has emerged as "a crucial site for the construction of social identity" as well as "a key terrain for ideological conflict."[52]

Not only has the attitude of intellectuals toward popular culture shifted dramatically since the intellectual primacy of the Frankfurt School, but it seems fair to say that in contemporary cultural studies, it is the work of Walter Benjamin, rather than that of, say, Adorno or Max Horkheimer, that has most influenced the study of popular culture. For Adorno, Horkheimer, and some of the other members of the Frankfurt School, popular culture was synonymous with mass culture: "a creature of ideological manipulation and imposition from above."[53] Mass culture was, therefore, repudiated by the Frankfurt School, which reasoned that it served the political function of encouraging passive conformism to the status quo. Horkheimer agreed with Adorno that technology in the service of the "culture industry" not only diminished "negative resistance," but actually reinforced authoritarian forms of government.[54] Unlike his contemporaries, however, Benjamin exhibited greater faith in the revolutionary potential of "art in the age of mechanical reproduction," and supported the "politicization of art" as a response to what he called the fascist "aestheticization of politics."[55] Arguably, then, for Benjamin, the technology of popular culture not only allows us to see its manipulations, but actually provides an opening for reinventing the self in culture. As Stuart Hall writes, even when popular culture "enters directly into the circuits of a dominant technology," it is an arena that is "*profoundly* mythic . . . a theatre of popular desires, a theatre of popular fantasies. It is where we discover and play with the identification of ourselves, where we are imagined, where we are represented [italics mine]."[56]

Popular culture and, in particular, media culture play a pivotal role in the contemporary cultural studies project. The intellectual's current relationship to media culture is one that is concerned to uncover the ways in which the public sphere can be manipulated by various desires that are encoded in media culture. Yet, while media culture appeals to repressed, regressive fantasies and reinforces race, gender, and class stereotypes, it also has the ability to deconstruct or subvert popular stereotypes, especially when these cultural forms (e.g., experimental audio and video media, music, film, dance, etc.) embody a self-critique. As Andrew Ross points out, the power of popular culture resides in its ability "to identify ideas and desires that are relatively oppositional alongside those that are clearly complicit to the official culture." It is in cultural critique that the intellectual as an interpreter of cultural forms and expressions (whether regressive or progressive) plays a central role.

Media culture, and the study of media culture, have clearly redefined our notions of culture, and it is in part the privilege and influence of popular culture in the cultural studies project that has served to dismantle the boundary between what is regarded as "high" (i.e., white, elitist, European) and "low" (i.e., popular, mass, [African–American]) culture. As Stuart Hall convincingly argues, black culture is by definition "a contradictory space" that cannot "be simplified or explained in terms of the simple binary oppositions that are still habitually used to map it out: high and low; resistance versus incorporation; authentic versus inauthentic; experiential versus formal; opposition versus homogenization."[57] In the elision of "folk" and "popular" in the contemporary cultural economy, black vernacular culture has become one of America's major forms of export capital in our transcultural and global economy.

If culture travels from the United States abroad, then theory travels to the United States from Europe. The institutionalization of cultural studies in the American academy represents the most recent of these transatlantic border crossings. Cornel West has emphasized the need to be aware of an American tradition of cultural studies and to establish a dialogue between British and U.S. traditions in cultural studies. In "The Postmodern Crisis of Black Intellectuals," West writes that "the traveling of cultural studies to the United States must be met with a critical reception—and by critical what I mean is an appropriation of the best: acknowledging where the blindnesses were, while discussing to what degree British cultural studies can be related to the U.S. context."[58] West makes the case for a redeployment of cultural studies that does not replicate the uncritical appropriation of European theory represented by the wholesale adoption of structuralism and poststructuralism into the American academy. Further, his remarks implicitly suggest an application of theory grounded in local contexts that have specific and practical relevance. Taken together, the essays by Manthia Diawara and Wahneema Lubiano elaborate the potential of West's claim. Diawara's genealogy of cultural studies warns of the dangers of reifying the methods and assumptions of British cultural studies in an African-American context, while Lubiano grounds this premise in the context of media culture.

The aim of the contemporary cultural studies investigator, as Stuart Hall puts it, is "not to generate another good theory, but to give a better theorized account of concrete historical reality."[59] Located at the borders of theory and praxis, the cultural studies analyst has the aim, as George Lipsitz describes it, of translating "cultural critiques . . . into cultural interventions by engaging dominant ideology at the specific sites where it may be articulated and disarticulated."[60] Thus, what distinguishes cultural studies from such contemporary projects as structuralism and poststructuralism is precisely the intellectual's commitment to and articulation of the relationship between theory and practice.

The mode of inquiry in cultural studies, then, entails an examination of concrete cultural practices; it also recognizes that the conditions of their production and reception entail a struggle of meaning. Influenced by the work of Jacques Lacan and Louis Althusser, filmic texts, in particular, have been constituted as both affirmation and critique of dominant and hegemonic cultural values. If, in autobiographical criticism, the focus remains on the subject position of the author, in contemporary filmic criticism the focus shifts to the spectator (viewer-reader), whose task it is to frame or locate "all the divisions of the text, thus providing them with an apparent unity."[61] Just as the border defines that space separating the inside from the outside of a country, a text, or a genre, the cinematic frame (at its most material level) defines that border separating the successive images or photographs of a strip of celluloid "whose repetitions (and slight variations) pass in front of the lens in order to project a motion picture."[62] Interestingly, the term "frame" itself refers both to the edges that contain each image and to the internal image contained by the outer borders. Thus the frame generates meaning through its internal arrangement of space as well as through its definition of the boundary between images.

Although frames and framing are associated with paintings, photographs, and the proscenium arch of the theater, it is the cinematic frame which has generated most critical attention (this in spite of, and perhaps because of, Derrida's work on the painting frame). So that while Gerald Mast, who views painting frames, photographs, and theater stages as "physical containers," may disagree with Derrida, who interrogates the frame as a fixed boundary, both would agree that the boundary "between what is inside and outside [the physical and focal limits of] the cinema frame is constantly shifting."[63] More central to our purposes, however, is Laura Rice's observation that "the act of 'framing' . . . conjoins the cultural, political, and personal assumptions we project onto the world—and the resistance of the world beyond us to being contained in a single image, a single framed space." Like Derrida, Rice is concerned with the "excess" that supersedes the frame: "Something is always beyond the frame; the image is always captive to the circle of assumptions we draw around it."[64]

Wahneema Lubiano's essay "Don't Talk with Your Eyes Closed: Caught in the Hollywood Gun Sights" focuses on the perceptual frame as well as the cinematic frame. Her reading explores "the phallocentric depth logic of certain deployments of black nationalism, including the positive-versus-negative image discourse around black film" in the context of *Deep Cover*, Bill Duke's film about the drug trade. Framed from "a particular black leftist and feminist" position, her project seeks to account for "the work of ideology in aesthetic practice and the dynamics of black spectator accommodation and resistance."

Addressing the issues of representation, spectatorship, and reception, Lubiano's reading confirms Andrew Ross' claim that popular culture remains both oppositional and complicit with dominant and hegemonic political formations. Lubiano discusses a film about a black undercover cop who exposes government complicity in his bust of a Latin American–based drug operation on the West Coast; her reading discloses how the film betrays "the nexus of a conventional master narrative of identity, family, and the making of a good patriarch" embedded in "a *black nationalist* narrative of identity, family, and the making of a good *black* patriarch."

Like several of the authors in this volume, Lubiano's self-location reflects her own political and social investments and, further, problematizes our perceptions about what is inside or outside the text. By exposing what Minh-

ha describes as the "social self (and selves) which necessarily mediates . . .
the viewing of the film," Lubiano brings to her analysis of the politics of
cultural production an unsentimental critique of what she found "pleasurable, dismaying, and interesting" about the film as well as "the problems
of that dismay, pleasure, and interest." To account for the problematic of
excess and lack in this transgressive pleasure ("however complicated or
attenuated that pleasure might be") and to untangle this "knot of pleasure
and dismay" in a film that reinscribes notions of patriarchy, racial essentialism, and conventional black femininity is the challenge that Lubiano
undertakes in her critical dissent. This negotiation of the relation between
the framer (viewer/spectator) and the framed (projected screen presences),
she discloses to be a complex metric of gains and losses. Reading the representation of race, class, gender, and sexuality creates a spectatorial dislocation
or repositioning that calls attention to the borders between the frames, those
sublimated "dark spaces" marking the presence of absence in the film—
specifically that of women and mothers (nurturers, teachers, and culture
carriers) in what Lubiano identifies as a "hysterical black nationalist revision
of a patriarchal family romance." Moreover, Lubiano examines the way
the black and female film spectator/reader is addressed in ways that are
both race- and gender-specific. But in showing how the black female subject
is hailed by simultaneously divergent forms of address, her work also affirms
the agency of the black female spectator, who brings to the cinematic frame
a reading that interrogates conventional or received frames of thinking about
the dialectics of race, gender, class, and sexuality.

Although much film theory has recently focused on the issue of gender,
little attention has been given to matters of race, class, sexuality, and ethnicity—and even less to the reading of gender within these contexts. Lubiano's essay focuses especially on these issues from the perspective of perceptual and cognitive framing within the subgenre of contemporary black
cinema. She examines the way in which film representation actually reinforces conventional race and gender roles. Rather than subvert these stereo-
typic representations of black women, such films, Lubiano argues, become
complicit in reinforcing racial and social norms when it comes to women
of color, thus reinscribing what Rachel Blau DuPlessis calls the "ambiguously
(non)hegemonic" position of a class—in this case black men—defined as
marginal from the standpoint of race, but dominant from that of gender.
As her reading makes evident, although black-directed films (whether
scripted by whites or blacks) may indeed break the frame in Inez Hedge's
sense of "upset[ting] our expectations about how films should look (the film
frame) as well as how experience is organized in film (the psychological or
cognitive frame),"[65] they not infrequently repress cultural specificity in their
appropriation and reproduction of the master('s) narrative. Lubiano's essay
finally addresses the need for investing black aesthetics with black cultural

specificity in the service of a more revolutionary agenda for cultural production. Unfortunately, the cost of desublimating the transgressive world of urban black life in the instance of this film is achieved only at the expense of repressing or killing off women and mothers who number among the casualties of such film logic. If Lubiano's reading *reframes the frame*, so to speak, it also speaks to a *frame-up* of the "dead, missing, or absent, black and Latina mothers."

It is appropriate that this volume of essays should conclude with an essay on cultural studies—a newly emergent academic discipline that redefines the boundaries delineating traditional disciplinarities. Cultural studies not only *reframes* the objects of inquiry, but constructs a broader *framework* within which to pursue alternative modes of inquiry. Cultural studies has shifted, redrawn, and sometimes even dissolved the lines demarcating conventional disciplinary borders by engaging in institutional and ideological analyses focusing both on "the material means and methods employed by institutions involved in the circulation of cultural objects and texts" and on the examination of "the ideas, feelings, beliefs, and representations embodied in and promulgated by the artifacts and practices of a culture."[66]

Thus, in Manthia Diawara's "Cultural Studies/Black Studies," a manifesto that calls for the construction of a new black cultural studies agenda, the four-sided frame collapses into the figure of the chiasmus.[67] What Peter Brunette and David Wills imagine as a collapsed frame that "erases the center and shoots off in four different directions" represents, for Derrida, "the thematic drawing of dissemination."[68] For our purposes, the collapsed four-square frame, or chiasmus, marks not so much the erasure or cancellation of borders as it does the unfolding of a newly visible and complex heterogeneity of internally divided borders. In Diawara's analysis, these shifting points of intersection (crossings and recrossings) make possible broader frame(work)s within which to pursue the question of identity as it emerges at the intersection of black and cultural studies. Mapping the broad terrain of cultural studies and its relation to ethnic studies, Diawara explores the possibilities of not only crossing putatively homogeneous disciplinary borders, but of recrossing heterogeneous interdisciplinary borders as well.

Diawara proposes a new frame(work) within which to locate black studies in the United States. Deploying Gramsci's notion of *elabore* to structure his inquiry into the problematics of black cultural studies, Diawara demonstrates the utility of *elaboration* as a means of recrossing—reframing or rethinking—the notion of cultural studies in a non-British context. Crossing the boundaries of the Birmingham school and the black British school of cultural studies, Diawara introduces the concept of *elabore* as a means of establishing between them a relationship of mutual interrogation, elaborating "the one in order to show the limitations of the other." The idea of cultural studies, Diawara suggests, cannot be imported whole cloth and wholesale; it needs to be elaborated within a local and particular context. (The assumption here seems to be that British theory does not always travel well!)

Thus, while acknowledging that black cultural studies in the United States must draw on the blindnesses and insights of both British models of cultural studies, Diawara's approach would establish a critique between and within these schools in order to clear a space for African–American cultural investigation. In looking to these two British schools to ascertain their importance for the development of black cultural studies in the United States, Diawara takes the position that the tools of British cultural studies need to be "elaborated" in order to ground cultural studies in the material conditions in the United States.

Just as "diasporic" black American texts "had to be articulated with black Britishness in such a way that they take on new forms," Diawara argues, so must black British texts be rearticulated in such a way that they take on new meaning. "Now it is the turn of black Americans to take the British cultural studies," writes Diawara, "and turn it into a cultural work that is capable of addressing [black American] issues." Rather than expecting the black British cultural analysts to show the way, Diawara invokes the Shlovskian concept of defamiliarization: "On the contrary, we must read them [black British cultural analysts] in such a way that they do not recognize themselves."

Insisting on the "anti-essentialist critique" of black cultural studies and the limitations presented by identity politics as an impediment to revolutionary struggle, Diawara calls attention to the particularizing and homogenizing assumptions prevalent in Black Studies. He then proposes that we abandon these studies in favor of an approach that emphasizes the performative aspects of black culture on the borders of the public sphere, a sphere that Cornel West has elsewhere aptly described as "a discursive and dialogical social space wherein the various 'publics' can find common ground."[69]

Diawara, then, distances his project of cultural studies from the traditional conception of Black Studies by relegating it (along with feminist and other ethnic studies) to the category of "victim" or "oppression" studies. Although Diawara's intent is clearly not to valorize a conservative agenda, his tactical appropriation of a conservative vocabulary for progressive ends is meant to affirm the performative dimension of diasporic aesthetics and culture so central to his project. [70]

Yet I would insist that Black Studies, as one of the primary oppositional discourses in the American political and social tradition, must be regarded in the context of its rich genealogy, a genealogy that derives in large part from artists and intellectuals such as W. E. B. Du Bois, Anna Julia Cooper, Alain Locke, Zora Neale Hurston, and Richard Wright, and has continued in cultural criticism by writers such as Ralph Ellison, Albert Murray, Angela

Davis, Henry Louis Gates, Jr., Houston Baker, Jr., Hortense Spillers, bell hooks, and Michele Wallace, among others. Reinforcing the connection between African–American Studies and cultural studies, Cornel West poses the crucial issue of race in this genealogy:

> How can the reception of cultural studies in the United States not . . . give [race] a tremendous weight and gravity if we're going to understand the internal dynamics of U.S. culture? . . . It's a different history than the formation of the British Empire. . . . How do we understand the moment of the intervention of Afro-American studies in the academy? Let's read that history next to the intervention of cultural studies in Britain.[71]

What cultural studies is to British Studies, West implies, is what African-American Studies is to the American academy.

Not only did the emergence of African–American Studies as a discipline in the academy in the seventies help deconstruct what George Lipsitz has described as "the consensus myth" of the fifties and sixties, but in some respects the argument that he makes regarding the relationship between American Studies and European cultural theory obtains equally for the relationship between African–American Studies and cultural studies. African–American Studies, I would claim, anticipated not only the "cross-disciplinary epistemological and hermeneutic concerns at the heart of contemporary European cultural theory," but also its concerns with comparative and cross-cultural work and, more specifically, its redefinitions of culture in the context of political contestation.[72]

Examining national, ethnic, and other coordinates of identity, Stuart Hall writes, "The great social collectivities which used to stabilize our identities— the great stable collectivities of class, race, gender and nations—have been, in our times, deeply undermined by social and political developments."[73] It has been what Hall calls these "great collective identities" that have, in the past, provided us with "a politics of location." But the (post)modern fragmentation of social and cultural identity in late capitalism has led to what might instead be described (Adrienne Rich notwithstanding) as a "politics of dislocation." In an increasingly complex and interdependent global economy, the boundaries of once-stable nation-states have been, as Hall points out, "increasingly besieged" and "reabsorbed into larger communities that overreach and interconnect national identities."[74]

If ethnic studies (like Women's Studies) continues to be associated with the notions of essentialism and particularism, then the notions of postmodern transnational or global culture also carry with them an equally suspect universalism. It is the aim of border studies as represented by the essays in this volume precisely to mediate between the dangers of particularism embodied in ideas of nationalism and ethnicity (or class and gender) on the one hand and the perils of universalism embodied in transnationalism and transculturalism on the other.

The question of identities and border crossings in the public sphere is brought closer to home when we consider the fact that as students, as scholars, as teachers, not only are we involved in certain forms of intellectual production, but as Henry Giroux reminds us, we are also uniquely situated in "border institutions,"[75] institutions that offer us the opportunity to be "engaged in daily acts of cultural translation and negotiation . . . [,] to become border crossers, to recognize that schooling is really an introduction to how culture is organized."[76] Giroux's notion of "border pedagogy" provides what some critics have called both a "spatialized [conception] of the way that power relations traverse our world and partition it" as well as a "pedagogy of hope."[77] What Giroux describes as "an insurgent multiculturalism" allows those of us engaged in intellectual inquiry as social action "to move between cultures, to travel within zones of cultural difference." At its best, border pedagogy results in the discovery of an idiom that facilitates dialogue in difference, that is able to articulate distinctions between cultures without promoting hierarchy and the norms of exclusionary stratification.

If the foregoing discussion seems to valorize border crossing without considering all of its social manifestations and political consequences, we would do well to heed Lati Mani's warning to "exercise analytic caution" before transposing analytical concepts from one culture or context to another. In metaphorizing the notions of border and borderlands, we must keep in mind "what losses of specificity—of class, power, and histories of oppression—[such a] transposition [might] entail."[78] Clearly, there are different places and ways of crossing the border: power relations and positionality shape the consequences and possible inequities resulting from such events. Border crossings move in different directions and from different locations, some from positions of centrality and dominance, others from positions of marginality and powerlessness. In the geopolitical context, colonized peoples frequently suffer border incursions that carry with them violent intent to colonize. Similarly, in the context of the academy, scholars who have worked to promote greater understanding and interest in fields such as Black Studies, Women's Studies, and Gay and Lesbian Studies may feel that the integrity of their newly constituted disciplines have been threatened by aggressive border crossings entailed in the professionalization and legitimation of cultural studies. Given its historical referents, the naive, facile valorization of border crossings must be deemed risky and unwarranted.

What we are proposing is "border crossing with a difference"—as an act of creation rather than one of violation. The essays in this volume suggest that academic trespass can result in the innovation and reconstitution of disciplinary edifices, with the consequence that the terms—and even objects—of analysis may look somewhat different when they are perceived in light of other disciplines. In methodological terms, remapping the borders between disciplines contributes to the larger intellectual project of rethinking culture, canon, and disciplinarity. In redrawing these lines, subjects and disciplines that were previously inconspicuous or uncharted are made visible and located according to their own coordinates. Border crossing yields what W. E. B. Du Bois calls "double-vision"—it expands our field of vision without being expansionist; it includes without consuming; it appreciates without appropriating; and it seeks to temper politics with ethics.

NOTES

I wish to express my thanks to Ned Lukacher, George Cunningham, Kathleen Diffley, and Donald Marshall, who read this essay at different stages of its development, as well as to Eva Bednarowicz, my research assistant, for her persistence and creativity.

1. From Gloria Anzaldúa, *Borderlands/La Frontera: The New Mestiza* (San Francisco: Spinters/Aunt Lute, 1987), 3.

2. From Trinh T. Minh-ha, *Framer Framed* (New York: Routledge, 1991), 218.

3. From Diane P. Freedman, *An Alchemy of Genres: Cross-Genre Writing by American Feminist Poet-Critics* (Charlottesville: University Press of Virginia), 31.

4. Jacques Derrida, *La Vérité en peinture (Truth in Painting)*. Translated by Geoff Bennington and Ian McLeod (Chicago: University of Chicago Press, 1987), 9–12. Derrida redefines this notion as part of a critique of Kantian self-presence. For commentary, see Mary Ann Caws, *Reading Frames in Modern Fiction* (Princeton, N.J.: Princeton University Press, 1985), and Peter Brunette and David Wills, *Screen/Play: Derrida and Film Theory* (Princeton, N.J.: Princeton University Press, 1989).

5. Jacques Derrida, "Living On: Border Lines," Harold Bloom *et. al.*, *Deconstruction and Criticism* (New York: Seabury Press, 1979), 83.

6. Trinh Minh-ha, 116, 218.

7. Michael R. Clifford, "Crossing (out) the Boundary: Foucault and Derrida on Transgressing Transgression," *Philosophy Today*, Vol. 31, No. 3/4 (Fall 1987). In invoking the notion of the "trespass" and its intellectual value, my intent here is less to enlist some modern and professionalized notion of a biblical "fortunate fall" than it is perhaps to privilege the classical and Promethean notion of trespass. "Trespass" introduces the notion of territory into the concept of border crossing, translating the Promethean theft into a kind of metaphorical crossing of boundaries that resulted in a new way of living for humankind. Not only does the Promethean trespass, then, break new ground, but the consequence is the expansion and remapping of specific borders that these essays aggregately reconstitute between the possible (mortal) and impossible (divine). In a modern evocation of this classical notion, I wish to suggest a notion of trespass as a way of crossing, intersecting, and interweaving that does not seek to colonize or imperialize, but to share and save cultures.

8. See Abdul R. JanMohamed, "Worldliness-Without World, Homelessness-As-Home: Toward a Definition of the Specular Border Intellectual," Michael Sprinkler (ed.) *Edward Said: A Critical Reader* (Cambridge, Mass.: Blackwell Publishers, 1992).

9. George Steiner, "The Responsibility of Intellectuals: A Discussion," *Salmagundi*, No. 70–71 (Spring-Summer 1986), 194.

10. Stuart Hall, "Cultural Studies and Its Theoretical Legacies," Lawrence Grossberg, Cary Nelson, Paula A. Treichler (eds.), *Cultural Studies* (New York: Routledge, 1992), 285.

11. See Emily Hicks, *Border Writing: The Multidimensional Text* (Minneapolis: University of Minnesota Press, 1991).

12. Hicks, xxv.

13. Hicks, xxvi, xxv.

14. Paula Gunn Allen's concept of "border studies" derives from the idea of "living on the borders," a concept complementing Gloria Anzaldúa's notion of "border culture" (as well as Abdul JanMohamed's). See Allen, " 'Border' Studies: The Intersections of Gender and Color," Joseph Gibaldi (ed.), *Introduction to Scholarship in Modern Languages and Literatures*, Second Edition (New York: Modern Language Association of America, 1992).

15. Edward Said, "Mind of Winter: Reflections on Life in Exile," *Harper's Magazine* (September 1984), 54.

16. Victor Turner, *From Ritual to Theatre: The Human Seriousness of Play* (New York: PAJ Publications, 1982), 25.

17. Turner, *From Ritual to Theatre*, 26.

18. Victor Turner, *Dramas, Fields, and Metaphors: Symbolic Action in Human Society* (Ithaca, N.Y.: Cornell University Press, 1974), 13–14.

19. Turner, *Drama, Fields, and Metaphors*, 13–14.

20. Turner, *From Ritual to Theatre*, 28. As Anzaldúa writes, "Living in a state of psychic unrest, in a Borderland, is what makes poets write and artists create." See *Borderlands/La Frontera*, 73.

21. JanMohamed, 98.

22. See Jane Marcus, "Alibis and Legends: The Ethics of Elsewhereness, Gender and Estrangement," *Women's Writing in Exile*, (eds.) Mary Lynn Broe and Angela Ingram (Chapel Hill: The University of North Carolina Press, 1989), 273.

23. See bell hooks, *Black Looks: Race and Representation* (Boston: South End Press, 1992), 157.

24. Marianna Torgovnick, *Gone Primitive: Savage Lives, Modern Intellects* (Chicago: The University of Chicago Press, 1990), 9.

25. hooks, 157–58.

26. Marcus herself articulates this problematic in her earlier piece, "Alibis and Legends," 271.

27. Marcus, "Alibis and Legends," 273.

28. Laura Rice defines translation as "an impossible task, suspended as it is between two disparate texts, each with its own world of assumptions," in "The Camera Always Lies," *The Women's Review of Books*, Vol. X, No. 6 (March 1993), 13.

29. Trinh Minh-ha, *Framer Framed*, 128. Further, Minh-ha reminds us that translation is "interpellated by ideology and can never by objective or neutral," 127.

30. Trinh Minh-ha, 128. What Ronald A. Sharpe observed of George Steiner can be said of the entire critical project, which, he proposes, "can be understood as translation, making as it does incursions across established borders into obscure territories which it illuminates by providing entryways, points of contact and connection, initial maps of the alien territory and, even more important, of our own realms, newly transformed by just these incursions and translations." Ronald A. Sharpe, "Interrogation at the Borders: George Steiner and the Trope of Translation," *New Literary History*, Vol. 21, No.1 (Autumn 1989), 153.

31. This is part of the larger project of grappling with the meaning of the term "postcoloniality" and defining borders of the discipline.

32. Edward Said, "Mind of Winter," 51.

33. Said, "Traveling Theory," *Inscriptions*, No 5 (1989), 237, quoted in JanMohamed, 100.

34. Amy K. Kaminsky, *Reading the Body Politic: Feminist Criticism and Latin American Women Writers* (Minneapolis: University of Minnesota Press, 1993), 60–61.

35. Mary Ann Caws, "Personal Criticism: A Matter of Choice," *Women of Bloomsbury: Virginia, Vanessa, and Carrington* (New York: Routledge, 1990); quoted in Nancy K. Miller, *Getting Personal: Feminist Occasions and Other Autobiographical Acts* (New York: Routledge, 1991), 21.

36. This is a form of criticism that has been been pioneered by women-of-color writers who have drawn on epistolary forms and the personal narrative. See, for example, the criticism of Barbara Smith, bell hooks, and the writers contributing to Cherríe Moraga and Gloria Anzaldúa (eds.), *This Bridge Called My Back: Writings by Radical Women of Color* (Watertown, Mass.: Persephone Press, 1981).

37. Thomas J. Farrell, "The Female and Male Modes of Rhetoric," *College English* Vol. 40, No. 8 (April 1979); quoted in Diane P. Freedman, Olivia Frey, and Frances Murphy Zauhar, *The Intimate Critique: Autobiographical Literary Criticism* (Durham, N.C.: Duke University Press, 1993), 2.

38. See Judith Kegan Gardiner, "On Female Identity and Writing by Women" *Writing and Sexual Difference* (ed.) Elizabeth Abel (Chicago: University of Chicago Press, 1982) and Nancy Chodorow, *The Reproduction of Mothering: Psychoanalysis and the Sociology of Gender* (Berkeley: University of California Press, 1978). See also Freedman *et al.*, "Border Crossing as Method and Motif in Contemporary American Writing, or, How Freud Helped Me Case the Joint," Freedman *et al.*, *The Ultimate Critique*, 13.

39. See Freedman *et al.*, *The Intimate Critique*, 5.

40. Jane Tomkins, "Me and My Shadow," Diane P. Freedman *et al.*, *The Intimate Critique*, 26.

41. Barbara Johnson, *A World of Difference* (Baltimore: Johns Hopkins University Press, 1987), 44.

42. Miller, 21.

43. See the discussion of cultural studies below in this introduction.

44. Of course, even when the signifying gesture of the signature becomes the vehicle of inscription, the authority and authenticity of the author-critic can still be called into question by the reader-critic. Elizabeth Abel's critique of white feminist readings of black women's texts seems to suggest that even other forms of criticism must be read as a gesture of self-disclosure on the part of the author-critic. See Elizabeth Abel, "Black Writing, White Reading," *Critical Inquiry* 19 (Spring 1993).

45. Minh-ha critiques "the theorist who continues to stand in a "safe place" to theorize about others." See *Framer Framed*, 123.

46. Cf. Minh-ha, who, in her evocation of poetical language, says that "there is no 'I' that just stands for *myself*. The 'I' is there; it has to be there, but it is there as the site where all other 'I's' can enter and cut across one another." *Framer Framed*, 122.

47. Andrew Ross, *No Respect: Intellectuals and Popular Culture* (New York: Routledge, 1989), 5.

48. Ross, *No Respect*, 50.

49. Ross, 50.

50. Of particular interest here is Adorno's well-known and controversial critique of jazz: "However little doubt there can be regarding the African elements in jazz, it is no less certain that everything unruly in it was from the very beginning integrated into a strict scheme, that its rebellious gestures are accompanied by the tendency to blind obeisance, much like the sado-masochistic type described by analytic psychology."

51. Dana Polan, "The Public's Fear; or, Media as Monster in Habermas, Negt, and Kluge," Bruce Robbins (ed.), *The Phantom Public Sphere* (Minneapolis: University of Minnesota Press, 1993), 35.

52. George Lipsitz, "Listening to Learn and Learning to Listen: Popular Culture, Cultural Theory, and American Studies," *American Quarterly*, Vol. 42, No. 4 (December 1990), 618.

53. Martin Jay, *The Dialectical Imagination: A History of the Frankfurt School and the Institute of Social Research, 1923–1950* (Boston: Little, Brown, 1973), 185.

54. See Jay, 216–17, for the Frankfurt School critique of mass culture, which was associated not with democracy, but with totalitarianism.

55. Jay, 211.

56. Stuart Hall, "What Is This 'Black' in Black Popular Culture?", Gina Dent, *Black Popular Culture* (Seattle: Bay Press, 1992), 26, 32.

57. Hall, 27.

58. West, "The Postmodern Crisis of Black Intellectuals," Grossberg *et al.*, *Cultural Studies*, 693.

59. Quoted in Lipsitz, "Listening to Learn and Learning to Listen," 621.

60. Lipsitz, 621.

61. Edward Branigan, *Point of View in the Cinema: A Theory of Narration and Subjectivity in Classical Film* (New York: Mouton Publishers, 1984), 3.

62. Peter Brunette and David Wills, *Screen/Play: Derrida and Film Theory* (Princeton, N.J.: Princeton University Press, 1989), 104.

63. See Brunette and Wills, "The Frame of the Frame," 99–137, and Gerald Mast, "On Framing," *Critical Inquiry* 11 (September 1984), 83, 85.

64. Laura Rice, "The Camera Always Lies," review of Trinh Minh-ha's *Framer Framed*, *The Women's Review of Books*, Vol. X, No. 6 (March 1993), 13.

65. Inez Hedges, *Breaking the Frame: Film language and the Experience of Limits* (Bloomington and Indianapolis: Indiana University Press, 1991), xiii.

66. Vincent Leitsch, "Cultural Studies," Michael Groden and Martin Kreiswirth (eds), *John Hopkins Guide to Literary Theory and Criticism*, (Baltimore: Johns Hopkins University Press, 1994).

67. From the Greek for *chi*, meaning the cross or letter "x."

68. Peter Brunette and David Wills suggest that this figure is "formed precisely when the four sides of the square or frame collapse to divide diagonally the internal coherence of whatever resides within that frame." *Screen/Play*, 118. The resulting image, as they point out, is a "crisscross double invagination"—an image deployed by Derrida in "Living On: Border/Lines."

69. Cornel West, *American Evasion of Philosophy: A Genealogy of Pragmatism* (Madison: University of Wisconsin Press, 1989), 105.

70. Even so, these labels are likely to be controversial for a number of readers. Ironically, in recent public debate, conservatives have habitually employed precisely this rhetorical code to critique diversity, difference, multiculturalism, and even cultural studies itself.

71. West, "The Postmodern Crisis of the Black Intellectuals," Lawrence Grossberg, Cary Nelson, Paula A. Treichler (eds.), *Cultural Studies* (New York: Routledge, 1992), 694.

72. Lipsitz, "Listening to Learn and Learning to Listen," 623.

73. Stuart Hall, "Ethnicity: Identity and Difference," *Radical America*, Vol. 23, No. 4, 12.

74. Hall, "Ethnicity, Identity, and Difference," 13.

75. Henry A. Giroux, "The Politics of Insurgent Multiculturalism in the Era of the Los Angeles Uprising," *Journal of the Midwest Modern Language Association*, Vol. 26, No. 1 (Spring 1993), 14

76. *Ibid.*, 15.

77. Marjorie Roemer and Vandana Sharma, review of Henry Giroux' *Border Crossings: Cultural Workers and the Politics of Education*, *Journal of the Midwest Modern Language Association*, Vol. 26, No. 1 (Spring 1993) 84.

78. Lati Mani, "Cultural Theory, Colonial Texts: Reading Eyewitness Accounts of Widow Burning," Grossberg *et al.*, *Cultural Studies*, 394.

PART I
CROSSING BORDERS:
EXILE AND LANGUAGE

1.

Bonding and Bondage: Nancy Cunard and the Making of the Negro Anthology

JANE MARCUS

BONDING AND BONDAGE

> It ought to be self-evident that Judaism in no way touches on the mass murder of Jews by Gentile Germans and their Gentile European helpers; nor is the Holocaust, though its victims were Jews, a product of Jewish history or civilization. Oppression belongs to the culture of the oppressors.
>
> Cynthia Ozick[1]

If it is true that oppression belongs to the culture of the oppressors, then it is also true that cultural historians need to remember that they are the ones who name and catalogue histories.[2] Blaming the victim has too often been the result of attributing oppression to those who were oppressed. For slavery continues to be studied as a problem in black history, when it is surely (firstly rather than also) a subject in the story of white cultures. Yet the identity of the historians and producers of knowledge about subject peoples has recently been scrutinized mercilessly for purity of motive and mind-set. Anyone who might possibly belong to the family of "oppressors" has been eliminated as an authority. Or at least I'm assuming that it was her gender, her color, her class, her politics and her several sexualities as a set of (shifting) identities which set all the red lights flashing on everybody's indicators of "political correctness" well before the popularity of the phrase but not the activity—to discredit Nancy Cunard as an intellectual historian of black culture. If slavery is not just a problem in black history, then why are a white European woman's extraordinary efforts to understand it and to write and circulate its many complex and overlapping different histories ignored or marginalized by black intellectuals and activists as well as white historians?

My project in this paper is to ask why Nancy Cunard (1896–1965) has been eliminated or discredited as a producer of knowledge in all the fields to which she contributed, why her voice has been silenced in the histories of the several modern(ist) discourses to which she contributed. Given her indifference to feminism, it would be ironic if the chief cause of the loss of Nancy Cunard's presence as a radical intellectual was her gender. She was not the kind of role model usually offered to aspiring young crusaders for social justice. She'd be a failure as a heroine in a "Lives of Great Women" series, and feminists will not find a long-lost champion of women's rights when her achievements are reviewed. Her life was not a happy one, nor was it stable in any sense. Women are supposed to live stably and provide stability for others. Nancy Cunard was a revolutionary, dedicating her life to political upheaval, committed to changing the world. But the standard narratives of revolutionary lives provide no pattern—except perhaps the lives of Russian upper class Anarchists. Revolutionaries are supposed to come from the working class. British intellectuals and historians of that class have not rushed to claim her as their own (The attitude is similar to the encouragement of class suspicion against Virginia Woolf's socialism and feminism. They are suspicious of her motives.) From the point of view of her birth, she was a class traitor, and so she is seen by biographers and spies for international intelligence agencies alike. Her other survival is as an eccentric, a stagey and flamboyant "character," like her fellow-poet Edith Sitwell. The place where she most deserves to be honored is the history of the struggle against racism in Britain and the U.S. She was a major figure from the Left in the British Black Liberation movement in the Thirties, Forties and Fifties. When the stories of African anti-colonial struggles are written, perhaps it is here that she will find her place in history.

Half-educated by governesses by her rich Irish-American mother (Maud Burke) and Sir Bache Cunard, inheritor of the shipping fortune, she renounced family and fortune and educated herself in the history of racial oppression and trained herself as a writer and publisher, journalist and anthropologist. As an English expatriate self-made "expert" on black culture and the history of slavery, she does not fit easily into the one anti-racist discourse which does exist, that created by white Englishwomen who worked in the anti-slavery movement, documented and analyzed by feminist intellectual historian Moira Ferguson in *Subject to Others*—unless it proves to be the case that the missing feminism in her story is really there and has been suppressed.[3]

Her name did her more harm than good. As brilliantly as her mother, Lady Emerald Cunard, had shone in her London literary and artistic salon with her (also married) lover Sir Thomas Beecham, Nancy's Hours Press office at 15 rue Guénégaud in Paris gave off a different sort of vibe, an antipatriotic glow made of blue notes and red flags and ivory bracelets,— a certain surrealist glamour composed of sex, primitivism, left politics and jazz. And there she staged a series of salons in the 20s and 30s around the intersections of surrealism, communism, avant-garde writing, African art and ivory artifacts, jazz and anti-fascism in Spain, a center where African intellectuals and political leaders and black artists from all over the world were apt to meet Beckett or Janet Flanner, Louis Aragon or George Moore.

But she was not a hostess or a lady with a salon, as a historian of women surrealists who had never heard of her assumed when she asked contemptuously, "Did she *do* anything?" Nancy Cunard was primarily what we used to call in the civil rights and antiwar movements, a full-time political organizer. She was a living network, a one-woman permanent walking demonstration against racism and fascism, and a celebrant of black culture in all its forms. She had a voice in shaping all the competing and conflicting discourses of modernism, but in their histories there is only the marginal trace of a husky whisper, a smudge like a streak of kohl across those hooded piercing eyes remembered in a malicious footnote. She was an autodidact, a self-made intellectual and political organizer. And she was very successful at her work. She produced an enormous amount of knowledge to combat racism and to invite Europe and the West to see Africa and Negro cultures as civilizations. Her work and the work of those she organized to produce the monumental *Negro* anthology, an international body of progressive intellectuals and artists of all races working together to produce and disseminate knowledge about black culture, was ridiculed, lost, dismissed, made fun of, ignored—and then it was done all over again. This is what gives me a chill. The case of the loss of the *Negro* anthology is an example of what happens to the histories of all oppressed groups when they have no institutions—universities, libraries, museums, art galleries—to protect and value, cherish and circulate them. (I always tell my students that my collection of books by women writers on feminism was bought in book sales by the university library. I was buying what the institutions of knowledge preservation were throwing away.)

Nancy Cunard is remembered as a bad bold body, the subject of some stunning photographs by Man Ray, Cecil Beaton and their colleagues in the visual avant-gardes of London and Paris. The problem with this limited role allowed on the margins of the numerous "fields" in which she worked, or, rather, the use of photographs of her to illustrate modernist texts and trends, is that her central generative activity is denied—as if Hemingway, for example, were remembered only in the louche snapshots of his friends and not for the shape and length of his sentences.

That body and its self-fetishizing is indeed one of my subjects. But I want to open up the question of what it means when a white woman of the mistress class stages herself as a slave, binds and shackles her body and her head in shameless and fashionable display of political solidarity which, contrary to her intentions, highlights difference. What happens when she revels physically in the primitivism she is articulating as modernism? How much irony is there in Cunard's costumes? Who shared it? And who shares it now?

We can begin to think about some answers when we acknowledge that it is not uncommon for the arc of desire to intersect with the arc of intellectual activity, for art and work to focus on exchanges between the body of the self and the other, especially in the encounter between surrealism and anthropology which generated so much of Cunard's cultural work. Hemingway's body might be studied along with his fiction and reportage. The sex life of the ethnographer has become the focus of recent genealogies of modernist anthropology and Michel Leiris has become a hero to his successors. But none of the writers cite Cunard. I believe her work was just as important as that of Leiris, who does in fact cite her political bravery and devotion to the cause of black culture, but then he had the protection of the institution of the *Musée de l'Homme* to allow for the playfulness of surrealist autobiography to mask the fact that he served the state in a daily job in which African and other forms of primitive art were collected, studied and displayed. He had an empire.[4]

If genealogy is history, then it is becoming clear that one of the ways hegemony is maintained in fields threatened by others, is the writing of the biographies of the great men in the field as a history of the field. For example, Lévi-Strauss made it clear that structuralism was founded by Jane Ellen Harrison; he continually acknowledged his debt to her pioneering work in inventing the discipline of anthropology as a materialist rather than a linguistic enterprise, where fieldwork and the study of objects in context was to replace the study of ancient texts alone. But his followers wished to eliminate her from history, to make Lévi-Strauss the founder, the father, of their field. Their genealogical persistence has effectively marginalized a central figure of modernist anthropology and a history is passed on of the great men and their great ideas yet again.

Is it that Nancy Cunard's lust to know and to reproduce and circulate what she found out by diligent research and a massive campaign of self-education offended or threatened everyone with a territorial interest in some aspect of the cultural history of modernism? Is it that, as Sabena Broeck argues, her desire and her politics were both centered on black men? Like Carl Van Vechten, Cunard was acknowledged as an important bridge figure between black and white cultures in Paris, London and New York. Why was it necessary to burn the bridges to build a black liberation movement? Or was it her "conflation of matriphobia and political radicalism," as Susan Friedman claims, which shocked her contemporaries most?

Was it that she raised "troubling questions about the mother-daughter bond within the psychodynamics of gender, race and class," by breaking the taboo of class loyalty and washing the Cunard family linen in public?

She died a raving alcoholic in a public ward in Paris, still working on her epic poem on world peace. Why is there such a taboo about the lives of women alcoholics?

Her biographer creates her as a misguided nymphomaniac, assuming that sexuality determined her politics just as her ex-lovers, black and white, attributed her lack of the monogamous impulse to a fundamental moral and intellectual flaw, when such behavior by themselves or their male friends was glamorous and enhancing to the image of the expatriate heroic artist. A strange posthumous as-told-to "autobiography" by her jazz musician ex-lover Henry Crowder circulates to discredit her role in the history of black liberation and in particular the amazing production of the *Negro* anthology—which he had inspired by his tales of life in the South and the history of slavery.[5]

Belittled by histories of the Harlem Renaissance, Nancy Cunard was left out altogether from the story of the culture she did so much to shape, the story of the Communist Party in Harlem in the 30s; she is basically a missing person in Valentine Cunningham's history of British writing in the 30s, barely mentioned in the histories of the English expatriates and the Spanish Civil War, ignored as a journalist and war-correspondent, marginalized as a modernist poet, erased from her role as organizer of the international protest movement on behalf of the Scottsboro boys, her Hours Press listed on the fringe of the small press and avant-garde publishing world (discovering Beckett, printing Pound's *Cantos*), reduced to a footnote in the biography of her lifelong friend Langston Hughes or demonized or left out of the lives of her former lovers like Louis Aragon, so that, incidentally, her role in the Paris Left as well as in Surrealism itself is summarily cut. Her role in collecting and showing African art in Paris early in the century and her pioneering of the revaluation of ethnic objects as art for museums and private collectors changed art history. Roger Fry is remembered, but even he is excluded from recent studies of primitivism. Where is Nancy Cunard? Her work for the *Negro* anthology revitalized the field of anthropology and introduced field-workers and ethnographers to each other's work as well as to positive ideas about Africa as civilized rather than savage cultures and had a major influence on French ethnographic practice, as Michel Leiris says in his memoirs.

But she exists neither in the history of art history's modernist turn to African images, nor in the history of the new participatory and positive practice of ethnography. Michel Leiris has become the hero of modern anthropology because he wrote his autobiography instead of an ethnography of the Africans he was sent to study. Nancy Cunard left no public autobiography and buried what personal memoirs she wrote between the lines of her biographies of the minor men of letters George Moore and Norman Douglas written in the 50s. Yet in her lifetime she was the princess of primitivism. Modernism in almost all its aspects could be explicated with a work of Nancy Cunard's, a poem, a broadside, a news item, a book, an African carving, a revolutionary pamphlet, an ivory bracelet, a photograph of her in a close-fitting leather costume or "solarized" with an elongated neck wound with beads and flung back as if awaiting the kiss of the vampire. Her body is here very much part of the history of the period, draped in tiger skins, wrapped in leopard, or backed by metal as in a Metropolis landscape of Thirties Berlin. Breastless, white and phallic, stretched in pleasure or perhaps it's pain, caught in soft cloth manacles, bound by silken scarves, held by ivory chains, she becomes a boy or an androgynous creature (a different kind of woman, the imaginary lesbian of Sapphic modernism?) from the African fertility figures with their pointed breasts which stand at the center of modernist primitivism.

Is this white woman's staging of herself as a prisoner or a slave the visual equivalent of feminism's use of the discourse of slavery to articulate its own demands for freedom? Does the cross-gendering and cross-sexualizing of these poses make racial divisions between reproductive and non-reproductive sex? Marking the black African woman's body for motherhood, modernism leaves a space for that other kind of boyish white woman's body which Man Ray and its photographers celebrate, in white top hat or cat's whiskers, in mask and cape and Spanish broad-brimmed hat or coat and tie and Eton-cropped hair, a body which breaks the rules of gender, a body which suggests sex without motherhood, interracial sex and intersexual race-ing. We know from our own lives that such fashionable cultural creations as our own bodies are perfectly compatible with intellectual careers and creative professional lives. Why do we deny this doubleness to women in history?

Nancy Cunard's monumental work, the oversized 855-page *Negro* anthology (with 385 illustrations), published in 1934 and paid for with the £1500 proceeds of lawsuits for interracial sex slanders against her in the English newspapers, was one of the first works to attempt the production of knowledge about blacks on a global scale. Two thirds of the 150 contributors were blacks, and the enormous volume (begun in 1930) covered every aspect of African art and civilization from individual African countries to the United States, the West Indies, South America, Haiti and Cuba. The object was to showcase the splendors of African civilizations at the same time as Europeans were being subjected to colonial exhibitions and fairs which treated Africans as cannibals and headhunters, savages who were subject to the campaigns of the military and the missionary invasions of Europeans. She and her team of scholars studied racism in the United States and the comparative history of slavery; they wrote about jazz, the blues and gospel. The Zora Neale Hurston pieces have still not been collected and made available. The articles are so fresh and comprehensive today that it is shocking to think that the work done for these essays was lost to the field. Questions raised and issues studied and documented here in the 30s were raised again in the 70s and debated as if this knowledge had never been accumulated. The loss in time and effort to progress in black Studies is enormous. If such a gap existed in physics or mathematics, the scientific community would be justifiably outraged. Was it the whiff of Communism which frightened readers off? Or was the massive press campaign to portray Cunard as an English heiress slumming in search of sex with black men effective in discrediting the intellectual importance of the book?

Only an autodidact could have imagined such a grandiose intellectual scheme (requiring immense amounts of research in primary documents in libraries all over the world) as Nancy Cunard's *Negro* anthology. Only a committed left-wing activist could have called up the worldwide ideals of cross-racial brother-and-sisterhood to bring such a project into being. Only a mad surrealist poet would have thought that its dynamite collections of artistic power and beauty would blow up in the face of bourgeoisies of all nations and colors and that the scales of prejudice would fall from their eyes at once. Only an intrepid Englishwoman in exile would have believed that she could bring it off, commissioning, cajoling, editing, revising, dealing with bruised egos and suspicious intellectuals, underground leaders, separatists and photographers and professors and anthropologists, folklorists and politicians, discovering new voices, letting controversial voices be heard, publishing manifestoes and always having the last word—editing the conservative Du Bois, arguing with Marcus Garvey, proclaiming in her fellow-travelling footnotes that the way and the only way of racial freedom was the Communist Party.

STRASBOURG PRIMITIVE: MISSIONARY KITSCH AND POSTCOLONIAL SHAME

Living in Strasbourg as a foreigner I notice that primitive folk motives decorate the village prints on tablecloths and aprons and casseroles for cooking regional dishes. These charming Alsatian designs in fabric and pottery are sold to the tourists, while the locals buy bright Turkish and Moroccan handicrafts and look to Paris for fashion. Peasant crafts denote purity, the natural and the exotic, and in exile one is aware of the competing claims of various foreign and homely primitivisms. Anthropologists have shown us how Africans carved figures of the anthropologists who came to study them and have given evidence of tribals who incorporate the debris of the modern world into their art forms. But I have seen some products of the clash of cultures which produce no smiles of assent or knowing nods.

All winter I have walked to market through the flea market, curious to see what's being bought and sold. It is full of strange representations of

Africa and Africans, of misshapen palm trees and sawed-off jungles. They look as if they were made by children or mental patients, by people with something missing in a sense of the beautiful, or lacking perspective. These odd and ugly drawings and paintings of African landscapes and people in clumsy, home-made wooden frames from the 20s and 30s are a version of the primitive I cannot place. On the blankets and tables of the local farmers they stand apart from the watercolors and oils of familiar rural scenes, wine-making peasants and snow on the Vosges Mountains. They are too childish to be kitsch, too earnest and grimly limited to compare to the naif/native productions from Haiti or Greece which entrance tourists. Sitting next to pornographic postcards of French soldiers with African women, they lack wit or élan or anything I can conceive of as "value" from my cultural perspective. They are unbelievably ugly.

I read that the French city of Nantes has produced an extraordinary exhibition this year, documenting its own carefully hidden history of centuries of extensive and enormously profitable slave trading. The cover-up is what interests me, the kind of cultural consensus which locks generations of people into living historical lies. What, I wonder, is the connection between Alsace and Africa?

Puzzled by these peculiar portraits of naked black women in exotic spaces and sensing their participation in some obscure discourse of professional pornography, a kind of Domestic Obscene, *I learn from a bookseller in Colmar that the region is rich in Africana, souvenirs of the Protestant missionaries who followed Albert Schweitzer, the local hero, to Africa. What's left in the flea markets is what serious collectors of Africana disdain.*

They were not at all what I had feared they were, the products of Christianized Africans who had lost their talent on conversion. I had assumed that these were unwanted and uncollected artifacts of Christian colonialism. They have none of the vigor and vibrancy of the folksy saints and sinners painted by Alsatian farmers on their walls and windows. They were made by white people in exile in Africa—missionaries who returned home with their homemade fetishes. This is the way some Alsatians saw Africa and Africans.

The ugliness of the "paintings" is exceeded by the ugliness of the carvings. The crudely hacked wooden objects appear to come from the Stone Age when compared with elegant, sleek, polished figures from Africa which fill the ethnographic museums of the West. The wood-carvers of this region make "primitive" figures of bears. But these bare-breasted African female figures look as if they were hacked out of firewood by butcher knives. The Brothers Grimm might recognize them as versions of "bears," as perhaps beasts from the jungle of Northern European dreams. They do nothing to delight the eye.

But it is not just a Schweitzer Protestant fertility figure I am seeing. For the Pères Blancs have their headquarters here too, Catholic Missionaires Africains. And they too return from exile.

When Roger Fry claimed in Vision and Design *(1920) that African carvings were the purest forms since the Greeks in the history of art, he echoed the modernist painters who had already begun to steal from the* Musée de l'Homme *to energize their moribund cultures. What he could not visualize, situated among the high modernists rushing to fill their paintings with the forms and colors of the Far East, Africa and Hawaii, was what would happen when "low" white European cultures appropriated the arts of their colonial subjects. Picasso and Matisse they were not.*

Inhabiting some as yet unmentioned site in the semi-ethnographic, the flea market fetishes which obsess me often have labels which mask their purpose as works of respectable scientific observation rather than objects of masturbatory fantasies for peeping priests. This dismal and lugubrious provincial primitivism disguises the eroto-religious rapacity of the missionary gaze. The awkwardness of the unskilled hackwork of the word-carvers and painters produces an embarrassment in this viewer—and yet I return again and again—that I will call post-colonial shame.

Neither the exquisite purity of form which Roger Fry found in African sculpture nor the ruthless genius of the appropriating modernist Picassos can be found in this messy detritus of cultural adventurism. For here at the level of popular culture or what we may call pop primitivism, there is a kind of missionary kitsch which deserves to be set alongside Tarzan *comics and* Tin-Tin *as a herald of the postmodern. The question is whether the invocation of fake anthropology on the part of these self-deceiving Christians was less socially damaging than real academic and institutionalized anthropology, disguising its service to empire and commerce?*

Determined to buy one of these strange carvings before leaving, I go back to the flea market. But the tourists are here and the missionary africana has gone back to the attic.

BONDAGE(S)

Something in Cunard's rejection of white culture and English imperialism was enacted in an exile more threatening than scholarly research into the history of slavery. By writing and publishing *Black Man, White Ladyship* (1931) she repudiated England as mother country in denouncing her American-born mother as a racist, mingling matriphobia with the idea of the struggle for black power. The sexualized black male body becomes the site of her political (and personal) rebellion, as she publicly gives up her inheritance both culturally and literally in a gesture which frightens everyone concerned, even her black lover. The version of this pamphlet currently in circulation in *The Gender of Modernism* is a reprint of the bowlderized pamphlet from Hugh Ford's *Nancy Cunard: Brave Poet, Indomitable Rebel*, and it leaves out her discussion of English homophobia and her relating of American lynchings to male concern with "white womanhood." This text also will repay study. In her role as undutiful daughter, Nancy Cunard gives us an alternative story of female development, a radical refusal of the reproduction of motherhood, a rejection of the mother in class and race terms as the representation of imperialism, and a declaration of the daughter's independence from the sacred bonds of mother-daughter love.

If Nancy Cunard were here today, doubtless she'd be dressed in some witty version of what French designers call the bondage dress—a series of crisscrossed bands similar to the chained/unchained images she performed for the avant–garde camera in the 30s. Nancy Cunard's reenactment of black slave bondage in the self-staging of her white body as a site for political protest against racism has not been read inside *her* semiotics, but instead as a perverse pornography, both political and sexual. But she really meant the performance of bondage to signify her political bonding with black culture. She meant it as literally as she meant to break the biological bond with her mother by publishing *Black Man, White Ladyship*.

The semiotics of exile which Nancy Cunard staged on her skinny, skeletal, emaciated body signal a motherlessness and lack of nurturing which we are used to constructing as anorexia. But she felt she was bonding with her black brothers when she was photographed as a white slave, her neck encircled by beads, her arms by bracelets. Even her leg warmers—this is the early 30s—are a form of chic shackles. She also almost always kept her head bound—in hats and scarves, veils and close bands or ribbons. (Her Twenties "permanent waves" and "marcel" curls bring her straight hair closer to the bounce and spring of "black" hair. Today she'd have beaded corn rows in an elaborate headdress. Think of how suspicious political commentators were of Hillary Clinton's headbands.)

While many of the most famous photographs of Nancy Cunard were taken by Man Ray and Cecil Beaton, some of the most interesting ones rediscovered by Val Williams in *The Other Observers*[6] were taken by Barabar Ker-Seymer, a German photographer working in London, and misattributed to the better-known photographers. Ker-Seymer used bold images from German cinema, leather, silver and corrugated iron to photograph glamorous gay London in the 30s, and Nancy Cunard's photos join those of Brian Howard, Raymond Mortimer and Eddie Sackville-West in her portrait gallery. After the scandal of *Black Man, White Ladyship*, in which she publicly denounced her mother's racism, Ker-Seymer suggested that she make "solarizations," negative prints which would make the white subject appear black. Ker-Seymer's solarizations of Nancy Cunard are an interesting visual parable of Cunard's desire for a black body. (Fig. 1) They also "expose" her neck and torso stretched with ropes of beads into an elaborate

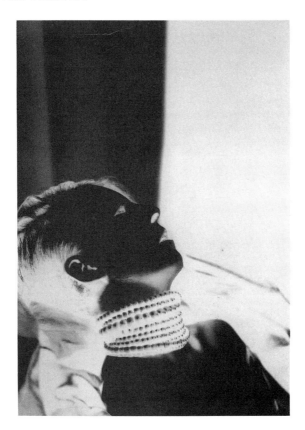

Fig. 1

mimicry of lynching, emphasizing in the thrown-back head, the red lips, dark nostrils and kohl-blackened eyes both the vampire's victim and the vampire herself. (Fig. 2) These images still have the power to confuse and disturb us. On the one hand it is outrageous that the white woman presents us with her tribalized body, appropriating African images of the elongated neck from ethnographic photographs of the exotic as in the semi-pornography of the pages of *National Geographic*, for fashion's pleasures. But the photos send other messages as well—messages about pain, sadistic torture, perhaps drugs. Her body looks drained. The straps of her dress are pulled down. Is she about to be raped or abused? Has she just had an orgasm and is that the open-mouthed edge of abandonment? Or does she just want to be fed? (Fig. 3)

Since Nancy Cunard, the crusading reporter and left-wing poet wrote so passionately against lynching and lynch mobs in America, protesting the violence against black men, the pictures are all the more disturbing. They suggest an absent violator of that exposed white female body—is the absent

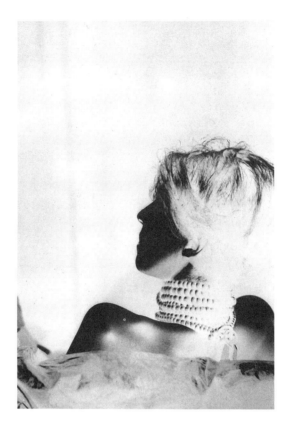

Fig. 2

rapist black? Her bound and exposed neck, along with the heavy make-up, make her melodramatically appear to be in thrall to an "evil" power. The brilliant Ker-Seymer photos of Nancy Cunard as the white woman appropriating the suffering of the lynched black man, the Southern racial and political martyr in the struggle for freedom, capture the ideological issues of the era as little else in art has been able to do—the white male construction of black manhood as only a violent threat to white womanhood, which justifies lynching and implicates white women in terrible crimes.[7] What does it mean when Nancy Cunard switches roles and performs "the white woman being lynched" when in reality black men were being lynched in the name of revenge for white woman's lost honor? Can the figure of the "white woman hanged, bound, manacled, enslaved" ever disrupt in performance the racial fears of sexual mixing she wants to explode? Or is she unaware of the act she is putting on? Having seen some examples of studio photos taken as late as the 50s of black men with tribal spears, feathers and drums from her own collection, I find it hard to think that she was unaware of the power of the performance of pain in these photographs. Can she enact the erotics of the white slave along with the politics of protest against racism? Are there kinds of "drag" which are not ethically permissible? I recall the fury of reviewers and audiences at Lina Wertmuller's representation of a German woman concentration camp commandant forcing a starving Italian prisoner to have sex with her. When a white woman claims the victim status of the lynched black man, can we read the performance of cross-racial and cross-sexual "lynching drag" as an attack on white males? Nancy Cunard's sexuality is very interesting and much more complex than her biographers have suggested. But the racial dimensions of that sexuality constitute no reason to doubt her utter political devotion to the cause of racial justice.

As I have argued in regard to Djuna Barnes' having herself photographed while being "forcibly fed," in order to experience the ordeal of the English suffragettes on hunger strike in prisons, there is a strange mixture of the political and the sexual in Cunard's public exhibitions of her pain.[8] Her bound head and limbs bring her body into play in a very complex crossing of sexual fetishism and commodity fetishism. Djuna Barnes' photographs of herself being forcibly fed show that the prison doctors were in fact

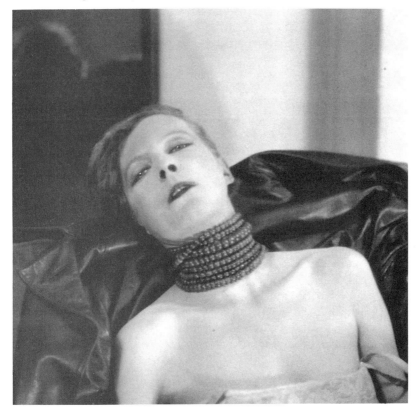

Fig. 3

Fig. 4

"raping" and violating the bodies of the hunger-striking suffragette women
political prisoners. But by choosing to be violated (and photographed in the
act, with all the paraphernalia of tubes and clamps invading the sheet-bound
body) in order to "feel what they felt," to vicariously experience the suffering
of the suffrage martyrs, Djuna Barnes, also a crusading reporter, calls into
play in 1917 a certain modernist high masochism which we are more used
to seeing in the works of male surrealists. It would be interesting to compare
the Barbara Ker-Seymer images with those of Man Ray which have become
classics. Both Barnes and Cunard put their bodies on the line, *exposed
themselves* in order to expose political evils. Photographs were weapons in
the struggle against sexism and racism for the women activist-reporters, but
they were also opportunities for erotic performance. The erotic performance
of pain of the victimization of blacks and women, slaves and sex objects,
may have allowed certain white women modernists empowerment through
fetishism.

The Ker-Seymer photograph shows Cunard (Fig. 4) lying uncomfortably
on a corrugated steel "bed," as if flung into the corner of a factory floor,

fully dressed, gazing with fear (and anticipation?) at an absent attacker, head bound, throat encircled with scarves, heavy ivory bracelets on both wrists. There is a particular kind of urban terror being invoked here, especially signalled by her large black glove, the melodramatic signifier of the murderer in the movies—is she both criminal and victim—caught in the act of stealing, perhaps, by an outraged employer—but just as easily an innocent victim grabbed on the street and thrown into a back corner of the Metropolis for who knows what purpose. Contradictory as the black leather glove is, the homeliness of the knitted leg-warmers above the elegant strapped and buckled pumps sends the viewer into further confusion. They, like the straps and bracelets and scarves, are about bondage. But what are these schoolgirl's skating socks doing with the figure's designer suit? They suggest that she is cold, has been there a long time, locked up. It is as if she is in prison in a modernist opera's set, a Lulu or Carmen in dancing shoes, exhausted after a steamy performance. Has a sympathetic warden smuggled in the home-made leg-warmers? Or do the stripes and straps and high-heeled shoes merely make her legs into a phallic fetish? Or like the heroine of *The Red*

Fig. 5

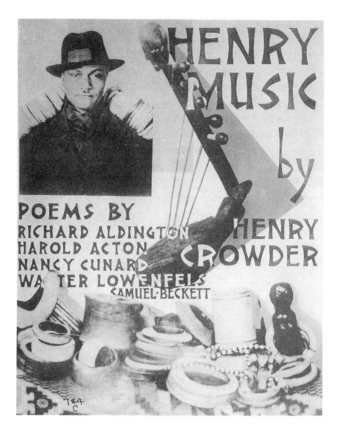

Fig. 6

Shoes, the woman artist in thrall to a puppet-master. The leg-warmers are incongruously homely and domestic, trading places with the corrugated steel "bed" on which she lies. The bed by rights should be soft and woolly like the leg-warmers, but shackles are supposed to be made of metal. As a series of substitutions, Ker-Seymer's picture places the white career-woman in the city at the scene of the crime. But Ker-Seymer refuses to tell us whether the woman is the victim or the perpetrator. They are uncanny in their staging of a certain gendered and classed homelessness.

Nancy Cunard (Fig. 5) certainly influenced museums to buy and display African art, to pay attention to primitivism. She was a walking advertisement for Pan-Africanism. She was a white signifier of "Black is Beautiful." The ivory bracelets which became her signature, worn from wrist to shoulder as a badge of exotic identification with African sexuality and power as well as of imprisonment, as reminders of the shackles of slaves and of the harem, were signs of the sincerity of her white negress act, however suspiciously the origins of the ivories and their cross-cultural meanings would now be regarded, however politically incorrect her seeming appropriations may appear. Visually her imprisoned arms retain their erotic charge. Though slaves died by the hundreds (and so did elephants) to satisfy the taste for ivory both inside Africa and in Europe, Asia, and America, Nancy Cunard's bracelets bound her like shackles to the history of slavery and the struggle for freedom. The ivory itself was a signature of her willing enslavement to the cause which she championed in her *Negro* anthology. It was—like her—off-white. How can one say that anyone's motives are pure? Or deny the agency Cunard earned by performing the bondage of blacks in dress, art, and sexual style as an aid to political bonding in the struggle against racism?

Her braceleted arms embrace the figure of Henry Crowder in Man Ray's brilliant collage for the cover of her 1930 Hours Press volume, *Henry-Music*. (Figs. 6 & 7) Her face does not appear. She stands behind her man in a form of simultaneous effacement and exhibitionism, saying "He is mine—but I'm not there." Part of her capture of Crowder, the jazz musician, consisted of insisting that he learn composition to write down his music, and she enlisted her friends Harold Acton, Richard Aldington, Walter Lowenfels and Samuel Beckett to produce poems to be set to his music. The

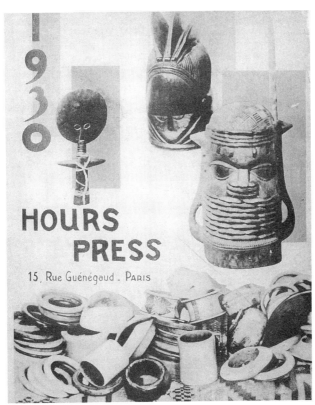

Fig. 7

essence of the style of Crowder's band, Eddie South and his Alabamians, was, of course, improvisation. One of the things that made it jazz was the difficulty of pinning it down. But she desperately wanted to capture all the energy of this dynamic music and "pin it down" to be passed on historically. So, in a way, *Henry-Music* is a rehearsal for the *Negro* anthology. Her own poem, "Equatorial Way," very much a part of '30s protest discourse, like her "Appeal for the Scottsboro Boys," seems to derive from the dramatic monologues of black poets. She writes in the voice of the redneck white sheriff, and one can sense her involvement with and adoption of techniques of black American folk and poetic forms. Like much angry black protest poetry of the period, "Equatorial Way" seems to anticipate rap. I read the poem in the Cunard Archives in Texas just as Ice-T announced that he would withdraw his song "Cop Killer" from his album and give it to his fans for free. The tradition in black culture which produced that song also produced Nancy Cunard's "Last advice to the crackers; Bake *your own* white meat—Last advice to the lynchers; Hang *your brother* by the feet."

EQUATORIAL WAY

For Henry

Not yet satisfied,
But I'll be satisfied
With the days I slaved for hopes,
Now I'm cuttin all the ropes—
Gettin in my due of dough
From [1] ofays that'll miss me so—
Go-ing . . . Go-ing . . .
Where the arrow points due south.

I dont mean your [2] redneck-farms,
I dont mean your [3] Jim-Crow trains,
I mean Gaboon—
I dont mean your cotton lands,
Ole-stuff coons in Dixie bands,
I've said Gaboon—
This aint no [4] white man's nigger
Nor was—but I've grown bigger
The further away from you
Further, longer away from you
My [5] cracker moon.

Doin my own stuff now,
Equator, Pole and Pole—
Fixin to board the prow

And let the Ocean roll and roll
And roll me over, even,
To where the Congo waters roll.

Wont take from the old lands
But twelve bottles of gin—
Wont leave on the old lands
But my cheque cashed in—
Then make clear to the Black Folks
They can't but win.

Goin to drink to the last damnation
Of the son o' bitch U.S.A.—
Goin to send for a conflagration
From down equatorial way—
Feelin kind just at this moment,
(Kind'a callin in my debts for pay.)

Last advice to the crackers:
Bake *your own* white meat—
Last advice to the lynchers:
Hang *your brother* by the feet.
One [6] sitting-pretty Black Man
Is a million-strong on heat.

Goin to beat up Fear on the octaves,
Tear the crackers limb from limb—
Goin to take on each-every vengeance,
Drum one blood-blasting hymn—
And laugh laugh LAUGH in the shadows
Louder'n Death—I'll be watching him.

Nancy Cunard, Henry Music, 1930

1—*Ofay;* white people
2—*Redneck;* appelation given
southern-states farmers, necks
scored by sun—petty tyrants.
3— *Jim-Crow trains;* in the southern
states no coloured person is
allowed in same compartment with
white people. A separate coach is
provided of which half is used for
baggage.

4—*White man's nigger;* A cringing or
dispirited Negro playing up to, i.e.
bullied by whites.
5—*Cracker;* southerners with violent
prejudice apt to explode.
6—*Sitting pretty;* lucky, well-placed, in
a good position.

Published by Wishart in London, the *Negro* anthology's printing was
paid for by Nancy Cunard herself, mostly from £1500 of legal fees earned

as a result of English newspapers' publication of slanderous stories from the American press connecting her with Paul Robeson while she was on her second research trip to Harlem in 1932.[9] It remains to be seen what role the United States and British governments had in these attacks. It is clear from her FBI file that spies in London reported to the United States on the preparation and publication of the *Negro* anthology. The censors intervened and insisted that René Crevel's "The negress in the Brothel," translated by Samuel Beckett, be removed from *Negro*. Undaunted, Cunard had the three pages set secretly by the radical Utopia Press and tipped them in while binding the volumes. The essay is not listed in the table of contents but is actually in the printed book—a reminder of her radical resourcefulness. She boasts of her conquest to Arthur Schomburg, but Hugh Ford apparently didn't notice this when he reprinted part of the anthology.[10] This subversive set of pages, significantly on black women's sexuality, there in the text but unmarked, surviving the censor in un-numbered pages, may serve as a sign of the suppressed referent of the *Negro* anthology itself, of Nancy Cunard's career as a white activist for the cause of black freedom, and this attempt to restore her to history as a producer of knowledge—the black woman's body. It increases the material value of the original volumes significantly to bibliophiles. And, unlike the resonance of the "blank page" in feminist critical discourse, it reminds us that along with the unwritten and unspoken, there is a great deal of cultural knowledge which was written but hidden, repressed, suppressed and forgotten, that the *Negro* anthology can be reinserted into cultural history.

"GONE NEGRO": THE FILES

Two of the U.S. State department files on Nancy Cunard have now been declassified, 800.00B Nancy Cunard, and 811.4016, Scottsboro. Secret Memorandum No. 1384 dated London, April 22, 1932, reports that Nancy Cunard has sailed to New York on the S.S. Albert Ballin and is now acting as intermediary between Ben Amis and a Negro Committee in New York and A. Ward of the Negro Welfare Association in London. Ben Amis was "one of the colored representatives" associated with Earl Browder and William Z. Foster on the National Executive Committee of the League of Struggle for Negro Rights. "This young woman has 'gone negro' in her sympathies and proclivities. She has been living at 18, rue Guénégaud, Paris, which she has made a sort of depot for negro 'art' and 'culture.' She has taken up both these and has been compiling a book about them. Politically she is now ultra-leftminded, and has been in touch with and furthering the interests of the League against Imperialism." Memo number 1388 says "this young lady gave orders to sell books and furniture in her negro shop in the rue Guénégaud and it is now closed. It is understood that her colored friend, Henry Crowder, preceded her to the United States." Other memos contain copies of her Scottsboro appeals and letters demanding that the passport of Ada Wright, mother of one of the Scottsboro Boys, who had been on a speaking tour in Europe, be revoked for "disloyalty," and inquiring about why Nancy Cunard, "British subject living among negroes" was allowed into the United States. Memorandum Number 1539, London, March 8, 1933, describes Cunard as widely known as a supporter of "negro . . . emancipation" and "concerned in the endeavor to set up a negro center in London."

The reporter has opinions: "There is now reason to believe that this young lady, owing to the stress of the times, no longer enjoys her former financial prosperity. She still proposes to bring out at her own expense and at the cost of some £600, the volume entitled *Negro*, on which she has been working, with colored collaboration, for some time, but it is thought that this is pretty well the last shot in her financial locker, at any rate for the present. Despite her financial situation, Miss Cunard appears to continue improvident and impenitent. She seems to be quite capable of sharing her last £10 with any organisation connected with the I.L.D."

In other files she is listed as "Nancy Cunard, Communist" and there are copies of letters to her from William Patterson of the International Labor Defence, regarding organizing in Britain, and especially colonial work. She gave "the negro Amis" $100 on April 4, 1933, for the Scottsboro case, from "collections made at dances, meetings etc. in England." Much remains to be done on these files on Cunard's work in England for the Scottsboro Defense and its part in the history of the British left's involvement in the struggle for black liberation.

THE *NEGRO* ANTHOLOGY

The book weighed eight pounds and had 250 pieces, including hundreds of photographs and illustrations. The oversized volume, a royal quarto on fine paper, the page measuring twelve by ten inches printed in Caslon Old Face type, is itself a semiotic signifier of both the dignity and gravity of the subject of international black culture(s). Hugh Ford's 1970 reprint (now out of print and also considered a rare volume, selling at $100) only covers half of a text which had 315 pages on Africa, an enormous section on America, the West Indies, the Carribean, and Latin America and a sixty-page section on Europe. This volume now brings $1,250 at Sotheby's or in the book trade if you can find a copy. The sections on African art, in particular and the long and detailed histories of slavery in various countries, as well as the naming and quoting and publishing of the works of black writers and political leaders, philosophers and rebels amount to an astonishing accomplishment. The book is an act of cultural work in its seriousness and international scope which is a tribute to Cunard's organizational and editing skills and the immense power of her own writing and research, as well as her ability to build international networks of scholars, historians, anthropologists, photographers, and poets to present this collective effort to the world.

Was it precisely because it was a collective effort that it has been lost to history? (Nancy Cunard's genius for collective efforts for the causes she believed in later extended to her Speak Outs of intellectuals' opinions, chapbooks of poems on the Spanish Civil War, and collections of poems for France in World War II.) We now often associate such monumental international cultural projects with feminism, as in the Arkin and Shollar *Longman's Anthology of Women Writers of the World,* which took ten years to prepare, or the massive Feminist Press volumes of the work of Indian women writers; but the *Negro* anthology is outstanding because it refuses to remain in the domain of art and ventures bravely (perhaps foolhardily) into politics, anthropology and history. People are suspicious of the motives of the organizers of such collective cultural efforts. But Nancy Cunard has not been accused of megalomania, merely of using the making of the anthology to work out her own exile from white Western culture.

Cunard did in fact enlist many people to help her, and Raymond Michelet is acknowledged for his assistance. Samuel Beckett, whom she is said to have "discovered" when she published his *Whoroscope* at the Hours Press, did many translations for the volume (and there is a faintly obscene echo of her name in *Waiting for Godot*). In sifting through what is left of her files and correspondence for the making of the volume (and what is left survived the fate of all her files used in the latrine and on the floor of her French village house when Nazi soldiers were billeted there) one is impressed by the sheer existence of her black literary and political networks all over the world. Holding these handmade scrapbooks in one's hand, the reader notes Cunard's pencilled reminders that the mud on these sheets came from Nazi boots, that much else was used as toilet paper or for target practice and that her famous collection of ivory bracelets was scattered in the nearby fields.

It is my opinion that Nancy Cunard was very much aware of the form of the anthology as cultural capital and that she produced a weighty and dignified tome with cultural market value in mind to participate in other economies driven by money and power as well as in the discourses and debates about race sparked by her fury at what she considered the neglect and denial of African art in the Colonial Exhibition in Paris in 1931. As a British subject (despite her exile in Paris) she was aware of the use of the anthology of poetry, especially Palgrave's *Golden Treasury,* as an instrument for the dissemination of ideology in the colonies, for insisting on the superiority of English culture to indigenous forms often constructed as the savage traces of all that was not culture or civilization. One thing Nancy Cunard strenuously opposed was the production of imitation Wordsworths all over the globe. What we now can see, sadly, is that the utopian production of such a cross-national tribute to black culture (we would now call this "multiculturalism") was practically meaningless if she could not secure the anthology's dissemination as well. The anthologies of English poetry were required reading in colonial schools all over Africa and India, cheaply printed and circulated widely, and people like us read and taught these works in the schools and colleges of the former colonies. Unless she could get the *Negro* anthology into those schools or into the hands of the readers who needed it, it was practically impossible to convince any but a handful of intellectuals (and some West Indian radicals who kept the banned book hidden under the bed during World War II) and those who had access to particular libraries that black culture was indeed culture and could, in fact, be compared to Wordsworth on its own terms. Instead it was banned in many African countries. The *Negro* anthology also got caught in the cross fire of local battles for cultural hegemony in Harlem, and Cunard herself seems to have been constructed as a white woman who steals black men or a frigid nymphomaniac with whom respectable black folks would not want to associate. The role of the FBI in savaging her reputation has yet to be determined, and the influence of agents or blackmail on friends is not to be underestimated. Friends of Langston Hughes have suggested to me that it was the combination of "communism" and unorthodox sexual practices which they shared which damaged the reputation of the book and its editor. Her witch status parallels that of Zora Neal Hurston, whose splendid essays inform the volume.

Or was the *Negro* anthology lost to history, basically ignored even though it was reprinted, because Cunard criticized W. E. B. Du Bois as well as publishing his essay? Because she wrote scornfully of the accommodationist NAACP and proclaimed for all to hear that the future of blacks everywhere was tied to the Communist Party? I suspect that the communist connection may be the real problem here, for although she published the works of all sides in her Harlem section, she marked the volume with the semiotic stamp of her left convictions, opening with "I, Too, Sing America," a Whitmanesque poem by the Langston Hughes, who like herself was not an actual member, but was very close to the Communist Party. She also opened the volume with Howard Lester's photograph picturing a black worker in a cap "An American Beast of Burden." She used her editorial privilege to mark her democratic inclusiveness by publishing articles she disagreed with and then disfiguring them with footnotes marking her differences with the author.

I suspect that Nancy Cunard's brilliant anthology (she first called it *Color*) was conceived as a work of propaganda for black liberation. She dedicated it to her lover, Henry Crowder, an Afro-American jazz pianist she met in Venice in the late 1920s, and claimed that by drawing her attention to the plight of blacks in the United States that he gave her life a purpose and shape. It is quite conceivable that this is true. Where the problem lies is in people's troubled and often hostile responses to her choice of cause and crusade. It is not possible for a white feminist in my position to claim the inaugural place for Nancy Cunard's *Negro* anthology that Alain Locke's *The New Negro,* a strictly artistic anthology of 1925, holds in Houston Baker's *Modernism and the Harlem Renaissance.* I may (and I shall) quote Alain Locke's letter to Cunard but my voice still does not have the authority of Houston Baker's. Whether the *Negro* anthology takes its place in cultural history will depend on whether or not black feminists take up Cunard's cause. Alain Locke's letter, dated April 14, 1934, begins as follows: "I congratulate you,—almost enviously, on the finest anthology in every sense of the word ever compiled on the Negro. When I saw the announcements, I feared a scrapbook, but by a miracle of arrangement, you have built up a unity of effect and a subtle accumulative force of enlightenment that is beyond all contradiction and evasion. . . . The serious analyses of Jazz by Antheil and Goffin are path breaking. You will have endless vindications in the years to come. Thanks for your discrimination in presenting my talented young friend, Zora Hurston."

A woman exile is an uncanny figure, I have argued elsewhere, for her very body means home and hearth; it signifies the womb/home of humankind. If a woman chooses homelessness, becomes a voluntary and even sometimes exultant exile, like Nancy Cunard, she frightens people. She certainly was a threat to "family values." She not only publicly repudiated her mother, her class and her country, Nancy Cunard never settled down, never made a home. Exile was her element and she exulted in it. For her home was where her press was, the instrument of her reaching the world with pleas for her political causes. Even before it was destroyed by the Nazis, her cottage in a Norman village near Paris was, to her friends, another example of her uncanny, unfeminine homelessness, a parody of the idea of home as a sanctuary for privacy. She had designed it while living with Louis Aragon, and it was a bizarre tribute to surrealism's radical attacks on home and family. One had to go through everyone's bedroom to get to the kitchen or common rooms, wrote Henry Crowder about Nancy's seduction of Michelet, the young French student who had run away from school and helped in the research for the anthology—under the very nose of her present lover, as it were. Women are supposed to be homemakers, and Nancy's restless wanderings, the very publicity of her life in the limelight or the cafe in the square made her seem unnatural. Her tragic death in Paris, drunk and raving lines from her last long poem pleading for world peace, was an exile's death.

Sometimes—in fact one might say all the time—she felt like a motherless child.

"A" TRAIN, CUNARD LINE

Working with modernism teaches one to wrestle with categories of periodization and geography as well as sexual identity and literary value. Accustomed as I was to challenging the hegemony of literary estates and biographers of writers from Virginia Woolf to Rebecca West, Djuna Barnes and Sylvia Townsend Warner, it was a shock to find that a healthy suspicion and a basic skepticism about received wisdom are equally necessary in reading (and believing) the biographers, autobiographers and literary historians of what is called the Harlem Renaissance. It seems obvious to me that naming the 1920s a renaissance constructs the 1930s and political activism as somehow anti-art. How can I reconstruct a modernist timeline which will highlight the publication of the *Negro* anthology in 1934? Working outside my field I find myself possessed with the mad desire to collate David Levering Lewis' *When Harlem Was in Vogue* with Mark Naison's *Communists in Harlem During the Depression*. I am confused by the marginalization of Nancy Cunard in odd footnotes and peculiar sideways citations in the lives of people like Langston Hughes and Claude McKay, who seem so central to her life in the period. As I work in the Cunard papers, I do not make copies of Langston Hughes' poems, expecting that they can be found in his *Collected Poems* in the library. But what am I to make of the fact that there is no volume of Langston Hughes' *Collected Poems* in the library? There are two separate but not equal volumes, one is "selected" and the other is marked "revolutionary." I read the biography. Langston Hughes, who figures in Cunard's life as a brother radical, a Communist Party fellow traveler like herself, a lifelong close friend and comrade whom she met in Paris, in the Soviet Union, in Harlem, and above all in Spain in the struggle against fascism, the Langston Hughes who was also the friend of her Latin-American radical writer friends, the Langston Hughes who shows up smiling with his arms around the comrades in her photo albums, the Langston Hughes I had assumed from his letters to her and her attitude to be homosexual like most of the men in her circles. This dynamic modernist figure is written out of history. By himself? By his literary estate? By the biographer who calls this lively, lusty figure asexual? In whose interest is Langston Hughes being de-sexed and whitewashed?[12]

Not only did I assume that homosexuality was part of the Hughes persona but that he and Claude McKay were linked to European modernists through some of the people in Cunard's gay radical circles. I also thought it would be an interesting problem in gay history to open that folder on writers and the Spanish Civil War in Cunard's papers at the Humanities Research Center to think about the relation between radicalism, race and homosexuality in the context of the Spanish Civil War. I am struck here with the tremendous gap between modernism as I was taught it and the modernism I teach. In that folder is W. H. Auden's handwritten copy of "Spain," along with Nancy Cunard's typescript for her volume, a typescript which is full of mistakes because she had trouble reading his handwriting. This is the poem Auden repudiated when he named the '30s that "low dishonest decade." It appears that he only sent the poem at the insistence of his and Nancy's mutual friend, Brian Howard. Are we to believe that Langston Hughes' heart was not in his poems for Spain either? Perhaps the 1990s is another low dishonest decade.

I am learning that it is necessary to chart these cultural journeys in both directions, to figure out whether or not we can get from here to there or from there to here. My questions began blithely with Nancy Cunard's exile from England. What would happen if one tried to take the Cunard line to Harlem, I asked. Does the "A" train still travel "express" to Paris? The historical problems are centered on recuperations of the aesthetics and politics of the '30s, not at the century's temporal extreme but always placed at the cultural extreme in a dualist dynamic which insists on setting up art and politics as natural enemies. Nancy Cunard's work as a poet, as an avant-garde publisher of the Hours Press (where she discovered Samuel Beckett and published Pound's *Cantos* and the work of many other major modernists), as the editor of the *Negro* anthology (1934), which I am claiming is the monumental internationalist forerunner of all our current work in cultural studies, as the organizer of several volumes of artists speaking out on the Spanish Civil War, as author of the *Scottsboro Appeal* and *Black Man, White Ladyship* and of a major contribution as a journalist for the Associated Negro Press reporting the Geneva meetings on Ethiopia, race issues in World War II and African questions through the '50s—has fallen through the cracks of several different maps of modernism in which one would expect to find her foregrounded. What are the reasons for this?

As one maps out any subject for inquiry, a center and periphery develop. If I examine my own process, will I be able to explain the cultural and historical processes which have denied Nancy Cunard recognition as a major intellectual and political figure of the twentieth century? *Why* is Nancy Cunard an embarrassment in black modernism or never mentioned at all when one could claim the *Negro* anthology as the inaugurating effort in claiming an African-American culture? The answers are not simple. But if I compare, for example, what feminists name and work against as the dominant texts, either as works of art or criticism, with those Houston Baker challenges in *Modernism and the Harlem Renaissance* or James De Jongh names in *Vicious Modernism: Black Harlem and the Literary Imagina-*

tion, there appears to be little agreement on what is hegemonic. One can say that white male modernisms, from the "Pound Era" to the "Auden Generation," include one white woman artist as monster—Woolf or Stein or Amy Lowell. When feminists have rewritten these narratives, as in Shari Benstock's *Women of the Left Bank,* Gilbert and Gubar's *No Man's Land,* or Bonnie Scott's *The Gender of Modernism,* new categories and paradigms emerge as in the subject of the sex war, "Sapphic modernism," or expatriate women writers. Race remains peripheral in many of these new modernisms as well (despite good intentions), and one of the critical or historical solutions for scholars has been to study What Has Been Left Out separately—engendering ethnic modernism in the United States, for instance, or looking at race as part of the passion for primitivism in European modernisms. But nothing seems to change in the way elite institutions teach an elite culture of "high" modernist texts and writers—women or blacks or gays or Chicanos may form alternative canons but never enter into or mess up the existing order of now "classic" texts and writers. They're "it." Everyone else is read and judged around or in relation to these texts. They may be allowed to form a separate order in themselves or in relation to one another.

Coming to Harlem via the Cunard Line in the '30s, I have different expectations and different cultural baggage than if I were coming to avant-garde Paris on the "A" train. But I already know that I would be allowed to write certain narratives about Nancy Cunard. In fact, I sketched out these familiar plots before writing this version of my tale. Nancy Cunard has been constructed as a nymphomaniac in order to explain her affairs with black men. This has called into question simultaneous claims that Cunard was an important radical intellectual and cultural historian. Even the category "nymphomaniac" only signifies heterosexual activity, though it becomes clear in cross-readings that Cunard had lesbian affairs, slept with younger men, older men, homosexuals, sailors, boxers, and appears to have been a third in some lesbian relationships. In Shari Benstock's *Women of the Left Bank,* Nancy Cunard is recuperated for a vision of radical modernism which stresses the vision of the Hours Press and her brave and committed journalism for Republican Spain. Benstock points out Richard Aldington's disgust at Cunard's publication of *Black Man, White Ladyship* and his creation of her repudiation of her class as a dangerous form of Bohemian eccentricity in a caricature short story called "Now She Lies There": "Its 'hysterical relish'," Benstock writes, "constitutes a stronger, more virulent form of an underlying assumption that women of a certain social class and economic background discovered in the expatriate experience a means of open rebellion against their families and a method of killing time" (*Women of the Left Bank,* 393).

Among Benstock's avant-garde expatriate women publishers, patrons, poets, journalists and editors on the Left Bank in the '20s and '30s, Cunard's left-wing politics, her commitment to the cause of blacks and the Spanish Civil War differentiate her from the surrealist fellow travelers whom she enlisted as allies in terms of her very seriousness. But, we ask, what is it that kept them (and us?) from a recognition of her seriousness, her intense hard work as a researcher and reporter and writer? Is it that her cause was not the enfranchisement of her own sex but rather the recognition of the claims of a whole downtrodden race across national lines and boundaries?

Lady Cunard's salon, un-Bohemian as it seems now, was a novelty in its day, and her unconventionality was protected by a cover-marriage. In some ways Nancy's outrageous artistic circles were extensions of her mother's social practices—she published in Edith Sitwell's collection *Wheels* and Virginia Woolf published her brilliant poem *Parallax* at the Hogarth Press in 1925; her 1921 poems were titled *Outlaws* and at the Hours Press she published surrealists, homosexuals and radicals from Louis Aragon to Laura Riding, Havelock Ellis to Brian Howard. But, as Claude McKay wrote to her from Tangier after his house and belongings had been destroyed by what he thought was the British Secret Service or International Police, it was one thing to stick to championing black arts and artists. Once she advocated political action for racial justice as in her international appeal for the Scottsboro Boys and publicly associated herself and the black cause with the Communist Party, she was bound to be hounded by the Yellow Press and bombarded with tons of sexually explicit hate mail (or hate-MALE as one of her American radical friends called it when he wrote from Max Eastman's Dutchess County farm that he had burned a bushel of it).

McKay was worried about how the adverse publicity would affect the reception of the *Negro* anthology, and yet the outside pressures on him succeeded in alienating him from Nancy and claiming in his memoirs that he did not contribute because she refused to pay him—when no one was paid for their collective work.

There is a great deal of work to be done on the history of the making of the *Negro* anthology and all of Nancy Cunard's writing on race. Nancy Cunard's route out of the hypocrisy and racism of her class is not to be easily dismissed. One cannot despise a woman who devoted herself to the cause of black liberation. Sex and race are dangerous subjects and very complex, especially when tangled in a woman's political life, as she and her friends lived and as we read their lives.

Where does my partisanship come from, I ask myself, realizing with a shock that black culture, politics, and music were my own route out of the stifling, Irish working-class Catholic school world of my youth. As Nancy Cunard claimed that when she was six years old she dreamed of blacks dancing and of herself joining the dance, and somehow knowing the steps, earning the eternal suspicion of biographers and critics, I'll have to risk saying it.

From the Jazz Priest Father O'Connor's Sunday afternoon Teenage Jazz Club sessions at Storyville, to surreptitious trips to clubs in Roxbury, hiding my school uniform under my trench coat, I came to the politics of race through music. Later, during the struggle for civil rights, I worked with my future husband teaching in freedom schools in Roxbury. We named one son for Malcolm X. This narrative has been suppressed in our family legends. The story has been the "how I became a feminist" story. It would be very interesting if it were true that like other white women from Aphra Behn to Virginia Woolf, I developed the sense of agency for a feminist identity through black culture and the struggle for civil rights.

NOTES

I am grateful to Dean Paul Sherwin and City College of New York for grants supporting the travel and research for this work. My interest in Nancy Cunard began in the Gender and Modernism Seminar at the University of Texas in 1990 with Holly McSpadden, who went on to write an M.A. thesis on Cunard. It began to focus more clearly in 1991 discussions with Christine Stansell on my concept of the politics of *Low Modernism* for the 1993 Berkshire Women's History Conference. The work of Mae Henderson, Hortense Spillers, and my daughter Lisa Marcus, has been crucial to the formation of my ideas.

Cunard's papers are at the Harry Ransome Humanities Research Center at the University of Texas, and I am grateful to manuscript librarians Cathy Henderson and Ken Craven. My thanks to Mr. A. R. A. Hobson for permission to quote from her papers and published work and to the Humanities Research Center, University of Texas, for permission to quote materials in its possession; my thanks as well to the staff of the HRC Photography Collection for their valuable help and permission to use the photographs. I am grateful to Cheryl Fish for research on the Cunard papers in the Arthur A. Schomburg Collection. Thanks to Michele Wallace and my students and colleagues at CUNY for responding to a version of this paper at "What Was the Twentieth Century?" in November 1992; to Sabena Broëck at the Institut fur England-und Amerikastudien, J.W. Goethe University, Frankfurt and her colleagues in the Women's Studies Seminar, April, 1993, the Women and Writing Seminar and the Social Anthropology Gender Seminar at Cambridge University and the London Modernism Seminar. A version was also given at Warwick, March, 1994, "The Politics of Identity, Secular Criticism and the Gravity of History."

1. Letter in *TLS*, July 5, 1991.

2. This essay marks the beginning of a larger project on Nancy Cunard and race. Nancy Cunard, editor, *Negro: An Anthology*. London: Wishart, 1934. Hugh Ford published an edited and abridged version. N.Y.: Ungar, 1970. See also Ford's edited volume, *Nancy Cunard: Brave Poet, Indomitable Rebel, 1896–1965*, which includes many memoirs and interviews with her friends. Philadelphia: Chilton, 1968. She first published in Edith Sitwell's *Wheels: An Anthology of Verse*. London: Longmans, Green, 1916. Cunard's published work includes *Outlaws*. London: Elkin Matthews and Marrot, 1921; *Sublunary*. London: Hodder and Stoughton, 1923; *Parallax*. London: Hogarth, 1925; *Black Man, White Ladyship: An Anniversary*. London: Utopia, 1931; editor *Authors Take Sides on the Spanish Civil War*. London: *Left Review*, 1937; with George Padmore, *The White Man's Duty*. London: W. H. Allen, 1943; *Men-Ship-Tank-Plane*. London: New Books, 1944; editor, *Poems from France*. Paris: La France Libre,

1944; *Grand Man: Memories of Norman Douglas.* London: Secker and Warburg, 1954; *G.M.: Memories of George Moore.* London: Rupert Hart-Davies, 1956; *These Were the Hours.* Carbondale: Southern Illinois UP, 1966. Her numerous essays and an immense amount of journalism have not been collected. The biography is by Anne Chisholm. *Nancy Cunard.* New York: Knopf, 1979; she is also discussed in Shari Benstock, *Women of the Left Bank: Paris 1900–1940.* Austin: University of Texas Press, 1986; and Susan Friedman in Bonnie Kime Scott, ed. *The Gender of Modernism.* Bloomington: Indiana University Press, 1990, 63–68, and Sabine Broeck, "Do White Ladies Get the Blues?" in *IEAS Women's Studies Newsletter,* No. 2, April, 1992, Frankfurt.

   3. *Subject to Others: British Women Writers and Colonial Slavery, 1670–1834.* New York, N.Y.: Routledge, 1992.

   4. See James Clifford, *The Predicament of Culture: Twentieth Century Ethnography, Literature and Art.* Cambridge, Mass.: Harvard University Press, 1988, and *Writing Culture: The Poetics and Politics of Ethnography,* eds. James Clifford and George E. Marcus. Berkeley: University of California Press, 1986; Michel Leiris, *Manhood: A Journey from Childhood to the Fierce Order of Virility,* trans. Richard Howard, Forward by Susan Sontag. Chicago: University of Chicago Press, 1984; Michel Leiris, *Journal 1922–1989,* ed. Jean Jamin. Paris: Gallimard, 1993.

   5. See Henry Crowder, *As Wonderful as All That?* Henry Crowder's Memoir of his Affair with Nancy Cunard 1928–1935 (with the assistance of Hugo Speck). Introduction and Epilogue by Robert L. Allen. (Navarro, California: Wild Trees Press, 1987). The typescript of this peculiar volume is now (1992) in the Humanities Research Center at the University of Texas. Ernest B. Speck, Emeritus Professor of English in Alpine, Texas, gave the unpublished manuscript to Allen after the death of his brother, a white journalist based in Paris in the 1930s for Universal News Service and Paris correspondent for *Variety.* They speculate that the book was not published for fear of a libel suit from Lady Cunard. My own hunch is that Speck took the disillusioned Crowder under his wing and produced the "as-told-to autobiography" as part of an effort to discredit Nancy's Left politics. The book is badly written but not consistently badly written; that is, it may have been produced by more than one author. Her FBI file shows that she was watched closely by British and American intelligence. The production of the *Negro* anthology was clearly viewed as subversive and its progress was reported. Without claiming that there was a conspiracy at work here, one may speculate on the extent of the perceived threat involved in the circulation of Negro poetry and history by a leftist. Letters in Texas from Claude McKay in North Africa about his contribution to the volume include descriptions of being watched and his house being destroyed by intelligence agents. These enthusiastic letters introducing her to his friends and family in the West Indies are hard to square with the portrait he paints later in his memoirs of a grasping white woman who refused to pay him for his contributions to the volume (when he knew that nobody was paid). I believe that Henry Crowder had a story to tell and that Speck helped him to tell it. What we don't know is who may have encouraged Speck to produce this slander on the reputation of Nancy Cunard. Harassment by intelligence agents and the collection of information on the sex lives of radicals was routine practice. The extent to which it may have been used against black poets like Langston Hughes remains to be seen. Henry Crowder's language justifying his attack on his ex-lover. He says he "owes it to (his) race" to "disclose all of the sordid details" because of "the dangerous and sometimes harmful nature of her activities." Right. Dangerous activities. He hopes the story may be of some value to colored men who become enamored with white women.

   6. Val Williams, *The Other Observers: Women Photographers in Britian 1900 to the Present.* London: Virago, 1991. The curator of the Photography Collection at the Humanities Research Center at the University of Texas identified many of these photographs as by Barbara Ker-Seymer. I am grateful for her help.

   7. See the catalogue *Alone in a Crowd: Prints of the 1930s–40s by African-American Artists.*

From the Collection of Reba and Dave Williams. American Federation of Arts, 1993. The lynching theme is represented very powerfully as a hanging tree with a waiting noose in the background of Charles White's "Hope for the Future," a 1947 portrait of a black madonna and child, p. 24, and in Elizabeth Catlett's "Mother and Child" (1946), p. 25.

8. See the introduction to my *Suffrage and the Pankhursts*. London: Routledge, 1987; and "Laughing at Leviticus: *Nightwood* as Woman's Circus Epic" in *Silence and Power: Djuna Barnes, a Revaluation*, ed. Mary Lynn Broe. Carbondale: University of Southern Illinois Press, 1991, 221–251; and "The Asylums of Antaeus; Women, War and Madness: Is There a Feminist Fetishism?" in *Feminism and Critical Theory: The Difference Within*, eds. Elizabeth Meese and Alice Parker. Amsterdam and Philadelphia: John Benjamins, 1988, pp. 49–81.

9. Further materials, typescripts of some articles, etc. for the *Negro* anthology are in the archives of the Atlanta University Center, Robert W. Woodruff Library. My thanks to Minnie H. Clayton for her help in locating them.

10. Nancy Cunard's correspondence with Arthur A. Schomburg is in the Archives of the Schomburg Center for Research in Black Culture branch of the New York Public Library (Microfilm R2798, reels 2, 6 and 10); thanks to Betty Odulashian for help in finding materials. My thanks to Lois Overbeck, associate editor of the Beckett letters, who also noticed that the essay on the "Negress in the Brothel" by René Crevel was not listed in the Table of Contents of *Negro* but had been separately printed and bound into the text without pagination.

11. One of the curators at the Humanities Research Center at the University of Texas told my class that the Hate Mail had included envelopes full of lead printers' slugs with no stamps on them. The receiver was supposed to pay for the postage. The vilification of the press, the lies and fabrications about a white woman who stayed in Harlem in the Grampion Hotel, deserves further study. The hate mail which the press outcry generated also should be looked at as a literary genre. The letters are predictable in their pornographic wishes for Nancy; their death threats and bad sexual puns on her name often come from those who sign themselves members of the Ku Klux Klan. Obviously presidents and movie stars and public figures of all kinds must receive a great deal of hate mail, but to my knowledge hate mail has not been studied as a literary genre. One of the most disturbing of these letters in the Humanities Research Center collection comes from someone who styles himself "Master of one of the fine steel monsters of the deep," a Cunard Line ship. He says he would sink the ship if she were on it, how could she sink so low, and so on. Nancy Cunard kept a batch of these letters and sometimes read them aloud to friends in later years, trying to figure out the psychology of the letter writers.

12. See Scott Braverman, "Isaac Julien's *Looking For Langston:* Hughes, Biography and Queer(ed) History," *Cultural Studies*, vol. 7, no. 2, May 1993, 311–323. For an alternative view than the biography's radical politics in Hughes' life, especially his struggles against fascism in Spain, see Cunard's *Three Negro Poets, Left Review*, vol 3, no. 9, 1937, 529–536, which includes the text of Hughes' speech before the Second International Writers' Congress in Paris. A student gave me a description from a bookseller's catalogue of a presentation copy of *Fine Clothes to the Jew* inscribed "For Havelock Ellis, with deep admiration, these songs and poems of a simple people. Sincerely Langston Hughes, Lincoln University, March 10, 1927." Included in the volume, which is offered at $1,500.00, is a letter to the sexologist, dated April 14, 1927, thanking him for his comments and for his own work: "Your books (the ones I've been able to get and read) have meant much to me. I feel that they have helped me better see and understand life."

2.

In Exile in the Mother Tongue: Yiddish and the Woman Poet

KATHRYN HELLERSTEIN

[Editor's note: the poems discussed in Kathryn Hellerstein's essay appear on pages 85 through 99]

A Jewish woman writing poetry in Yiddish during the first half of the twentieth century, at the very moment when she was moving from Eastern Europe to America, could be described as an exile, in exile, in the mother tongue.[1] As a Jew living *in goles* (the traditional Jewish term for the Diaspora), the woman was part of the historical exile of the Jewish people from the Land of Israel, that is, the geographical dispersion and the spiritual exile. Her native language, Yiddish, called colloquially by its speakers *mame-loshn*, mother tongue, was the cultural paradigm of that historical exile, a language that migrated with the Jews, first from Western to Eastern Europe, in the late Middle Ages, and then to America, in the late nineteenth century. And insofar as the woman's actual home was, say, Eastern Europe, when she emigrated to America, she went into still another, more personal exile, and not infrequently wrote, or dreamed of writing, poems about her new dispersion in Yiddish, that language in perpetual exile.

And her exile did not stop here. She was also caught in a convoluted cultural exile. Wherever she was, when she wrote in Yiddish, this poet was cut off from readers and writers in the culture of her host country—in Eastern Europe, Poland or Russia, and in America—and its native language. These majority cultures might seem to offer a Yiddish poet a true home, a cosmopolitan refuge for secular spirituality. Yet Yiddish poetry could not live there; it was hardly known to exist. Although Yiddish poets were often versed in Russian, Polish, and German literature, few writers in those languages read or spoke Yiddish.

At the same time, a woman writing secular Yiddish poetry was exiled—to use the word more figuratively—from the inner culture of traditional Judaism. It is undeniable that women have always been an integral part of Jewish life and values. Because traditional Jewish law governs every detail of daily life, from food preparation to observance of holidays to child-rearing to marital relations—those domains of the female—women observing these laws have ensured that Judaism is transmitted and survives into the next generation. Yet, as the law was practiced in Eastern Europe, traditional Judaism literally placed women behind the *mekhitse* or screen in the synagogue, banished their prayers from the *minyan*—the quorum of men needed for public prayer—and muffled women's voices, preventing them from fully participating in the liturgical ceremony held in the high, sacred language of Hebrew.

In this figurative sense, traditional Judaism might be said to have exiled women from the *loshn-koydsh*, the Sacred Tongue, from Hebrew and Aramaic, the languages of the Bible and the Talmud. The system of education that made virtually all Jewish boys, throughout all regions and from all social strata, literate to some degree in Hebrew and Aramaic generally excluded Jewish girls. Daughters in some wealthy families may have learned Hebrew from a private tutor or a doting father, and some very exceptional girls taught themselves Hebrew. But according to the cultural norms of a millennium, the women's domain was the vernacular language of Yiddish. Girls or women who had learned the letters of the alphabet could read Yiddish. And together with their mothers, they read in Yiddish the large body of devotional literature—suppticatory prayers, translation-adaptations of the Bible, and sermons—that had been composed for their edification. If they could not read, then they listened to their more literate sisters read to them.[2]

In order to make her voice heard in the larger community, however, a modern woman Yiddish poet literally had to remove herself from the women's section. She had to transpose the language of women's private prayers into the poetry of modern Yiddish literature. Again, one might think that in this modern, even modernist, literature, the woman Yiddish poet would at last have found a home for herself. But, in fact, despite the program of equality and freedom officially advocated by the fathers of modern Yiddish literature,[3] a woman poet found herself not in the mainstream of the Yiddish literary culture, but pushed onto its margins.

The reasons for the woman poet's predicament are complicated. Partly they lie in the history of the cultural movement that established Yiddish literature as a secular, modern, and essentially male entity. In the 1860s, proponents of the Haskalah, the Jewish Enlightenment, which in Eastern Europe was the main vehicle for secularizing and modernizing Jewish life for the betterment of the Jews' political, economic, and social conditions, discovered that the dominant language of Jewish literacy, Hebrew, which was frozen in the formulations of the Bible and the rabbis, was an ineffective medium for spreading new ideas to the Jewish masses. As these Haskalah authors began to write didactic fiction in Yiddish, they sought to excise from their works any connotation of what was, in fact, the largest body of previous Yiddish writings, namely, the devotional works "for girls, women, and ignorant men," (as the title pages for many such books proclaimed), which had been printed profusely since the sixteenth century. Thus, even as Yiddish became a language of worldly literature, for the Haskalah writers and their successors—the Labor Poets in the 1890s and the moderns of the early 1900s—it still retained a taint which was identified with being female and ignorant.

Although its proponents acknowledged Yiddish as a treasury of the folk imagination, and while Yiddishists declared it the locus of hope for the Jewish nation, as an alternative to Zionism (at the Czernowicz Yiddish Conference of 1908), Yiddish writers themselves tended to view their own language with a sexually charged ambivalence. On the one hand, the formulation *mame-loshn* (literally, mother tongue) took hold in the early twentieth century, when immigration and assimilation seemed to justify a nostalgia for one's own native language. This locution, with its homey, Germanic *mame* and eloquent, Hebraic *loshn*, embodies the hybrid etymology of Yiddish, that new entity born when the intimate mother embraced the articulate tongue of patriarchy. A repository for both the old culture and the new nationalism, *mame-loshn*'s positive femaleness protected and preserved Jewishness in the flux of modern change. Yet, the gendered strength of *mame-loshn* was disempowered, deracinated, even exiled from women's minds and words. Although no exact origin for the term is known, the foremost historian of Yiddish, Max Weinreich, unblinkingly attributed it to an archetypal Jewish boy, who presumably learned Jewish legends in Yiddish from his mother and Biblical/rabbinic texts in Hebrew from his father. Even the eighteenth- and nineteenth-century precursors, the loftier *muter-loshn* and *mutershprakh*, come from male-directed ideologies of Jewish peoplehood.[4] On the other hand, when the so-called grandfather of modern Yiddish literature, Sh. Y. Abramovitsh, popularly known by his pen name Mendele the Bookpeddler, explained why he had turned from Hebrew to Yiddish, he used what the critic Dan Miron calls "a highly suggestive analogy," and depicted Yiddish as the Biblical harlot, "a strange woman." Her bastard children were the earlier Yiddish writings, which Abramovitsh legitimated when he "wedded" himself to the language. "In short," Miron writes, "Abramovitsh conceived of his resort to Yiddish as a promiscuous affair redeemed by marriage and by orderly procreation."[5]

Personifying Yiddish as female, male authors expressed the desire to dominate and suppress that aspect of the language.[6] They extended their ambivalence about their en-gendered language to their female colleagues, the women who also had come under the influence of the Enlightenment and who, by the end of the nineteenth century, were writing Yiddish poetry (and some prose) in a secular mode. Although powerful literary men like I. L. Peretz and Sholem Aleichem encouraged and published young women authors, a residual prejudice lingered in the ways works by women were read. Possibly, Yiddish poems written by women were still too strong a reminder of the old-fashioned, "female" aspects of the Yiddish language that the worldly moderns attempted to appropriate and transform. But whatever the reason, male poets and literary critics only grudgingly acknowledged writing by women. Much more frequently, they dismissed it.[7]

To be sure, any man writing modern poetry in Yiddish—rooted in the Diaspora—also inevitably alienated himself from the old Hebraic tradition and all its religious laws and ways, as well as from the Hebrew-centered nationalist movement, Zionism. But a woman writing modern poetry in Yiddish had already been excluded from that mainstream of Judaism. She had to define her poetry against both the Yiddish devotional culture of women and the Hebraic culture of traditional Judaism. She was also chastised by her male colleagues to distance herself from so-called female literary patterns and conform to male poetic standards, at which she was doubly bound to fail.[8] By choosing to write poetry in Yiddish, she placed herself in a web of exclusion that exiled her self in the world at large and her gender and language within Judaism.

No woman Yiddish poet exemplifies this multiple exile better than Kadya Molodowsky. Perhaps the most prolific and influential of all the women poets, Molodowsky was born in 1894 in the shtetl of Bereza Kartuskay, White Russia, and died in 1975, in New York City. As a young woman, she lived in Kiev and later in Warsaw, where she taught in the secular Yiddish schools. Her first three books of poems, published in Warsaw and Vilna between 1927 and 1935, won critical notice, although her poems for children established her literary reputation. In 1935, she left Europe for the United States, where she settled in New York. There, she published four books of poetry, a novel, plays, short stories, essays, and journalism. She helped found and edit the literary journal *Svive*, which first appeared in 1943–44 and later from 1955 to 1974. In 1971, Molodowsky received the Itsek Manger Prize, the most prestigious award in the world of Yiddish letters.

Although accomplished and successful, Molodowsky was always a poet of exile. In her first book of poems, *Kheshvndike nekht* (Nights of Heshvan), published in Vilna in 1927, she described the struggle of an enlightened young woman, like herself at odds with the traditions of her maternal ancestors, yet unable or unwilling to shake loose from them. The best of all these early poems, the sequence "Froyen-lider" (Women-Poems), figures

the ambivalent spiritual exile of a Yiddish woman poet in a pattern of
Hebraic diction against which the Germanic syntax of the Yiddish struggles.[9]
Yet only in the poems she wrote in the 1930s did Molodowsky finally
develop a poetics of displacement. In her third book, *Freydke*, and her
fourth, *In land fun mayn gebeyn* (In the Country of My Bones), published
immediately before and after her immigration to America in the middle of
that decade, Molodowsky's poems began to evolve from an explicit narrative
treatment of exile to a submerged semiotic system, in which the very elements
of language—words and letters—became fragmented signs of the poet's
exile. This disintegration of *mame-loshn*, the medium in which the poet,
the woman, the immigrant/exile, and the Jew find a single expression, marks
the matrix of what Jane Marcus calls, comparing Virginia Woolf and Walter
Benjamin, "their radical homelessness as woman and Jew."[10] The radical
homelessness of this particular Jewish woman is compounded and complicated in Molodowsky's progressive self-exile from the coherence of her
mother tongue.

The title poem of Molodowsky's 1935 book *Freydke* is a *poeme*, a sixteen-
part narrative. Freydke is the poem's heroine, a Jewish woman who, by
peddling eggs in Warsaw, supports herself and her young daughter, Reyzl.
Although her name means "joy," Freydke is the archetype of grim, Jewish
survival amid poverty. Capable, strong, intelligent, Freydke, the poet tells
us, could have been a sailor, an astronomer, a builder, but, caught up daily
among "Hundreds of thousands and thousands of steps, / Uncounted, /
Uncautious, / Spilling onto the street," she is bound to her basket of fragile
eggs and to her tattered wallet with its few copper pennies. While the
wallet, "A legacy passing from father to children," represents the communal
poverty, it is also a disgraceful mark of identity, "Like the medieval patches
of yellow,"[11] and thus an emblem of Jewish exile and endless geographical
displacements. Freydke herself, though, is not going farther than the street,
where she sells eggs door-to-door.

In the course of her daily peddling, Freydke encounters the gamut of
Jewish religious and political pieties within Warsaw; yet among her custom-
ers, Freydke remains an outsider, and she has always been one, as the
poem's narrator recounts her history. A recent arrival in Warsaw from
Vilna, Freydke initially worked in a sweatshop, until she and her fellow
workers, all women, were locked out by the shop's greedy owner. Faced
with poverty, Freydke turned to peddling eggs while her closest friend,
Sheyndl Kanerey, whose name literally means "Pretty Canary," was de-
ported from Poland for leading a strike and took illegal refuge in France.
The heart of the poem contrasts Freydke's economic travails in Warsaw
with Sheyndl's fugitive life in Paris as the archetypal political exile. Separated
from her husband, who, like Sheyndl, was expelled first from Poland and
then from Paris, Freydke, at home in Warsaw, is estranged and entrapped.

This quick summary barely does justice to the poem's rich and nuanced narrative and, especially, its vivid portrait of the life of a Jewish woman exiled within the economy of the 1930s Jewish community in Warsaw by dint of her politics, her class, and her gender. Freydke's choices are limited: either she can remain an economic exile at home or, like her friend Sheyndl and her husband, become a fugitive abroad. The poem suggests that there is only little difference between these two states of exile. Writing this poem in a didactic mode, Molodowksy used Freydke as an example to expose the predicament of young working-class Jews, and especially women. Although its program is more subtle than most political poetry of the day, "Freydke" calls out for political and social reform.

Lest one think, however, that this poem was in any way autobiographical, it is important to note that Molodowsky herself wrote it from a position of relative personal security. A schoolteacher by profession, not a factory worker,[12] she had a steady salary, even if it was so small that she was obliged to hold two positions simultaneously—teaching Yiddish in a Bundist school[13] in the mornings and Hebrew in a Jewish community school in the evenings.[14] And while she closely observed the poverty of Jewish Warsaw through her students' eyes,[15] Molodowsky herself was hardly in desperate straits. Married to an intellectual, the historian Shimke Lev, and without children, she early on enjoyed a good measure of literary success. Her first book of poems had been published by a prestigious Vilna house, B. Kletskin, and was well received. Her second book, children's poems, *Geyen shikhelekh avek, vu der velt hot nor an ek: mayselekh* (Little Shoes Walk Away, to Where the World Will End One Day), published in 1931, was awarded a cash prize by the Jewish community of Warsaw and the Yiddish Pen Club.[16] And her third book of poems, *Dzshike gas* (Dzshike Street) had just been published, in 1933.

Given these facts, why would Molodowsky have written the dismal story of Freydke? Partly, no doubt, it was the desire to be *engagé*, to participate in the causes of the day, which was one of the strongest and most strongly male conventional duties that Yiddish poets, particularly of the Labor Poets school, felt an obligation to assume, if only to expose the injustices and despair of the Jewish masses.

There may, however, be a deeper reason. It is possible to read "Freydke" as a kind of allegory for the Yiddish woman poet's exile. Both Freydke, the joyless working-class woman in Warsaw, and Sheyndl Kanerey, the songbird in exile abroad, may be seen as figures for the woman poet. In Freydke and in the image of Freydke's basket of eggs, Molodowsky conflates the exiles of gender and class. Locked out of the sweatshop, the woman worker resorts to selling eggs, which are, of course, a product of female sexuality, a source of nourishment, and a promise of procreation, even a hint of rebirth (particularly in Jewish folklore), but also a symbol for a woman's poems. In the

Yiddish world, poems by women were regarded as the products of feminine sexuality by male critics, who often praised and blamed women's writing with metaphors of courtship, intercourse, and childbirth.[17] Indeed, Molodowsky herself had brilliantly appropriated and subverted the patriarchal sources for this trope in her early sequence of poems, "Froyen-lider" (Women-Poems),[18] some eight years before.

At the time she was composing "Freydke," Molodowsky may have felt the female sexual associations attached to women's poetry painfully driven home to her by male critics. In her second book of poetry, *Dzshike gas,* published two years before *Freydke*, Molodowsky had described her alienation from the working class as a woman poet:

> And I—they point at me with their fingers:
> "There she is—the lady singer,
> The devil take her mother—
> She hangs around here all the time
> And out of our despair braids rhymes."[19]

The book in which this poem appeared received several scathing reviews in the Warsaw Bundist press in 1933. One reviewer, a man, complained of an overdose of feminine aestheticism in the poet's politics. His charge that most of her poems were "sweetly charming, daintily feminine love-songs"[20] may have inspired Molodowsky to write "Freydke," a poem of near-epic proportion that makes two working-class women the heroine/victims and includes a paean to the French Jewish garment workers' strikes.[21] Yet, this politically corrected poem may also conceal a portrait of the poet as a woman writing in *mame-loshn*, a woman deliberately "braiding rhymes" in a context where rhymes should be forged. If Freydke and Sheyndl together represent the poet, then this poem is about how the woman poet, like the egg-peddler and the singing fugitive, has been colonized by the system—read male critics—and ultimately sent into a kind of "cultural exile," a radical homelessness, a state *between* being expelled from her own voice and being coerced by a male mode of writing. In this case, Molodowsky makes that homelessness productive. Unlike the character Freydke, forced by her simultaneous imprisonment/exile to face "the hard, close truth," and unlike Sheyndl, who survives on idealism, the poet finds exile a fertile ground for creating the kind of new poem epitomized by "Freydke," which at once conforms by teaching the correct politics and mirrors its own author's exile within Yiddish poetry.

While still at home in Warsaw, Molodowsky transformed her internal exile as a woman poet into the occasion for writing a poem that depicted what Susan Hardy Aiken, in an essay on Isak Dinesen, calls "woman's irrevocable status as a foreigner within androcentric culture and discourse."[22] But when Molodowsky placed herself in literal exile from her homeland, the feminism that had surfaced in "Freydke" as a response to that foreignness submerged itself, and another kind of response ensued.

Until now, I have assumed a difference between inner and outer exile. One tends to think of inner dislocation, the dislocation of the spirit, as more significant than a move from one place to another. What I will now argue is that this is not really the case, that geographical uprooting may, in fact, cause dislocations of the psyche that even poetry cannot heal. In traditional Judaism, the term *goles* (*galut* in Hebrew), the Exile, points to two separate aspects of exile: one geographical and the other spiritual. Geographically, the world is divided into the Land of Israel and the Diaspora, where the Jews were dispersed after the fall of the Second Temple. From the viewpoint of traditional Judaism, all of the Diaspora, vast and variegated as it may be, is homogeneous; it is all "not-Israel." Spiritually, *goles* is the condition and feelings of alienation, uprootedness from the national homeland and from its attendant Divine Presence.[23] As long as a Jew is not spiritually redeemed (as long as the Messiah has not come), then it does not matter where in the geographical *goles* he/she lives.

Hypothetically speaking, then, if Kadya Molodowsky had been a traditional Jew, her move from Poland to America should not have upset her spiritually, for she would have simply shifted from one place of exile to another, as she had done her whole life, moving from region to region within Jewish Eastern Europe. But the fact of the matter is that she was alienated from the tradition (although that alienation is itself one version of spiritual exile in Judaism), and precisely because of that spiritual alienation, that is, modernity, secularization, her physical dislocation from Poland to America was far more disruptive than any inner feeling of exile. Kadya Molodowsky, during her years in Eastern Europe, may have been living *in goles*, but like millions of others, she did not feel it as exile. She felt at home there, partly because Yiddish, her language, thrived there.

What then, is the real difference between inner and outer exile? Is the dichotomy between outer and inner, between geographical and spiritual exile, itself a mystification that needs to be collapsed? One likes to think that the conflicts of outer exile are resolved by finding an inner home, and vice versa. One likes to think so, but in fact, what we will see in Molodowsky's poems is that for this Jewish woman, it did not work this way. Rather, her poems record the incurability of exile.

Molodowsky emigrated to America in 1935, and two years later she published her fourth book, *In land fun mayn gebeyn* (In the Country of My Bones).[24] The poems in this book redirect her concerns with exile inward. Lyrical, obscurely symbolic, intensely private, these poems represent an internalization of exile, as the poet, who observed the exiles of Freydke with dispassion and compassion, now is compelled to confront her own exiles from her geographical home in Lithuania and Warsaw, from her own language, Yiddish, and from her very self.

In land fun mayn gebeyn (In the Country of My Bones), the very title of the collection, suggests the ambiguity which is at the heart of the book's poems. Where—or more accurately, what—is "the *country* of my bones," from which the poet speaks? Is it her birthplace, the land where her bones were formed, a "motherland," suggesting a kind of return, via the imagination, to the homeland where she presumably no longer resides, to the womb of gestation? Or is it the country of *my* bones, that is, her own body, now mother to herself, which is all that she has as a homeland? Or is it the land in which she will be buried, that is, the land of her skeleton, her remains, which, neither her birthplace nor the land of herself, is a place of pure alienation, pure exile? The very ambiguity here signals the book's central concern with the problem of exile: how does one find, let alone recover, a place in the world?

In order to follow Molodowsky's progress in answering this question—how does one find a place for oneself *in* exile—I would like to consider five lyric poems from this book, in their original order. Before looking at the poems themselves, let me sum up what I believe is the progression they imply. In the first poem, the poet seeks to find herself and justification for her writing in the act of reinventing the story of her life. In the second poem, the poet, after immigrating to New York City, comes to terms with her new residence by seeking her old homeland within her bones. What she finds there, though, is, comically, a fierce debate between a shtetl cottage and the Empire State Building. In the third poem, the poet imagines a kind of ideal national homeland (Birobidzshan), which turns out, in the end, to be located in the realm of pure language. The fourth poem focuses directly on the letters of the Yiddish and English alphabets, on elements of language itself, as literal signposts of the familiar and the alien. Finally, in the fifth poem, the poet finds her inheritance in exile, but now in those very letters of the Hebrew alphabet that exist solely for their own sake. What one sees here, then, is a progression from autobiographical narration to a kind of semiotic system in which inscribed letters become signs of the only points of stability which the poet can find for herself within the instability of exile.

Let us now look at these poems in somewhat greater detail. The first poem, which is also the longest, and to my mind most interesting, of the five poems, entitled "Mayn artsi-biografye," actually requires an entire essay to unpack the allusions—personal, cultural and literary—through which Molodowsky develops an *ars poetica*. The initial mystery the poem poses is its title. What is an *artsi-biografye*? The word is not the same as *oytobiografye*, the standard Yiddish term for autobiography, a genre that first appeared in Yiddish prose with the Enlightenment writers of the mid-nineteenth century.[25] Not an autobiography, Molodowsky's *artsi-biografye* is actually an ironic neologism for the essence of life, the *ultimate* life. (The Yiddish prefix *artsi* denotes "arch" with a positive connotation, as in "archbishop" [*artsibiskop*], while the variant *artse* has a negative connotation, as in "arch-villain" [*artseroshe*].)[26] By replacing the self of *oyto* with the extreme state of *artsi*, this poetic biography, then, seeks to distill the essence of life, which in this case, happens to be the essence of exile.

The speaker in this poem is in a constant state of displacement:

> un a shprukh zol mikh valgern iber der velt,
> azoy az di hor zoln shtekhn kapoyr.
> in midbar fun fremdn un tunklen feld,
> un unter di fis grobt zikh unter a tkhoyr.

> in langonikn vander, in trukenem gang,
> vi hastik di ban zol nisht gebn a ris,
> gey ikh say-vi a vakhe indroysn farbay
> mit borvese, shtendik-fartilikte fis.

> And let a spell send me to wander the world.
> A charm so terrific, my hair stands on end.
> In some faraway desert of alien fields,
> Under my feet, a skunk burrows in sand.

> In endless wandering across arid ways,
> No matter how quickly the train passes by,
> I'm always outside, walking by watchfully,
> With battered, bare feet, half-destroyed.

In her wandering, the speaker must constantly perform and sell her art: "like a peddler," she lugs "thin, measured-out bundles of culture." This figure, the poet as peddler, recalls Freydke, the egg-peddler, but the persona of "Mayn artsi-biografye" is a far more cynical and self-conscious practitioner of her occupation. Suddenly, ". . . in the midst of a noisy, staring hall,"—it is not clear where this happens, perhaps in a poetry reading, where she is trying to sell her "thin . . . bundles of 'culture,' "—the speaker abruptly descends into her authentic self, the self of the past, "where the holes shine through my shoes, . . . where my idiotic nightingale sings" (17–20).[28] The image of the nightingale recalls Sheyndl Kanerey, the poet as fugitive, but for this poet, "idiotic," her memory becomes a site of exile (23–24).

First she remembers childhood scenes: two children playing "horsey," the speaker acting the part of Queen Esther in a Purim-play, and several other episodes, each of which rises to the surface like a submerged memory from the deepest self. Suddenly, the child playing the horse warns her driver that they are both headed toward death. "Onward, my ultimate biography" (72) becomes the refrain with which the speaker drives the poem onward, descending still deeper into memory for the sources of her self and her art, but never quite finding them. She connects her urge to tell stories with two figures from her early life, the schoolteacher of Sorok and Shloyminke the Blacksmith, a landlord whose stories were so good she would trade them for "the whole of New York." However, a sudden apocalyptic vision makes her "darling ultimate biography / [Burn] up in smoky gloom" (91–92) and returns the poet to the present moment, when a nameless person, in the American manner, asks her birthdate. The poet replies:

> (In our family, a battle raged
> Stubbornly over me each year—
> From Elul [September] my grandmother counted my age,
> My mother calculated it from Iyar [May–June].

> But both knew for certain—
> And this is what quieted their zeal—
> That unquestionably on that morning
> It was a heavy rain that fell.) (100–107)

To understand this exchange, it is essential to know that among Eastern European Jews, it was not unusual even for mothers not to be able to recall the precise month in which their daughters were born. (Sons' birthdays were remembered because they had to be known in order to celebrate the bar mitzvah at the proper time.) In America, of course, everyone, no matter what gender, knows his/her birthday! Even what seems to be an essential, unarguable fact, a birthday, is, then, culture-bound. And so, the conflict between the American desire for absolute fact and the Eastern European vagueness about dates (but certainty about weather) turns out to be a cultural clash, a signal to the poet's real problem, which is her need to redefine herself in America, in exile, her reason for having to write this ultimate biography for herself. By accounting for her life, she hopes to make a new life in America. And where will she find inspiration for composing that life? She concludes:

> mayn artsibiografye, s'iz bashert dir
> di hiltserne strunes a shpan ton: farfaln.
> shtep, mayn zingeruvke, hiper nisht—
> es makht nisht oys, oyb s'zshavern abisl di pedaln.

> My ultimate biography, it is your fate
> That the wooden strings stride forth: for naught.
> Stitch, my sweet Singer, but don't skip—
> It doesn't matter if the pedals rust a bit. (108–111)

"My Singer" (in Yiddish, *mayn zingeruvke*, where *zinger* is given a feminine and diminutive Slavic suffix), the poet's muse and instrument, is actually a bilingual pun. It means both the singer as poet, and more literally, a Singer sewing machine. Because the "*hiltserne strunes*," "wooden strings"—that is, instrument strings made of wood like the spokes of a wagon wheel (a very private image in the poem for the source of the folk voice in the poet's childhood, a voice that now may well be mute)—no longer "step forward" with purpose, it is now to the static, functional pedalling of the sweatshop machine that the poet's ultimate biography, her life, it seems, is decreed.

Between this poem and "Freydke," one can glimpse what has transpired since Molodowsky's immigration. The last lines in the poem allude to "Freydke," where the working-class woman is a trope for the woman poet, with its implied alignment of gender and class. There is also a line of continuity between the two poems in the very idea of *artsi-biografye*, telling a life, which harkens back to the narrative mode of "Freydke." Yet at the same time, one is equally aware of the profound differences between the two poems. In fact, "*Mayn artsi-biografye*" is not a linear narrative, as is "Freydke," but rather an assemblage of lyric moments that emblematize the nature of a life, not its story. Here, narrative continuity has been reconstructed as juxtaposed or overlapping bits of episodes. With Molodowsky's ocean crossing, a sea change has occurred.

The transformation is epitomized in the bilingual play on *zinger*/Singer (sewing machine)/singer (poet). The pun conflates the poet's art and the laborer's machine, but it also interleaves Yiddish language and American culture.[29] As the narrative becomes increasingly fragmented and layered, it draws attention to its language, and as the language itself becomes dense and self-referential, it metamorphoses into territory. In "Freydke," Molodowsky used the situation of exile as material for a symbolic narrative about herself, a woman poet in exile. In "*Mayn artsi-biografye*," the condition of the poet in exile is summed up in the one word "zingeruvke," which becomes a bilingual sign of exile, an element in the semiotics of exile. This density of language results from the change that coming to America has forced on Molodowsky.

This movement away from symbols and toward signs continues in the next two poems in the series. The second poem, "In the Country of My Bones," begins with a nostalgic snapshot of the Old Home, "A cottage [that] struggles against gray poverty / Like a hearty plant against drought"

(10–11), where the mother's words transform poverty into plenty.[30] Coming to America, though, the poet sees "people and cities / Through a crooked and fluid mirror" (28–29). In these lines, the mirror that reflects one's own image becomes a distorting window, a surface that affords the poet a glimpse of the outer world through a vanishing vision of herself. Along with the disappearing self, the power that words once had in the Old Country to change things diminishes and becomes a sign of the disjunction between the two cultures. In an unhappy situation, the poet finds herself in linguistic limbo, dangling between two untranslatable idioms, which epitomize two contrasting cultural responses to adversity:

> der yenki volt af dem gezogt: o-key.
> der litvak zogt: es toyg af a kapore.

> About this, the Yankee would say: Okay.
> The Litvak says: It's fine if you're a scapegoat.[31] (36–37)

Finally, the poet relates how the Old World cottage and the New World skyscraper appropriate the act of writing:

> A cottage met up with the Empire State Building
> And one curved in a question-mark across from the other:
> The Empire State Building openly, impudently
> Pointed with its highest tower
> And wrote brilliantly and unexpectedly
> As lightning in the darkness of a storm:[32] (41–46)

This surreal exchange, which takes place within the poet's psyche, makes the Empire State Building and the cottage into the ultimate signs of the poet's dis-ease in her new land. The obviously phallic Empire State Building signals a submerged sexual dialogue in the poem between its male, appropriating self and the shtetl cottage, associated with the mother, the poet's girlhood, a garden, and the inhabitants of domesticity—the cat, the hen, the goose. Although the New World phallus inscribes a new meaning on the Old World, here rendered as female, the cottage is not shaken or silenced by such bullying and continues to counsel the poet. In the concluding lines, though, the poet returns to her writing, not as a creator, but as a dutiful recorder of her "mistakes," her cultural misunderstandings. Inscribing the errors, the errings, and the wanderings of exile becomes the poet's sole occupation.

The third poem, "In My Hand, Two Pheasant Feathers," further advances the semiotic movement. The poet turns from nostalgia over the past to an idealized reverie on the future promise of a national homeland in Birobidzs-han, the Jewish autonomous state that the Soviets decreed in 1934.[33] The poet's enthusiasm for this failed project may seem today naive, but no matter. This reverie focuses on specific objects, two pheasant feathers, which, as the poet holds them in her hand, are overtaken by the very words that name them. These words become signs for all words—English, Yiddish, and Russian—which, through an intricate play on idiom and exoticism, replace the actual things that locate the speaker either at home or in exile.[34] Here, for once, as language replaces the material world, the poet seems to find a momentary place for herself.

The fragmentation of language intensifies, however, in the fourth poem, "Oysyes" (Alphabet Letters), where not words, but letters become signs for the condition of exile the poet resigns herself to in America. The poem tells a story that is relatively clear-cut and coherent, in comparison to the preceding poems:

> In branks, in bruklin un nyu-york siti,
> hobn mayne shvesterkinder kromen.
> zibn shvesterkinder mit zibn kromen, vi gebotn.
> bizneslayt mit lange tsetlen fun bankrotn.
> un mayn familye-nomen hot a kuk geton af mir fun zeyere shildn
> mit a blik—a fremdn un a vildn.
> es hot der flamediker "mem" (fun moyshe un fun marks)
> gehipet af a grinem fisl.
> der "alef" hot blank gevunken tsu der gas.
> der "lamed" hot oysgeshlayft zikh vi a tlie.
> un s'hot der "alef-beys" geshrien in ayzernem gebrazg fun shtot:
> —bankrot, bankrot un nokhamol bankrot.
> nor untern shild zaynen der feter mikhl un di mume sore
> breyt gevorn, keyn ayen hore.
> zi—a bloye zaydene fas,
> un er—a groye, shtolene sprunzshine.
> un di kinder: dzshuli, bitris, meks un karoline,
> hobn shtolts getrogn afn pleytse oysyes vi shtern,
> tsu velkhn kortn-klub un boy-skaut zey gehern.[35]

> In the Bronx, in Brooklyn and in New York City,
> My cousins all have stores.
> Seven cousins with seven stores, like commandments.
> Business people with long lists of going bankrupt.
> And from their signs my family-name peeks
> At me with wild and foreign looks.
> The flaming *mem* (of Moses and of Marx)
> Skips on one green foot.

The *alef* winks glossily at the street below.
The *lamed* loops a knot like a gallows.
And the alphabet shrieks in the iron uproar of the city:
—Bankrupt, bankrupt and bankrupt, what a pity.
But beneath the sign, my Uncle Mikhl and Aunt Sore
Have grown wide—evil eye, stay away—*keyn ayn hore.*
She—a blue silk barrel,
And he—a gray steel spring.
And their children—Julie, Beatrice, Max and Carolyn—
Proudly wear letters like stars on short sleeves and long,
Showing card clubs and Boy Scout troops to which they belong.

Mem, alef, lamed,—the individual letters of the first syllable of the family name, Molodowsky—inscribed on the signboards of the immigrant cousins' failed businesses, mock the speaker, who has padded her poem, ironically or desperately (one cannot be certain), with Americanisms. However, the bankrupt status of these cousins belies their acculturation in America. Disembodied letters of the English alphabet, namely, the Boy Scout and club insignia, adorn the sleeves of the immigrants' American-born children and indicate the degree to which they have successfully assimilated in American culture. Thus, while the Yiddish letters spelling out a fragment of the family name point toward the immigrant generation's failure in America, the English letters on the sleeves of children with American names seem to point in the opposite direction. But, in fact, the letters spell nothing. Unanchored signs in the poem, floating free of language, they point beyond exile. And, in contrast to her Americanized relatives, the poet herself is letterless. She has no idea as to where in America she belongs.

The system of signs in the preceding four poems has added layer by layer to the poet's disenfranchisement from her life, her country, her writing, her language. The last poem in the series, "Yerushe" (Legacy) completes this movement:

a himl iz do—zaynen shtern faran.
un ikh—halb a badkhn
un halb oriman.

ver veys tsi a shvindler, ver veys—a poet
in antliene shikh—
in farblondzsheter bet.

keyn zakh nisht keyn simn—
keyn zakh nisht bavayzt.
s'ken zayn s'iz dos lebn ingantsn fargrayzt.

nor di gramen shtoltsirn mit goldener smikhe
fun shindlnem dakh
mit tserisener strikhe.

in praysn geven, un abisl fartshadet,
mit a posek farshleyert,
mit a late farlatet.

nor di oysyes zaynen geyorshnt voylgibik,
fun dem altn melamed
leyzer-ber mitn tsibek.[36]

Here is a sky—stars are there.
And I—half jester,
Half pauper.[37]

Who knows if a poet, who knows if a fraud
In borrowed shoes,
In a wandering bed.

No thing is a symbol—
Nothing to reveal.
Maybe life is all wrong, a raw deal.

But in gold ordination, rhymes proudly sputter
From a shingled roof
With a torn gutter.

Was in Prussia, asphyxiated a bit, unattached,
Veiled with a verse,
With a patch, patched.

Only alphabet letters are bequeathed, plentiful, ripe,
By the old schoolteacher
Leyzer-ber with his pipe.

In this poem, the reality of the sky and the stars is certain, but the speaker's reality, her authenticity, becomes entirely open to question. The self-doubt is fueled by the fact that the speaker is in exile, where there are no signs, no symbols, where life itself, like a corrupt text, may be "fargrayzt," full of errors and inaccuracies. In exile, "rhymes proudly sputter" like ordained rabbis, with official sanction and pretension, but they are meaningless, because they spurt their pride from a broken roof. In the penultimate stanza, we have a glimpse of autobiographical narrative, a previous moment of the speaker's exile in Prussia; but anything that this exile might have revealed is suffocated, veiled, patched over. Poverty and exile have no meaning for this speaker; the Biblical verse ("posek") masks suffering; poetry is not a form of revelation. In the last stanza, all that is left to inherit are alphabet letters, abundant but decontextualized, no longer part of a written text. These Hebrew/Yiddish "oyseyes" signify nothing but their remnant selves.[38]

The semiotics of textual disintegration here is linked to the speaker's definition of self. Twice over in "Legacy" she divides herself in two. First, there is the dichotomy between the "badkhn," the old-style songster who entertained at Jewish weddings throughout Eastern Europe, and the pauper; and then between the "poet" (modern, high-culture) and the fraud. These dualisms recall the split self-portrait of the artist as egg-peddler and fugitive songbird in "Freydke," but in the present poem, the dichotomy is even more distorted for Molodowsky, because these double images of herself are also male. Even the source of her heritage, the old schoolteacher of Hebrew to young boys, with his old-fashioned Yiddish name and his phallic pipe, is male, no longer the haunted "mothers" with their Yiddish prayers, whom Molodowsky had invoked as her past in her earliest "Women-Poems" ("Froyen-lider"). Why does Molodowsky assume a male persona here? Why does she figure herself, in this moment of crisis, in the dominant, masculine strain of Jewish culture? What has become of the female persona of the early poems? Where is the woman teacher of Yiddish to small children that Molodowsky herself was in Warsaw? In "Legacy," Molodowsky has been subsumed by the male precedent of traditional culture and, at the nadir of her exile, has lost herself. If she is trying to retrieve the patriarchal tradition for her own ends, she has failed.

What we see in these five poems, then, is a full circle. Having to leave Poland, her actual home, utterly transformed Molodowsky's poetry about exile. The forms of the poems change from allegorical narrative about the exile of the woman poet to poems pieced together like collages from fragments of memory and language, the remnants of the self, to which the poet clings for dear life. We begin to see Molodowsky's own development within these poems not as an allegory for exile but as a semiotics of exile, in which the poems themselves become signs. Initially, things had been material objects: the strikers in "Freydke" dismember actual sewing machines. Then, things became the poet's words (the sewing machines become a pun on Singer/singer), which in turn, become words authored by the inanimate things (the Empire State Building) that are no longer under the poet's control. And eventually, words split into syllables (the commercial signs of acculturated immigrants), until, finally, syllables become random letters that point in opposite directions, at the two cultures that fail to be reconciled within the poet. The more atomized these things become, the more one feels that they are operating within a semiotic system, but one that, as it becomes increasingly fragmented, also becomes more abstracted, less tangible, less real.

At the same time, the more things are broken into the elements of written language, the more susceptible the poet herself becomes to the dislocations of exile. In the last poem, "Legacy," the self-doubt created by exile has entirely undermined the semiotic system: all that is left are the alphabet letters, no longer signs, but a legacy without significance. With or without meaning, though, the letters may be said still to exist as whole units, unlike the speaker's divided, amorphous self.

This latter distintegration might be called the price the woman Yiddish poet paid for her multiple exiles. To be sure, the five poems I have discussed are only part of the 1937 book. Molodowsky did not stop writing poetry with "Legacy." However, after this book appeared, Molodowsky did not publish another collection of poetry for nine years, although she did publish prose fiction and essays. And even though her autobiography, serialized in the journal she edited during her last decade (1965–74), tries to smooth over this period of crisis as a poet, it nonetheless indicates the depth of the breakdown Molodowsky suffered.

Meanwhile, history intervened, in the form of the Nazi destruction of European Jewry. Molodowsky's next book of poems, *Only King David Remained* (New York, 1946), is no longer about exile, but about grief, loss, and rage. The impact of the Holocaust was even greater than she feared. Entire Jewish populations were destroyed, as was the culture of *Yiddishkayt*, from which the language and literature of Yiddish had come. And after that destruction, Molodowsky as a woman Yiddish poet was no longer an exile. She was a survivor.

In the book that she finally published after the Holocaust, Molodowsky turned, in her Yiddish poems, from the exile of Yiddish in America to the Hebrew texts of traditional Judaism—Bible and liturgy—with which she subverted the covenant in outraged anti-prayers. In her final book, *Light from the Thornbush* (Buenos Aires, 1965), the Yiddish poems look to the redemption from exile promised by the Jewish state of Israel. In these two last books, the poet moves increasingly into a public persona that speaks powerfully and representatively for the Jewish people. It is as if the conforming aspect of the younger Molodowsky that, writing "Freydke" as a political poem, submitted to the male criticism of her second book as too "womanly," now takes over the author's subversive side that made Freydke and Sheyndl Kanerey into the embodiments of a woman poet's exile. Sacrificing her private self for a public persona, Molodowsky takes flight from the crisis of exile.

In her final work, her prose autobiography, *Fun mayn elterzeydns yerushe* (From My Great-grandfather's Legacy),[39] Molodowsky turned to Zionism, the secular answer to Jewish exile, and to the state of Israel, where Yiddish was superseded by Hebrew and officially fossilized as the Diaspora language. In telling her life story from this vantage point, Molodowsky smooths over the entire period of her exile in America.[40] But this turning to Zionism was from one perspective a self-destructive act, because during the 1950s Zionism was predicated on *shelilat hagola*, the denial of the Diaspora and exilic Judaism. The Zionist movement extolled Hebrew at the expense of Yiddish. There was (and still is), of course, a significant Yiddish community in Israel, but in those years it was seen as an anachronism, no matter how it thrived.

Autobiography, as we know, is always structured according to some agenda of the author's reconstruction of a self and a life, whether conscious or not.[41] It is no accident that Molodowsky concludes her life story with a lengthy account of her visit to Israel in the 1950s as the editor for a short-lived Yiddish journal there called, significantly, *Heym* (Home).[42] In light of its submerged theme of the absolute loss of Yiddish Eastern Europe, the emphasis Molodowsky gives to this episode makes it stand out as the culminating experience of her life. But, in fact, Molodowsky herself did not actually move to Israel. (For all her Zionism, she probably felt too old to move, to go into exile still another time, even if that exile were a kind of homecoming.) This editing of experience shapes Molodowsky's account of her life in the United States. In the end, Molodowsky's America, the place she settled for the last forty years of her life, is not *dos goldene land*, the fantasied land with streets paved with gold, nor the hard pavements of the tenement neighborhoods, the New Home with which other immigrants learned to come to terms. Rather, Molodowsky's America was a place of real exile, a liminal place, a threshhold prolonged into a lifetime of alienation for herself and for Yiddish.

"I came to America saturated with different exiles." "The poems in this book bring out the sorrow that lay in my bones." So Molodowsky wrote in her autobiography, describing how she composed the poems in her book *In land fun mayn gebeyn*. As we have seen in this paper, Molodowsky found it harder to assuage that sorrow than even she would admit in her public accounting of her life. And reading these poems today, that sorrow must seem even deeper, as do her various exiles. Nineteen years after her death, Molodowsky's poems are hardly known, except to small circles of Yiddish devotees and scholars in America, Australia, and Israel. In Israel, her children's poems are still celebrated, but only in Hebrew translation. (Many people there who know these poems think that Molodowsky wrote them in Hebrew!)

And even here, among literary scholars in America, these poems can be read almost exclusively as they are translated into English. In this way, we might say that we, too, collaborate in placing the poems into a state of exile from the very material of which they were made, the poet's mother tongue.

My translations are intended to bring you closer to a Yiddish poet's exile in her native language, but they inevitably remove the poems further from their source. From another perspective, though, we might say that we are helping the poems immigrate into the present. Without our efforts, the poems would simply turn to dust. In this conflicted way, we perpetuate their exile in our mother tongue.

Texts for
"In Exile in the Mother Tongue:
 Yiddish and the Woman Poet"

The poems that follow appear in both English and transliterated Yiddish. English versions appear on left-hand pages while the Yiddish transliterations appear on the right.

My Ultimate Biography

My darling, ultimate biography,
Dear papas, dear mamas, dear hearts, I say—
Ah, it's not nice, and ah, it's not kind
To treat a person this way.

The last thing in the world that I need
Is to deal in poems at the boisterous fair.
So, may my crazy-quilt market-stall
Wobble like a shop full of ready-to-wear.

And let a spell send me to wander the world,
A charm so terrific, my hair stands on end.   10
In some faraway desert of alien fields,
Under my feet, a skunk burrows in sand.

In endless wandering, across arid ways,
No matter how quickly the train passes by,
I'm always outside, walking by watchfully,
With battered, bare feet, half-destroyed.

I lug thin, measured bundles of "culture"
Like a peddlar with crates on his shoulder,
And in the midst of a noisy, staring hall,
I suddenly plunge from the boards. Down I fall.   20

And down? Where is down?
Out there, like a-one and a-two,
Out there, where the holes shine through my shoes,
Out there, where my idiotic nightingale sings.

Just like my mother, the vendor of kvass,
Onward, biography, bold and bluster—
Bottles are ringing, ringing like bells,
And here I am—a drenched kapellmeister.

(Keep ringing, ringing bottles,
Green and fresh and clear,   30
In a trough of water—
Ringing meteors.

Keep ringing, ringing, bottles,
All bundled up together,
Keep ringing, ringing, bottles,
Mother's been sent off somewhere.

Mayn Artsi-Biografye

mayn tayerinke artsibiografye,
tatelekh, mamelekh, hartsele, kroyn—
akh, vi nisht fayn, un akh, vi nisht sheyn,
azoy bahandlen a parshoyn.

nokh dos hot mir tsum ruml gefelt—
mit lider handlen afn hilkhikn yarid.
es zol mayn kolirter stragan*
zikh vaklen, vi a kreml mit shnit.

un a shprukh zol mikh valgern iber der velt,
azoy az di hor zoln shtekhn kapoyr.
in midbar fun fremdn un tunklen feld,
un unter di fis grobt zikh unter a tkhoyr.

in langonikn vander, in trukenem gang,
vi hastik di ban zol nisht gebn a ris,
gey ikh say-vi a vakhe indroysn farbay
mit borvese, shtendik-fartilikte fis.

un dare, gemostene bintlekh 'kultur'
tsetrog vi a pedler afn aksl di skrines.
un inmitn a royshikn, oygikn zal
mit trask gey ikh plutsling arop fun di shines.

un vu arop? un vu?
ot dort take, vi eyns un tsvey,
ot dort vu s'shaynt di lokh fun mayne shikh,
ot dort vu s'zingt mayn tamevater solovey.

ot punkt vi bay der kvasnitse der mamen,
foroys mayn artsibiografye, drayster—
flesher zaynen hilkhike glokn,
un ikh—a naser kapelmayster.

(klingt nokh flesher,
grine, yunge, klore,
in a korete mit vaser
klingendike meteorn.

klingt nokh fleshlekh,
ayngebundene tsuzamen,
klingt nokh fleshlekh,
s'hot geshikt ergets di mame.)

*Mark-geshtel (Molodowsky's note)

Look lively, Yezepke, and start up the cart,
Make it move quick with a smack of your lips.
The front wheels strum their wooden strings—
The two back wheels both dreamily squeak.   40

A penny a mile,
And three pennies a day,
As always, the morning
Comes up with the day.

In the chilly blue,
In the boiling sun,
The children speak,
One to one:

Now, let's change places,
And you push the cart.   50
Shout "giddy-up" so
It hits my heart.

But wheels, being wheels,
Spin out a psalm,
Repeat and repeat
A round holy-poem:

Shmelke-Tsalke, eenie meenie,
On Purim I'll be Esther Queenie,

Queen Esther with her golden shoes—
The wheels squeak sha-reek and sha-rooz.   60

As the wheels squeak sha-reek and sha-rooz,
Queen Esther walks in her golden shoes.

With her baize dress all fastened with buttons,
And before her, as always a silver flute trumpets.

Trill, trill, and trill—la-la-la.
The horsey in front shouts:
Stop! Stand still! Whoa! Whoa!

Don't you see? Where are you?
We're sinking in loam.
Ahead lies a graveyard,   70
And behind lies a stone.

nu, gib dort, yezepke, a munter dos vegl,
un gringer zol zayn—gib a tsmok mit di lipn.
di fodershte redlekh mit hiltserne strunes—
di hintershte—tsvey farkholemte skripen.

a groshn a viorst,
un a drayer a tog,
der frimorgn, vi shtendik,
geyt oyf mit fartog.

mit bloykayt, vos keltert,
mit zun, vos brit,
zogt eyn kind tsum tsveytn,
a kind tsu a kind:

itst lomir zikh baytn
un du shtup dem vagon,
un shray mir het-ta,
az in piate vet shlogn.

nor redlekh, vi redlekh,
zey dreyen a mizmer,
zey zogn un zogn
a rundikn pizmen:

hayda-ruda, shmelke-tsalke,
purim kh'vel shpiln in ester hamalke,

in ester hamalke mit goldene shikh—
skripen di reder tshi-rikh un tshi-rikh.

skripen di reder tshi-rikh un tshi-rikh,
geyt ester hamalke in goldene shikh.

mit kneplekh farshpilyet di bayene kleyd,
un foroys, vi geveynlekh, trumeytert a fleyt.

triler, un triler, un triler—la-la.
shrayt dos ferdl un fornt:
—blayb shteyn un het-ta!

du zest nisht? vu biztu?
mir zinken in leym.
fun fornt—a grub,
un fun hintn—a shteyn.

Onward, my ultimate biography,
But how can we ever move on without
The braid-tugging Blacksmith Shloyminke?
He has a tale to tell me about a goat.

Who can resist the wonderful tale
(Of a goat and a wolf and a head of kraut)?—
I'd give the whole of New York City
For the familiar gallop of his cart.

And for the schoolteacher of Sorok,   80
For his beard, mixed-up, wavy,
When he strides across the market between terms
With a brand-new, bright tinny laver.

And by no means on account of his wages
Does his face gleam, pensively glare;
At dawn he saw the sun and the moon
Masquerade in the pelt of a bear.

And wrestle—like schoolteachers over a post—
With a bearish paw raised high,
Until dust fell onto the shtetl   90
When flaming storm-clouds raced by.

My darling, ultimate biography,
Burned up in smoky gloom.
I laugh until my ribs crack
When they ask when my birthday will come.

My birthday—from a cherry-tree twig
A luminous, patched shirt depends,
I send you my most courteous words
For each of your birthdays, my friends.

(In our family, a battle raged
Stubbornly over me each year—
From Elul my grandmother counted my age,
My mother calculated it from Iyar.

But both knew for certain—
And this is what quieted their zeal—
That unquestionably on that morning
It was a heavy rain that fell.)

foroys, mayn artsibiografye,
vi kon zayn do on shloyminke dem shmid?
ot tsit er mikh fest bay di tseplekh,
er hot a mayse mit a tsig.

ver kon bayshteyn dem vunderlekher mayse
(fun a tsig un a volf un a kepl kroyt)—
es meg zikh nyu-york zikh farbahaltn
far galop fun a heymisher boyd.

un bloyz farn soroker melamed
far zayn tsetumlter, khvaliker bord,
ven er shpant afn mark beyn-hazmonem
mit a nayer a blekhener kvort.

un nisht azoy vayt tsulib fardinstn
iz zayn ponem fartrakht un tsehelt,
er hot gezen fartog di zun un di levone
in berene peltsn farshtelt.

un zikh geshlogn—vi tsvey melamdim far a knelung—
un a berene lape a farhoyb,
un es yogn zikh flamike khmares,
azsh es falt afn shtetl a shtoyb.

mayn tayerinke artsibiografye
in roykhikn umet farbrent.
lakh ikh azsh het biz di ripn,
az me fregt mayn geburtstog iz ven.

mayn geburtstog—af a karshnboym-tsvaygl
a hemd a farlatete shaynt,
ikh shik aykh mayne heflekhste verter
tsu ayer geburtstog, mayne fraynt.

(in unzer mishpokhe hot geflakert
a farakshonte shlakht vegn mir—
di bobe hot getseylt mikh fun elul,
di mame hot gedenkt, az fun iyar.

nor beyde hobn gevust, un af rikhtik—
un dos hot geshtilt zeyr bren—
az in yenem frimorgn bli sofek
iz a regn geven.)

My ultimate biography, it is your fate
That the wooden strings stride forth: for naught.
Stitch, my sweet Singer, but don't skip—   110
It doesn't matter if the pedals rust a bit.

In the Country of My Bones

There, where my eyes' horizon ends,
Rises the country of my bones.
Thoroughly kneaded with ten fingers,
Flown through in a metro,
And snagged near a white cherry tree.

Good morning! It's a sunny Monday,
It's a Tuesday of windy rain,
(How amazing, that people's feet
Can stroll through so many days and ways.)

A cottage struggles against gray poverty   10
Like a hearty plant against drought.
The doors cut the day open with a rattle,
The cat awakens, and the hens, and the goose.
Hope awakens that cucumbers in the garden will suddenly turn
    green,
And a hen will lay an egg.
My mother—a clever general—ordered
That no one should want for *tsimmes* and tea.
No, no! All you need do is ask for it,
Cucumbers turn green, the world is bright.
My feet tremble toward distant, sunny races,   20
But now a familiar command arrives:
—Look, the goose! Where has she waddled away to?
Maybe into Khayim Gedaliah's lettuce-patch.
The blue ribbon in my braid trembles
And the sunniness is extinguished and the swaying butterfly.

The waves saw away at one another, the waves
Of all the seas that I have floated through.
And it seems to me: I have seen people and cities
Through a crooked and fluid mirror.
I hoisted my silk shirt to flutter as a flag,   30
And went off into the world in a shirt of hard labor,
I seem always to be in debt to everyone,
And the hardest complaints are always sticking out at me.

mayn artsibiografye, s'iz bashert dir
di hiltserne strunes a shpan ton: farfaln.
shtep, mayn zingeruvke, hiper nisht—
es makht nisht oys, oyb s'zshavern abisl di pedaln.

In Land Fun Mayn Gebeyn

dort, vu s'endikt zikh der horizont fun mayne oygn,
hoybt zikh on dos land fun mayn gebeyn.
mit tsen finger durkhgeknotn,
durkhgefloygn in a metro,
un farhakt zikh lem a vaysn karshn-boym.

a gut morgn! s'iz a zuniker montik,
s'iz a dinstik mit a vintikn regn,
(s'ara vunder s'iz, vos fis fun mentshn
kenen durkhgeyn durkh azoyfil teg un vegn.)

es ranglt zikh a shtibele mit groyer oremkayt,
vi mit trikenish a shtarker flants.
shnaydn af dem tog di tirn mit a khripe,
khapt zikh af di kats, di hiner un di gandz.
khapt zikh af a hofenung, az s'veln ugerkes in gortn zikh
     tsegrinen,
un a hun vet leygn an ey.
s'hot di mame—a kluger general—geheysn,
men zol nisht veln keyn floymen-tsimes un keyn tey.
neyn, iz neyn! ver darf zikh nokh dem fregn,
es grinen agresn, di velt iz hel.
es tsitern di fis tsu vayte, zunike geyegn,
nor do kumt on a heymisher bafel:
—zeh, di gandz—vunhin hot zi avekgepadet?
shoyn arayn mistome tsu khaym gedalyn in salate.
git a tsiter dos bloye bendl in mayn tsop
un s'lesht zikh oys di zunikayt un der tsevigter flater.

es zegn eyns dos andere di khvalyes
fun ale yamen, vos ikh bin durgeshvumen.
un s'dakht zikh mir: kh'hob mentshn un kh'hob shtet gezen
durkh a shpigl a flisikn un krumen.
ikh hob mayn zaydn hemdl oyfgeflatert af a fon,
un in der velt avek in hemd fun shverer horevanye,
bin ikh grod geblibn alemen bal-khoyv,
un tsu mir shtelt men aroys di shverste tayne.

This is clear.
The clearest of all.
About this, the Yankee would say: Okay.
The Litvak says: It's fine if you're a scapegoat.

Strange as the sun is naked, and it's naked to consider this.
A threatening cloudiness hangs in me
And obscures a soft summer day.   40
A cottage met up with the Empire State Building
And one curved in a question-mark across from the other:
The Empire State Building openly, impudently
Pointed with its highest tower
And wrote brilliantly and unexpectedly
As lightning in the darkness of a storm:
—See, with my highest copper tip
I've cut a harrow in the sky,
And your grandfather, unhappily, with trembling hands
Blessed the new moon!   50

—See, at my most delicate cornice,
Formed by fingers in fever and dread,
Sits, placing one leg upon the other
New York's greatest bastard?

And the cottage, as usual, asks how you are,
And calmly says to me:
—There's none of the bee's venom in honey—
I improve such mistakes in the country of my bones
And record them in my writings.

In My Hand, Two Pheasant Feathers

In my hand, two pheasant feathers.
From the young country of Birobidzhan.
In my hand, two pheasant feathers—
Slender,
Thin.
There is in them the wonder
Of tomorrow's light-filled state.
Of cities and unexpected names.
Of a new turn in history.
But my memory, the old crow   10
That still carries the old drum of generations to me,
Is already here.

azoy iz klor.
dos klorste shebeklore.
der yenki volt af dem gezogt: o-key.
der litvak zogt: es toyg af a kapore.

modne vi di zun iz naket, un s'iz naket dos klern.
es hengt a khmarnekayt in mir
un dekt a zumer-tog a veykhn.
es hot zikh a kleyn shtibele bagegnt mitn empayr-steyt
un eyns antkegn andern zikh oysgeboygn in a frage-tseykhn:
der empayr-steyt hot ofn, frekh
geteytlt mitn hekhtstn turem
un geshribn blank un umgerikht,
vi a blits in finsterkayt fun shturem:
—zest, mit mayn hekhstn kupernem shpits
hob ikh farshnitn in himl a brone
un umzist hot dayn zeyde mit tsiterike hent
mekhadesh geven di levone!

—zest, bay mayn eydlste gezims,
mit finger gefuremt in fiber un forkht,
zitst farleygt a fus af a fus
der grester paskudnyak fun nyu-york?

un dos shtibele, geveynlekh, fregt zikh vos men makht,
un zogt mir ruik:
—in honik iz nishto fun bin di giftn—
farbeser ikh di toyesn in land fun mayn gebeyn
un fartseykhn zey in mayne shriftn.

Bay mir in Hant Tsvey Feder fun a Fazan

. . . .
un mayn zikorn, di alte kro—
zi hoyert iber mir shoyn do,
ot itster, in nyu-york, in branks.   25
s'iz do a lebn, azoy tsu zogn, oykh a kranks.
di zelbe vog. di zelbe hendlerishe late.
s'iz nisht keyn krom, es iz a stor.
s'iz nisht keyn berdiker, nor a gegolter tate.

I am called by name—
An old voice.
A low and narrow, limping little table.
A five-penny lamp smokes and burns.
And old hands pluck feathers.
Bunches of feathers, speckled, gray.
It's the languishing, childhood sadness of late autumn.
And crooked shutters   20
On rusty hinges
Terrify with night and with Slavic pogroms.

And my memory, that old crow,
Hovers here, above me
Even now, in New York, in the Bronx.
It's a life here, that is to say, a sick life, too.
The same scales. The same mercenary patch.
No longer a "*krom*", it is a "store."
No longer a bearded but a shaven father.

In my hand, two pheasant feathers.   30
Although the word "pheasant" rings
Too foreign, too refined.
It's not like "*mamzer-gonoruk*,"
(the gander's gonorrheal bastard)
And certainly not like "*katshke-dreydl*"
(lucky-ducky, spin the top, you will win where it will stop).
But it rings like tractor, Bire, Tiga—
Hearty, armed words
That have shaken off those old worries.
Strong and unexpectedly emerging—   40
The first autonomous Jewish region.

And although I have never seen the Tiga area
Or the river Bire—
And I dreamed up this entire country
From a thousand miles away—
I listen: it shouts out
With woods and waters,
With tanks,
With armoured, steel seagulls
The song of all songs: 50
And the wolf shall dwell with the lamb.

bay mir in hant tsvey federns fun a fazan.   30
khotsh s'klingt dos vort fazan
tsu fremd, tsu eydl.
s'iz nisht vi mamzer-gonoruk,
un shoyn avade nisht vi katshke-dreydl.
es klingt ober vi traktor, bire, tayge—   35
verter muntere, bavofnte,
un oysgetonene fun alter dayge.

. . . .

Alphabet Letters

In the Bronx, in Brooklyn and in New York City,
My cousins all have stores.
Seven cousins with seven stores, like commandments.
Business people with long lists of going bankrupt.
And from their signs my family-name peeks
At me with wild and foreign looks.
The flaming *mem* (of Moses and of Marx)
Skips on one green foot.
The *alef* winks glossily at the street below.
The *lamed* loops a knot like a gallows.   10
And the alphabet shrieks in the iron uproar of the city:
—Bankrupt, bankrupt and bankrupt, what a pity.
But beneath the sign, my Uncle Mikhl and Aunt Sore
Have grown wide—evil eye, stay away—*keyn ayen hore.*
She—a blue silk barrel,
And he—a gray steel spring.
And their children—Julie, Beatrice, Max and Carolyn—
Proudly wear letters like stars on short sleeves and long,
Showing card clubs and Boy Scout troops to which they belong.

Legacy

Here is a sky—stars are there.
And I—half jester,
Half pauper.

Who knows if a poet, who knows if a fraud
In borrowed shoes,
In a wandering bed.

No thing is a symbol—
Nothing to reveal.
Maybe life is all wrong, a raw deal.

But in gold ordination, rhymes proudly sputter   10
From a shingled roof
With a torn gutter.

Was in Prussia, asphyxiated a bit, unattached,
Veiled with a verse,
With a patch, patched.

Only alphabet letters are bequeathed, plentiful, ripe,
By the old schoolteacher
Leyzer-ber with his pipe.

Oysyes

In branks, in bruklin un nyu-york siti,
hobn mayne shvesterkinder kromen.
zibn shvesterkinder mit zibn kromen, vi gebotn.
bizneslayt mit lange tsetlen fun bankrotn.
un mayn familye-nomen hot a kuk geton af mir fun zeyere shildn
mit a blik—a fremdn un a vildn.
es hot der flamediker "mem" (fun moyshe un fun marks)
gehipet af a grinem fisl.
der "alef" hot blank gevunken tsu der gas.
der "lamed" hot oysgeshlayft zikh vi a tlie.
un s'hot der "alef-beys" geshrien in ayzernem gebrazg fun shtot:
—bankrot, bankrot un nokhamol bankrot.
nor untern shild zaynen der feter mikhl un di mume sore
breyt gevorn, keyn ayen hore.
zi—a bloye zaydene fas,
un er—a groye, shtolene sprunzshine.
un di kinder: dzshuli, bitris, meks un karoline,
hobn shtolts getrogn afn pleytse oysyes vi shtern,
tsu velkhn kortn-klub un boy-skaut zey gehern.

Yerushe

a himl iz do—zaynen shtern faran.
un ikh—halb a badkhn
un halb oriman.

ver veys tsi a shvindler, ver veys—a poet
in antliene shikh—
in farblondzsheter bet.

keyn zakh nisht keyn simn—
keyn zakh nisht bavayzt.
s'ken zayn s'iz dos lebn ingantsn fargrayzt.

nor di gramen shtoltsirn mit goldener smikhe
fun shindlnem dakh
mit tserisener strikhe.

in praysn geven, un abisl fartshadet,
mit a posek farshleyert,
mit a late farlatet.

nor di oysyes zaynen geyarshnt voylgibik,
fun dem altn melamed
leyzer-ber mitn tsibek.

NOTES

1. I am grateful to the Stroum Foundation and the Jewish Studies Program in the Jackson School of International Studies at the University of Washington for providing me with the stimulating context in which I wrote this paper, during the winter and spring of 1992. I wish to thank the following friends and colleagues for their extremely helpful remarks, questions, and criticisms on earlier versions of this essay: Yael Zerubavel, Shulamit Magnes, Mae Henderson, David Rosenthal, Martin Jaffee, Joe Butwin, Naomi Sokoloff, Pat Hurshell, Esther Helfgott, Ia Dubois, and Elizabeth Tenenbaum. My thanks to Miriam Waddington and David Roskies for their coments on my translation of "Mayn Atsi-Biografye." I am especially indebted to my husband, David Stern, for his bountiful help and support.

2. On the Yiddish devotional literature for women, see Chava Weissler, "The Traditional Piety of Ashkenazic Women." In *Jewish Spirituality: From the Sixteenth-Century Revival to the Present*, ed. Arthur Green. New York: Crossroads, 1987, 245–275.

3. Benjamin Harshav calls modern Yiddish literature "a secular extension of the traditional authority of the 'fathers.' " Benjamin Harshav, *The Meaning of Yiddish*. Berkeley: University of California Press, 1990, 3.

4. See Max Weinreich, *History of the Yiddish Language*, trans. Shlomo Noble and Joshua A. Fishman. Chicago: University of Chicago Press, 1980, 263, 271. Weinreich locates the origins of the term *mame-loshn* within the dichotomy of the Yiddish and Hebrew learning of a hypothetical Jewish boy: "The *agode* (legendary) material was more likely derived from the mother, that is, in Yiddish, from the Tsenerene and the moralistic books. . . . But biblical passages and Loshn-koydesh sayings were more likely to come from the father, and the boys accompanied their father to the synagogue. We have here explicitly a long-lasting attachment of Yiddish to the mother and Hebrew to the father." The assumption by Weinreich that even the most primal self-awareness of the Yiddish language occurred only from a male point of view, reveals a gender bias within the field of Yiddish studies.

In his thumbnail sketch of the concept of mother tongue in Yiddish, Weinreich further exposes how the Yiddish language was engendered as female by male writers: "The term *muter-loshn* (mother tongue) was apparently an innovation of Aaron son of Samuel of Hergershausen [a proponent of prayers in the mother tongue, rather than in Hebrew and author of *Liblikhe tfile* . . . (Delightful Prayer) . . . (Fürth, 1709), a collection of Yiddish prayers that was possibly banned (p. 263)]; *mutershprakh* (mother tongue) is a still younger term in Yiddish, introduced in the course of Westernization, in the struggle for a Jewish school system in connection with the nationality problems of the twentieth century. But we may say with certainty about *mame-loshn* (mother tongue), with all the warmth that the concept breathes, that it derives from the Ashkenazic tradition, although the expression appears in writing perhaps no earlier than the beginning of the twentieth century."

5. Dan Miron, *A Traveler Disguised: The Rise of Modern Yiddish Fiction in the Nineteenth Century*. New York: Schocken, 1973, 13–14.

6. Male authors, who personified the Yiddish language as negatively female and expressed the desire to subordinate that perceived aspect of the language, did so in part as a reaction to the figurative misogyny of nineteenth-century anti-Semitic writings, where assimilated Jewish men were depicted as "womanish." Paula Hyman explains that "male Jews defined an identity that not only distinguished themselves from women but that also displaced their own anxieties upon women." (Paula Hyman, "The Sexual Politics of Jewish Identity." Chapter 3 in *Gender and Assimilation: Roles and Representation of Women in Modern Jewish History*. The third of three Stroum Lectures in Jewish Studies, University of Washington, March 16, 1992, pp. 1–2 of typescript. Quoted with permission of the author.) Hyman argues that this displacement was a reaction to "the coincidence of antisemitism and misogyny," in which anti-Semites perceived "modern Jews and modern women" as disrupting their "vision of a smoothly function-

ing, ... hierarchical social order" (Hyman, 3, quoted by permission of the author). The Enlightenment writers who turned to Yiddish were caught in a conundrum, for they advanced the modernization of Jewish letters by reverting, as it were, to the language of female literacy. Their identification and personification of the language as female provided them with a way to conquer and then colonize it in their own, male terms.

Although unlike the Jewish men who aspired to middle-class business and professions in Western Europe through assimilation, these Yiddish writers in Eastern Europe were engaged in an activity that was *like* assimilation in certain respects. As they strove to define and justify a modern Yiddish literature, these men invented retrospectively a secular literary tradition for Yiddish, which borrowed from the models of English, German, and Russian literatures. Rather than assimilating into the dominant cultures' literatures, these writers were trying to make their own, unique tradition in the Jewish vernacular recognizable as a world literature. Still, the desire to appear worldly and to evade the anti-Semitic depictions of Jewish men as "womanish" may have fueled the efforts of these writers to distance themselves and their work from the associations with the female, with ignorance, with old-fashioned and superstitious faith that the Yiddish language held for the enlightened. Well into the twentieth century, the feminization of the Yiddish language continued to make the male Yiddish writers uneasy about the very medium in which they were so at home.

7. As a result, significantly fewer women than men published poems in the journals and papers of the day, and most women poets published no more than one volume of poetry during their lifetimes. Thus, women writers were essentially outsiders to the Yiddish literary world.

Yael Zerubavel, at the University of Pennsylvania, reminded me in a conversation that women Hebrew writers, too, were outsiders, and wondered whether such exclusion is a part of Jewish tradition. The difference is that women writing secular poetry in Hebrew were treading on the traditional male linguistic domain, while women writing in Yiddish were within the traditional female domain which had been transformed by men. This comparison needs to be treated fully.

8. See Celeste M. Schenck, "Exiled by Genre: Modernism, Canonicity, and the Politics of Exclusion." In *Women Writing in Exile*, eds. Mary Lynn Broe and Angela Ingram. Chapel Hill: University of North Carolina Press, 1989, 226–250. Schenck redefines "the double bind of the woman poet . . . for the female Modernist [as] her simultaneous exile *from* and *to* poetic form." Yiddish women poets were often faulted both for "writing like a woman" and for not adequately mastering the poetics of men.

9. See Kathryn Hellerstein, "Hebraisms as Metaphor in Kadya Molodowsky's 'Froyen-lider I.' " In *The Uses of Adversity: Failure and Accommodation in Reader Response*, ed. Ellen Spolsky. Lewisburg, Pennsylvania: Bucknell University Press, 1990, 143–152.

10. Jane Marcus, "Alibis and Legends: The Ethics of Elsewhereness, Gender and Estrangement." In *Women's Writing in Exile*, eds. Mary Lynn Broe and Angela Ingram. Chapel Hill: University of North Carolina Press, 1989, 276.

11. Kadya Molodowsky, "Freydke: poeme," I, in *Freydke*. Second Printing. Warsaw: Literarishe bleter, 1936, 5–8. All translations are by Kathryn Hellerstein, unless otherwise noted.

12. Although Molodowsky was not a factory worker, she tells in her autobiography how she studiously learned hat-making at a factory as soon as she had decided to accept an invitation to America as a literary tourist. She states that she never had to use her hat-making skills to earn her living. See Kadya Molodowsky, "Fun mayn elterzeydns yerushe." *Svive* 36 (April 1972) 62.

13. She taught in a school known as TSISHO, an acronym for Tsentrale Yidish Shule Organizatsye—Central Yiddish School Organization, on Tvarde Street, in Warsaw.

14. A Hebrew school run by the Jewish community or *kehillah* of Warsaw. Molodowsky's father, a teacher of Gemorrah, had tutored her in Hebrew when she was a girl.

15. Molodowsky, "Fun mayn elterzeydns yerushe," *Svive* 36 (April 1972), 61.

16. *Ibid.*, 57.

17. Such as Melekh Ravitsh in his literary column, reporting back to Warsaw about the literary scene in New York, "Literarishe felieton: Yidishe dikhterins in nyu-york." *Vokhnshrift* (Warsaw) 44 (193) (October 25, 1934), 5. Ravitsh used the metaphor of birth to compliment Celia Dropkin on her poem "The Circus Lady": "Nor zaynen di lider aleyn shoyn gornisht fun a hayskul-kind, eyns fun zey, vos vert oft tsitert iz efsher eyns fun di laydnshaftlekhste lider, vos a yidishe shrayberin (zint sore bas tovim) *hot af papir—geboyrn*. Dos iz dos lid fun der tsirkus-dame" (emphasis mine). (But the poems themselves are nothing by a high school child, one of them, that is often cited is perhaps one of the most passionate poems that a Yiddish female writer [since Sarah Bas Tovim] has given birth to on paper. This poem is "The Circus Lady.") The childbirth metaphor had been used by Yiddish critics since 1915 (by A. Glanz) and recurs in other articles by Melekh Ravitsh on women poets (in *Literarishe bleter*, 1927 and 1928).

18. See Kathryn Hellerstein, "A Word for My Blood: A Reading of Kadya Molodowsky's *Froyen-lider* (Vilna, 1927)." *Association for Jewish Studies Review*, vol. 13, nos. 1–2 (Spring–Fall 1988), 47–79.

19. Kadya Molodowsky, "Dzshike gas." In *Dzshike gas*. Warsaw: Literarishe bleter, 2nd printing, 1936, 5–6. Trans. Kathryn Hellerstein, "Dzshike Street." *Bridges* 2, 1 (Spring 1991), 54–55.

20. Kh. Sh. Kazdan, "Di dikhterin af der dzshike gas" (The Poetess on Dzshike Street). *Vokhnshrift* 22 (122) (June 9, 1933), 2. Kazdan blasts Molodowsky for the section "Dzshike Street" of her book, saying that it is too aesthetic, that the poet is unable to deal with the poverty but is "in love with life." He can't understand how her "pure lyricism," which he admits is a strength, can coexist with her distaste for the street of poverty. The reviewer praises her children's poems and says they have no equal in Yiddish, but then asks, "ober s'iz tsu bavundern, vi oykh dos ay a mekhitse far zikh" (but it's to wonder whether this is also a synagogue screen for herself), and criticizes her for calling the book *Dzshike gas*, when most of the poems are "tsentliker, prekhtike ferzn. zis-kheynevdeke, froyish-tsarte libelider . . ." (delicate, gorgeous verses. sweet-charming, womanly-dainty love-songs . . .).

21. See Paula Hyman, *From Dreyfus to Vichy: The Remaking of French Jewry, 1906–1939.* New York: Columbia University Press, 1979, 98, 106: ". . . restrictive legislation was imposed upon immigrant workers, artisans, and merchants, beginning with the law of August 10, 1932, which limited the ratio of foreign workers to be employed in any industry or trade to 10 percent of the total. . . . the impact of this decree upon the Jewish trades was particularly severe, and the number of immigrant *faconniers* ["home workers, who were provided with raw material by an entrepreneur and who often subcontracted their work to other laborers," 98] increased substantially as workers attempted to evade the provisons of the decree and its successors in 1934 and 1935."

See also Nancy L. Green, *The Pletzl of Paris: Jewish Immigrant Workers in the Belle Epoque.* New York: Holmes and Meier, 1986, 125–149. (This is about the 1910s, much earlier.) David H. Weinberg, *A Community on Trial: The Jews of Paris in the 1930s.* Chicago: University of Chicago Press, 1974, 103–170. Jonathan Boyarin, *Polish Jews in Paris: The Ethnography of Memory.* Bloomington: Indiana University Press, 1991, 46–53 (on illegal entry into France from Poland).

22. Susan Hardy Aiken, "Writing (in) Exile: Isak Dinesen and the Poetics of Displacement." In *Women's Writing in Exile*, eds. Mary Lynn Broe and Angela Ingram. Chapel Hill: University of North Carolina Press, 1989, 115.

23. H. H. B.-S., "Galut," *Encyclopedia Judaica*. Vol. 4, 276–294.

24. The reasons for and circumstances of Molodowsky's departure from Poland are ambiguous. According to her autobiography, *Fun mayn elterzeydns yerushe* (From My Great-grandfather's Legacy), published in *Svive* 36 [April 1972], 60–64), Molodowsky decided rather casually

to leave Poland for the United States, where her two sisters and father had settled, by accepting a 1935 invitation from the Sholem Aleichem Folk Institute as a visiting writer. That this "visit" enforced a three-year separation from her husband renders the casualness of this retrospective account suspect. The gaps in Molodowsky's narration of her departure from her husband and brother, the focus upon marginal details, and the oddly cheery tone all suggest an intentional obfuscation of the actual reasons for her emigration. My sense of this ambiguity was confirmed in a conversation on March 19, 1993, with Anna Gonshor, a master's candidate in Jewish Studies at McGill University, whose yet-unpublished research reveals that Molodowsky was very likely motivated to leave Poland because of conflicts in her political activities on the Jewish left.

25. On a Jewish woman's autobiography as "representative of the experience of Jewish women" during the Haskalah, see Shulamit Magnus, "A Woman's Experience of Enlightenment: History and Memory in the Memoirs of Pauline Wengeroff," unpublished article presented at the Jewish Studies Colloquium, Stanford University, February 11, 1992, 1–17. On Hebrew autobiographies, see Alan Mintz, *Banished from Their Fathers' Tables.* Bloomington: Indiana University Press, 1989, 3–24. The most famous examples of Yiddish autobiographies are by Sh. Abramovich (Mendele Moykhr Sforim), *Reb Khayims Yosl* (translated as Of Bygone Days), and Sholem Ravinovich (Sholem Aleichem), *Funem yarid* (From the Fair).

26. Uriel Weinreich, *Modern English-Yiddish, Yiddish-English Dictionary.* New York: YIVO Institute and McGraw-Hill, 1968, 78.

27. Kadya Molodowsky, "*Mayn artsi-biografye.*" In *In land fun mayn gebeyn.* Chicago: L. M. Stein, 1937, 8–11.

28. *Ibid.*

29. Adele Baker, Professor of Slavic Languages at the University of Washington, informed me on May 26, 1992, that the Singer sewing machine represented "America" to residents of Vilna in the late nineteenth and early twentieth centuries, for it was one of the few American imports. This made her wonder if the Singer sewing machine at the end of the poem reflects a double image of America—the America Molodowsky "saw" from Warsaw and the revised vision of America she sees now that she is in New York.

30. Molodowsky, "In land fun mayn gebeyn." In *In land fun mayn gebeyn*, 46–48.

31. *Ibid.*, 47.

32. *Ibid.*, 47.

33. Birobidzshan, a province in the far eastern part of the former USSR, was designated by the Soviet government as an autonomous "Jewish state" in 1934, although it more or less failed to catch on.

34. In "In My Hand, Two Pheasant Feathers," various kinds of Yiddish diction spark the speaker's vision of a homeland. The speaker meditates upon the two pheasant feathers from Birobidzshan that she holds in her hand:

> un mayn zikorn, di alte kro—
> zi hoyert iber mir shoyn do,
> ot itster, in nyu-york, in branks.
> s'iz do a lebn, azoy tsu zogn, oykh a kranks.
> di zelbe vog. di zelbe hendlerishe late.
> s'iz nisht keyn krom, es iz a stor.
> s'iz nisht keyn berdiker, nor a gegolter tate.
>
> bay mir in hant tsvey federn fun a fazan.
> khotsh s'klingt dos vort fazan
> tsu fremd, tsu eydl.
> s'iz nisht vi mamzer-gonoruk,
> un shoyn avade nisht vi katshke-dreydl.
> es klingt ober vi traktor, bire, tayge—

verter muntere, bavofnte,
un oysgetonene fun alter dayge.

And my memory, that old crow,
Hovers here, above me
Even now, in New York, in the Bronx.
It's a life here, that is to say, a sick life, too.
The same scales. The same mercenary patch.
No longer a "*krom,*" it is a "store."
No longer a bearded but a shaven father.

In my hand, two pheasant feathers.
Although the word "pheasant" rings
Too foreign, too refined.
It's not like "*mamzer-gonoruk,*"
(the gander's gonorrheal bastard)
And certainly not like "*katshke-dreydl*"
(lucky-ducky, spin the top, you will win where it will stop).
But it rings like tractor, Bire, Tiga—
Hearty, armed words
That have shaken off those old worries.

The speaker's initial complaint that, in New York Yiddish, the Americanism "*stor*" has replaced "*krom*" evolves into an evaluation of language as a reflection of class. The speaker considers the bird name of the feathers she holds, "fazan," pheasant, "Too foreign, too refined[,]" and compares it with two regional Yiddish phrases deeply rooted in the folk: "mamzer-gonoruk" and "katshke-dreydl." I've been hard-pressed to find a translation for either of these words, despite my badgering numerous colleagues, friends, and informants, but the first seems to be a Warsaw curse or insult that names a bastard as perhaps gander-like and/or gonorrheal, while the second is probably part of a children's nonsense rhyme having to do with ducks. In any case, the names of birds—pheasant, gander, duck—unify these lines on the symbolism of language. The word "fazan" is as exotic as the Slavic names of the Tige region and Bira River, as the word "traktor," the machine of modern farm labor, yet all these words promise to the idealistic speaker a Jewish homeland, free from the "old worries" of Jewish life in capitalism.

35. Kadya Molodowsky, "Oysyes." In *In land fun mayn gebeyn*. Chicago: L. M. Stein, 1937, 75.

36. *Ibid.*, 82.

37. *Badkhn* denotes generally a joker and specifically the traditional wedding joke-maker or professional jester, who would be hired to appear at a wedding to compose rhymed satires and sentimental songs about the bride and bridegroom. *Oriman* denotes a pauper.

38. It's important to note how flat Molodowsky's final image of the alphabet letters is, when compared to other Yiddish poems, where the letters of the Hebrew alphabet are infused with spirit and meaning. Especially relevant is Mark M. Warshawsky's (1840–1907) "Afn pripetshik" (On the Hearthstone), a song so popular that it was "folklorized," that is, it was commonly assumed to be a folk song. In this sentimental song, an old schoolteacher tells his pupils that all of Jewish life and history in exile is contained within the letters of the Hebrew alphabet. The last two stanzas read:

Az ir vet, kinder, elter vern,
vet ir aleyn farshteyn,
vifl in di oysyes lign trern,
un vi fil geveyn.

Az ir vet, kinder, dem goles shlepn,
oysgemutshet zayn,

zolt ir fun di oysyes koyekh shepn,
kukt in zey arayn!

Children, when you grow older,
You will come to know,
How many tears lie in the letters,
And how much sorrow.

Children, when you come to bear the exile,
Weary, worn, and spent,
May you derive strength from the letters,
Look into their content!

Mark M. Warshawsky, "Oyfn pripetshik" (At the Fireplace). In *Mir trogn a gezang: The New Book of Yiddish Songs*, Eleanor Gordon Mlotek. New York: Workmen's Circle Education Department, 1972, 2–3. See also, for contrast, a modernist's use of this motif: A. Glanz-Leyeles, "Der got fun yisroel" (The God of Israel). In *American Yiddish Poetry: A Bilingual Anthology*, ed. Benjamin and Barbara Harshav. Berkeley: University of California Press, 1986, 76–79.

39. Kadya Molodowsky, *Fun mayn elterzeydns yerushe* (From My Great-grandfather's Legacy), chapters 48–51. *Svive* (Environment) 36 (April 1972), 53–64. Chapters 52–54. *Svive* 37 (September 1972), 55–63.

40. Perhaps the best way to make this point is to read Molodowsky's account of how she composed the poems of *In land fun mayn gebeyn*, keeping in mind the semiotics of exile we saw in five poems from that book. In September 1972, she writes:

In my wanderings, I saw the Jews of Kiev, of Minsk, after the Russian Revolution, beaten away from their livelihoods. I saw the helplessness of the Jews in Poland, their poverty, their struggle for a piece of bread in the country of Polish oppression. I travelled through Germany in the beginning of Hitler's reign and sensed the mute fear that lay over the Jews of Germany. I came to America saturated with different exiles. A perilous storm drifts above Jewish roofs. I gave this book the name "In the Country of My Bones." The poems in this book bring out the sorrow that lay in my bones. L. M. Stein told me that he would buy new type so that the book would look nice. The book appeared in the year 1937. (Molodowsky, "Yerushe." *Svive* 37 [September 1972], 61–62)

The salient feature of this passage is the catalogue of Jewish communities—Kiev, Minsk, Poland, Germany—and their sufferings, all emblems of Jewish exile, political, economic, and cultural, at the mercy of Communism and Nazism. This list, a litany of victims, echoes the conventions of Jewish writings in response to catastrophe that go back to the Middle Ages and thereby converts the speaker into a spokesperson for the collective experience. And it is this role of spokesperson that Molodowsky retrospectively assumes, in the stunning sentence, "I came to America saturated with different exiles." What is missing here is the personal Molodowsky, her sense of her own exile. When she writes, "The poems in this book bring out the sorrow that lay in my bones," she has transformed the communal exiles into an internal sorrow. Typically for the autobiography, she does not linger on introspection; she concludes with details of cheerful pragmatism: the publisher's new font to make the book look pretty, the date of its appearance. Molodowsky's autobiography conveys the experience of exile as communal, not individual, and thereby coherent and seamless; it exhibits little of the internal conflict that marks the poems she wrote at the time.

41. On the shaping of autobiography and definition of self, see Georges Gusdorf, "Conditions and Limits of Autobiography." In *Autobiography: Essays: Theoretical and Critical*, ed. James Olney. Princeton, N.J.: Princeton University Press, 1980, 28–48. On gender and autobiography, see Shari Benstock, "Authorizing the Autobiographical." In *The Private Self: Theory and Practice of Women's Autobiographical Writings*, ed. Shari Benstock. Chapel Hill: University of North Carolina Press, 1988, 10–33. Also see Susan Stanford Friedman, "Women's Autobio-

graphical Selves: Theory and Practice." In *The Private Self: Theory and Practice of Women's Autobiographical Writings*, ed. Shari Benstock. Chapel Hill: University of North Carolina Press, 1988, 34–62. Also Jane Marcus, "Invincible Mediocrity: The Private Selves of Public Women." In *The Private Self: Theory and Practice of Women's Autobiographical Writings*, ed. Shari Benstock. Chapel Hill: University of North Carolina Press, 1988, 114–146.

42. Molodowsky, *Fun mayn elterzeydns yerushe Svive* 39 (May 1973), 55–63; *Svive* 41 (April 1974), 50–54. I say "the 1950s" because, as it is worth noting, Molodowsky provides very few dates in the autobiography, which absence contributes to the mythic, representative sense of her life story.

3.

Comparative Identities: Exile in the Writings of Frantz Fanon and W. E. B. Du Bois

ANITA HAYA GOLDMAN

The question of political identity—of the mutual dependence and jeopardy that are the result of our engagement with the political world—has been greatly complicated in recent years by the sheer variety of terms in which it has been addressed. What is immediately striking about the current literature on identity is the growing need for interdisciplinary dialogue and comparative work.

This discussion will compare and contrast two conceptions of identity, each of which derives from a distinctive tradition in political thought. The first is the model of African-American identity figured in Du Bois' *Souls of Black Folk* (1903), and elaborated by Dr. Martin Luther King, Jr.—a model which registers Du Bois' inheritance of philosophical writings by Emerson and Alexander Crummell. The second is the analysis of identity set forth in the work of Frantz Fanon. In *Black Skin, White Masks* (1952), *A Dying Colonialism* (1959), *The Wretched of the Earth* (1963), and *Toward the African Revolution* (1967), Fanon established a framework for thinking about identity which forms the basis for critical writings on colonial and postcolonial literatures.

A brief comparative look at the writings of Fanon and Du Bois immediately reveals their many similarities. Both writers refuse what Fanon refers to as the logic of "either-or"[1] and explore a central contradiction, or difference within, that is constitutive of the self. Both are adamantly concerned with the effects of racism and invoke a politics of solidarity, opposition, and liberation. And both express a critique of liberal nationalism, a tradition in which the discourse of rights has been used to mask the surreptitious violation or compromised extension of rights. But looking back over the past two and a half decades, it is the profound difference between these two thinkers which seems to be of the most vital significance. In the United States, at least, the struggle for black liberation was, and indeed still is, shackled by indecision regarding these two radically different, irreconcilable, and equally memorable visions of the self and society—between haunting justifications for defensive violence on the one hand, and on the other a desire to believe in the political efficacy of civil disobedience and love.

In the pages that follow, I will focus on a subject that is fundamental to both Fanon's and Du Bois' grappling with the question of black identity: the experience of exile, of life in the interstices between cultures,[2] what Du Bois refers to as "the world-wandering of a soul in search of itself" (*Souls*, 361).[3] Both Fanon and Du Bois were intimately familiar with the isolating discontinuities associated with exile as geographical dislocation—Fanon, we know, never returned to his native Martinique; and Du Bois emigrated to Ghana in 1961. Understanding what is unique in each theorist's conceptualization of exilic space should lead to a better understanding of their project as a whole: the task of representing exile not only shapes Fanon's and Du Bois' distinctive theories of race, their respective critiques of identitarian thought, and the development of their poetics; it is also foundational to the expression of their utopianism. This sustained deliberation over exile and identity as inseparable subjects culminates in the utopian symbology of the lifted veil: at the very outset of Du Bois' career in *Souls*, and in Fanon's meditation on the unveiled Algerian woman in *A Dying Colonialism*. The hoped-for benefits of this comparative analysis is that it will ultimately contribute to new interdisciplinary work on identity, and facilitate a dialogue between literary scholars who are interested in African–American and other "ethnic" American identities, and those whose primary theoretical researches are directed toward the colonial and postcolonial context.

There is a vast literature on the subject of exile in which theorists have variously described its effects as either beneficial and inspirational, or as mutilating.[4] In current literary discussions, there has been a rather misleading tendency to use the term metaphorically, so that the experience of exile has come to mean, more broadly, the experience of difference and estrangement in society; and most broadly, an aspect of what is most human in all of us.[5] Used in this metaphorical sense, the preoccupation with exile is obliquely registered in both Fanon's and Du Bois' writings as their critiques of available discourses on identity: for Fanon, exile may be regarded as a narcissistic withdrawal from the world into the self;[6] for Du Bois, it marks the tragic limitation of sentiment or sympathy;[7] for both writers, exile represents a failure of Hegelian recognition.[8]

For the purposes of this comparative analysis, however, it may be useful to begin by juxtaposing two substantive, detailed scenes of exile in Fanon's *Black Skin, White Masks* and in Du Bois' *Souls*, both of which contribute to the work of articulating a theory of race by accounting for the social formation of racial identity. Fanon describes the effects of race as visibility, the lived experience of the black, when he recounts the experience of being exiled from the white world upon the first occasion of his hearing the familiar phrase "Look, a Negro!" and "meeting the white man's eyes" (*BS,WM*, 109, 110). On that day, he tells us, he was "completely dislocated, unable to be abroad with the other, the white man, who unmercifully imprisoned me" (*BS, WM*, 112).

> While I was forgetting, forgiving, and wanting only to love, my message was flung back in my face like a slap. The white world, the only honorable one, barred me from all participation. . . . I was told to stay within bounds, to go back where I belonged. (*BS,WM*, 114–15)

Fanon's reflections upon the scene of exile as the moment of his constitution as a visible, racial subject—the moment at which he was seen and barred from all participation—bring to mind the opening pages of Du Bois' *Souls*. Du Bois recalls the day when, as a young boy, he was exiled by the glance of a white girl who peremptorily refused to accept his visiting-card. "In a wee wooden schoolhouse, something put it into the boys' and girls' heads to buy gorgeous visiting-cards—ten cents a package—and exchange," he writes.

> The exchange was merry, till one girl, a tall newcomer, refused my card,—refused it peremptorily, with a glance. Then it dawned upon me with a certain suddenness that I was different from the others. . . . Why did God make me an outcast and a stranger in mine own house? The shades of the prison-house closed round about us all: walls strait and stubborn to the whitest, but relentlessly narrow, tall, and unscalable to sons of night who must plod darkly on in resignation, or beat unavailing palms against the stone, or steadily, half hopelessly, watch the streak of blue above. (*Souls*, 214)

Fanon's conceptualization of exile resembles Du Bois' insofar as both theorists consider the phenomenology of the gaze—the exile's discovery that he is, as Fanon puts it, "the slave . . . of . . . appearance" (*BS,WM*, 116).[9] But beyond this, an important point of difference emerges. In contrast to Fanon's relatively brief, passing reference to the fact that he was "barred from all participation," Du Bois casts the remembered event of his exile as an elaborately wrought scene of his exclusion from a sexual economy of written self-representation that is itself inextricably bound up with the material possibilities of American liberal market culture: the visiting-cards cost ten cents a package.

Although Du Bois' recollection of exile as racism in the classroom does not involve the actual infringement of legal rights, the passage discloses an attribute of exile that is central to his thinking about identity, and which will be my primary point of focus for this discussion: namely that for Du Bois, African-American exile consists in an impaired relation to the state; it represents a deprivation of rights. The importance of this conception of exile becomes more apparent when we consider the fact that for Du Bois, the exile's political position bears a striking resemblance to that of the civil disobedient: for the African-American exile, as for the disobedient, the experience of dissatisfaction with the state justifies an act of resistance that is in turn constitutive of political identity. By contrast, as we shall see, Fanon's exploration of the meaning of exile exhibits none of Du Bois' engagement with existing political institutions or, in particular, with the oppositional, liberal rights rhetoric deployed by writers such as Thoreau, Gandhi, and King; unlike Du Bois, Fanon dismisses the conceptual possibilities of civil disobedience as a framework for social cohesion. Instead, he emphasizes the importance of existential knowledge, of bringing the fact and sources of exile into consciousness, an inner transformation that necessarily precedes any willed passivity or action (including radically violent action) with respect to social structures. In order to trace the consequences of this central difference in Fanon's and Du Bois' thinking about exile, I will now turn to the conceptual linkage of exile and rights as Du Bois invokes it in *Souls*.

Representations of exile recur throughout *Souls*, and provide an underlying structural coherence to Du Bois' narrative: the bleak historical reality of exile emerges in Du Bois' analysis of the diminishing numbers of black landowners and the subsequent migration to northern cities in "The Quest of the Golden Fleece"; it surfaces again in his imaginative exploration of Crummell's "weird pilgrimage" (*Souls*, 361) or twenty years of wandering after having been exiled from Bishop Onderdonk's diocese on account of his race; and again in "The Coming of John" when John returns home and finds it impossible to teach and thus "to find his place in the world about him" (*Souls*, 373).

The gradual accumulation of these images over the course of many pages discloses a second attribute of Du Bois' imaginative exploration of African–American exile: that this experience of exile may be effectively depicted as physical mobility; as the act of traveling over land. In *Souls* Du Bois' portrayal of exile as movement over land illustrates his ambivalence between, on the one hand, his love for and identification with the world around him; and, on the other, the scientific objectivity that is entailed by the nature of his sociological work. This ambivalence, which structures all of Du Bois' successive representations of exile, is visible in "Of the Faith of the Fathers," when Du Bois describes his walk down a country road on his way to observe a Southern Negro revival. "It was out in the country, far from home, far from my foster home, on a dark Sunday night," he recalls.

The road wandered from our rambling log-house up the stony bed of a creek, past wheat and corn, until we could hear dimly across the fields a rhythmic cadence of song,—soft, thrilling, powerful, that swelled and died sorrowfully in our ears. I was a country schoolteacher then, fresh from the East, and had never seen a Southern Negro revival. To be sure, we in Berkshire were not perhaps as stiff and formal as they in Suffolk of olden time; yet we were very quiet and subdued, and I know not what would have happened those clear Sabbath mornings had some one punctuated the sermon with a wild scream, or interrupted the long prayer with a loud Amen! (*Souls*, 337–38)

Du Bois' narrative rendering of exile is governed by the logic of this ambivalence, his contradictory wish both to repudiate and embrace the natural and cultural forms which evoke in him the fervor of religious revival. At the same time that Du Bois' lingering description of movement through the landscape mirrors his total involvement in the lovely cadences of song that take hold of his imagination, he also abruptly reminds us of his strangeness to the scene: his home is but a foster home; in Berkshire religious practices are quiet and subdued. Similar moments of ambivalence recur throughout *Souls*, as in "Of the Quest of the Golden Fleece," when Du Bois weighs the difficult question of why black agricultural laborers in Dougherty County, Georgia, are drifting to town, and breaks from this sociohistorical analysis in order to alert us to the fact that he is traveling through the Black Belt by car: "Why do not the Negroes become land-owners, and build up the black landed peasantry, which has for a generation and more been the dream of philanthropist and statesman?" he writes.

To the car-window sociologist, to the man who seeks to understand and know the South by devoting the few leisure hours of a holiday trip to unravelling the snarl of centuries,—to such men very often the whole trouble with the black field-hand may be summed up by Aunt Ophelia's word, "Shiftless!" They have noted repeatedly scenes like one I saw last summer. We were riding along the highroad to town at the close of a long day. A couple of young black fellows passed us in a muleteam. . . . Shiftless? Yes, the personification of shiftlessness. And yet follow up those boys: they are not lazy; to-morrow morning they'll be up with the sun; they work hard when they do work, and they work willingly. . . . They are careless because they have not found that it pays to be careful; they are improvident because the improvident ones of their acquaintance get on about as as well as the provident. (*Souls*, 314)

Here again, the ambivalence of exile is brought forward as the image of movement over land: at the same time that Du Bois discloses the depth of his insight into life in the Black Belt by distinguishing his methodology from that of the ordinary sociologist, he also presents himself as sitting behind that car window, gazing from a safe, objective distance at the terrible poverty which is the object of his investigation.

The repeated emphasis Du Bois places on the image of exile as movement over land registers, above all else, his belief that exile entails the deprivation of civil rights. Throughout *Souls* he situates his personal recollections of exile in relation to this sociohistorical fact of African-Americans' lack of access to the benefits of political life. For Du Bois, the exile's stance is one of resistance and ongoing struggle to assert legal and human rights: the right to vote; the right to ownership and self-ownership; and the right to freedom, which he defines as freedom to work, to think, to love, and to aspire (*Souls*, 220).

In "The Railway Emergency Brake: The Use of Analogy in Legal and Political Argument,"[10] Elaine Scarry explores the idea that political obligations or the bonds of citizenship are tacitly assumed by voluntary, willed movement of the body along a public highway. In particular, Scarry calls attention to John Locke's description in his *Second Treatise of Government* of the citizen's tacit consent as "consent . . . [that] is detached from property rights and attached to the voluntary motion of 'travelling freely on the highway' " (7). Scarry's insight with regard to the representation of consent as free movement on the public highway—and, in particular, her concern with the legal definition of the public highway as a democratic space in which the enjoyment of civil rights is protected regardless of race—has clear applicability to Du Bois' imaginative rendering of exile as the act of walking on the public highway.

Du Bois' haunting realization that in the South a black person may be deprived of his rights of citizenship even in that most democratic of spaces, the public highway, is crucial to understanding his account of exile in *Souls*. The inseparability of Du Bois' vision of exile and his preoccupation with rights is explicitly articulated in "The Quest of the Golden Fleece," when he observes that "a black stranger in Baker County . . . is liable to be stopped anywhere on the public highway" (*Souls*, 313). In "The Meaning of Progress" this image of exile is brought closer to home when Du Bois describes himself as a stranger walking along a Tennessee highway, looking for a job. "I see now the white, hot roads lazily rise and fall and wind before me under the burning July sun," he writes.

I feel the deep weariness of my heart and limb as ten, eight, six miles stretch relentlessly ahead; I feel my heart sink heavily as I hear again and again, "Got a teacher? Yes." So I walked on and on—horses were too expensive—

until I had wandered beyond railways, beyond stage lines, to a land of "varmints" and rattlesnakes, where the coming of a stranger was an event, and men lived and died in the shadow of one blue hill. (*Souls*, 253)

On the one hand, Du Bois is continually drawn to the land and the collective history it represents, because his identity as a teacher, a sociologist, and an exiled stranger emerges only insofar as he is symbolically situated in relation to it. On the other hand, Du Bois resists the threat inherent in his very nearness to the poverty, unemployment, and discrimination that are the subject of his analysis. At the same time that Du Bois describes his intimacy with and movement within the barren landscape, he also works at every moment to distance himself from the prospect of violated rights, economic immobility, and years of suffering it inevitably brings to mind— the fact that, as he tells us, in this land men lived and died in the shadow of one blue hill. Like a blues song, *Souls* explores the symbolic possibilities of exile—and, more specifically, the ambivalence embedded in the image of walking along the public highway—for the verbal work of self-creation.[11]

The relationship between exile, movement over land, and the deprivation of civil rights culminates in the image of train travel in *Souls*.[12] In "The Coming of John," John leaves his home and family on a train that "noisily bore playmate and brother and son away to the world" (364), and returns once again to Altahama, seated on another train which Du Bois specifically presents as a space of political exile.[13] "John rose gloomily as the train stopped," Du Bois writes, "for he was thinking of the 'Jim Crow' car" (*Souls*, 370). Indeed, earlier in *Souls*, Du Bois confronts his own difficulties of exile when he invites his reader to ride the Jim Crow car in this famous passage from "Of the Black Belt":

But we must hasten on our journey. .... If you wish to ride with me you must come into the "Jim Crow Car." There will be no objection,—already four other white men, and a little white girl with her nurse, are in there. Usually the races are mixed in there; but the white coach is all white. Of course this car is not so good as the other, but it is fairly clean and comfortable. The discomfort lies chiefly in the hearts of those four black men yonder—and in mine. (*Souls*, 286)

In *From Behind the Veil*, Robert Stepto has accurately described Du Bois' transformation of the Jim Crow car, a "despised and imposed conveyance, employed rather ingeniously to inflict the stasis of social structure upon blacks in motion, into something of a ritual vehicle for *communitas*."[14] Du Bois' refusal to cast his experience of discrimination in purely personal terms results not only in his articulation of a collective, because heartfelt, experience of exile for African-Americans; it also leaves open the possibility that this exilic discomfort may be communicated to any reader, regardless of race, who accepts his invitation to enter an exilic narrative space, represented by the image of the train rolling on through the Black Belt.[15]

Finally, the image of train travel through the Black Belt provides Du Bois with yet another occasion to gaze out through a windowpane at the landscape: "Out of the North the train thundered, and we woke to see the crimson soil of Georgia stretching away bare and monotonous right and left," he writes.

Yet we did not nod, nor weary of the scene; for this is historic ground. Right across our track, three hundred and sixty years ago, wandered the cavalcade of Hernando de Soto. . . . Here sits Atlanta, the city of a hundred hills. . . . Just this side of Atlanta is the land of the Cherokees and to the southwest . . . , you may stand on a spot which is to-day the centre of the Negro problem,—the centre of those nine million men who are America's dark heritage from slavery and the slave-trade. (*Souls*, 285)

Just as, when he describes a couple of black men in a mule team seen through his car window, Du Bois discloses his powerful identification with life and labor in the Black Belt at the same time that he asserts his distanced scientific objectivity; so, here, the ambivalence of exile has been put in service of historiographical work. Du Bois' omission of any reference to his personal experience of exile in the Jim Crow car works against the generic conventions and premises of autobiographical narrative: in this passage, Du Bois symbolically situates himself in relation to the landscape by conceiving of it in historical terms, as the collective history of nine million exiles, the history of what he calls "the Negro problem."

I have called attention to the ambivalence of exile—the fact that Du Bois is forever balancing his attachment and aversion to the social world, a world that takes on an incontestable reality in Du Bois' writings only as he tirelessly records his observations and movement through the landscape—because this ambivalence manifests itself in connection with Du Bois' thinking about rights, and in particular his critique of the liberal tradition in identitarian thought. We have seen that at the same time that Du Bois identifies with black history and culture, America's dark heritage, he also distances himself from the economic immobility and violated rights that constitute the historical burdens of identification. For Du Bois, this ambivalence of exile, the experience of being doubly exiled from the beneficial intimacies of both race and citizenship, is famously articulated in his innovative theory of African-American identity as double-consciousness. "The Negro is a sort of seventh son, born with a veil, and gifted with second-sight in this American world,—a world which yields him no true self-consciousness, but only lets him see himself through the revelation of the other world," Du Bois observes.

It is a peculiar sensation, this double-consciousness, this sense of always looking at one's self through the eyes of others. . . . One ever feels his twoness,—an American, a Negro; two souls, two thoughts, two unreconciled strivings; two warring ideals in one dark body. (*Souls*, 215)

Du Bois' vision of exile in this passage is best understood as part of his larger critique of the liberal concept of personhood as self-possessed citizenship. For Du Bois, exile results in a model of identity as double-consciousness which enacts a critique of rights as a framework for thinking about political identity: the discourse of rights, like race, is necessary but insufficient to represent the self. Each time he demonstrates the flexibility, the untold capacities, and the necessity of democratic language, Du Bois also alerts us to dangers of this rhetoric, the fact that rights have often been invoked to mask their compromised extension or violation. Viewed in these terms, the model of black identity as double-consciousness that emerges from Du Bois' conceptualization of African–American exile is one that allows him to profit from the oppositional possibilities of liberalism and racialism without being enslaved to these identitarian categories as artifacts of white Western culture.[16]

Du Bois' critique of liberalism, his strategic disavowal yet simultaneous commitment to rights, calls our attention back to the fact, and consequences, of this fundamental difference with Fanon in his thinking about exile: unlike Du Bois' vision of exile in *Souls*, Fanon's writings exhibit an outright rejection of liberalism. Fanon's profound dissatisfaction with the discourse of rights, his awareness of the insufficiencies of the liberal framework to account for the experience of exile and oppression, is most readily apparent in *Wretched of the Earth*. "The characteristic feature of certain political structures is that they claim abstract principles but refrain from issuing definite commands," he writes.

The entire action of these nationalist political parties during the colonial period is action of the electoral type: a string of philosophico-political dissertations on the themes of rights of peoples to self-determination, the rights of man to freedom from hunger and human dignity, and the unceasing affirmation of the principle: "One man, one vote." The national political parties never lay stress upon the necessity of a trial of armed strength, for the good reason that their objective is not the radical overthrowing of the system.[17]

For Fanon, the liberal vocabulary of rights is language which has, in his words, been "hammered into the native's mind" by a corrupt colonialist bourgeoisie (*WE*, 47); it is language which has forever lost its referential capacities by having been put to bad use. In *Wretched of the Earth*, Fanon calls for the invention of a new political vocabulary, hence new forms of social organization, that will present radical alternatives to liberalism. "The very forms of organization of the struggle will suggest . . . a different vocabulary," he concludes. "Brother, sister, friend—these are words outlawed by the colonialist bourgeoisie, because for them my brother is my purse, my friend is part of my scheme for getting on." (*WE*, 47)

This difference concerning Fanon's and Du Bois' critique of liberalism is reflected in their different approaches to the historical matter of emancipation in their writings. Although in *Souls* Du Bois does not, as he would thirty-two years later in *Black Reconstruction*, emphasize the fact that bearing arms was essential to the acquisition of American citizenship on the part of freedmen, he does acknowledge the active participation of blacks in the process of political self-transformation. For example, in the chapter titled "Of the Dawn of Freedom," Du Bois calls attention to the experience of blacks during Sherman's raid through Georgia: "Some see all significance in the grim front of the destroyer, and some in the bitter sufferers of the Lost Cause," he writes.

But to me neither soldier nor fugitive speaks with so deep a meaning as that dark human cloud that clung like remorse on the rear of those swift columns. . . . In vain were they ordered back, in vain were bridges hewn from beneath their feet; on they trudged and writhed and surged, until they rolled into Savannah, a starved and naked horde of tens of thousands. (*Souls*, 225)

In contrast to Du Bois' acknowledgement of black agency in the process of political self-transformation, Fanon insists in *Black Skin, White Masks* that "historically, the Negro . . . was set free by his master" (*BS,WM*, 219). During the course of his discussion, Fanon makes an explicit distinction between the history of emancipation for American blacks and the experience of "the French Negro," who "did not fight for his freedom" (*BS,WM*, 219): "The former slave needs a challenge to his humanity, he wants a conflict, a riot," he observes.

But it is too late: The French Negro is doomed to bite himself and just to bite. I say "the French Negro," for the American Negro is cast in a different play. In the United States, the Negro battles and is battled. . . .
    . . . For the French Negro the situation is unbearable. Unable ever to be sure whether the white man considers him consciousness in-itself-for-itself, he must forever absorb himself in uncovering resistance, opposition, challenge. (*BS,WM*, 221–222)

For Fanon, then, this programmatic process of reconstructing the historical particularities of emancipation necessarily determines conceptual possibilities for thinking about identity and exile, and underscores the fact that he is uniquely situated with respect to a tradition in identitarian thought. While, as we have seen, Du Bois' views on black emancipation in the United States fit well with his critique of liberalism and his representation of exile as the deprivation of rights, Fanon's historiographal rendering of emancipation entails a concept of the French Negro's exile as an unbearable situation of doubt as to "whether the white man considers him consciousness in-itself-for-itself."

We know that Fanon read widely in works of existential philosophy and literature which were popular in postwar France.[18] In particular, he was influenced by Sartre's writings on identity such as *Anti-Semite and Jew* and *Being and Nothingness*. But the work that had the greatest impact on Fanon's thinking about exile was Sartre's *Black Orpheus*, which Sartre wrote as an introduction to Leopold Senghor's *Anthologie de la nouvelle poésie nègre et malgache de langue française*. In this essay, Sartre dwells at length on the relationship between exile, language, and the emergence of identity in the colonial context. The aspect of Sartre's poetics that is most relevant to this discussion, and which warrants a brief unfolding here, is Sartre's invention and use of a rich symbology of geographical displacement.

Exile as political displacement is often experienced as geographical displacement: as Said puts it, "Exile is the unhealable rift forced between a human being and a native place, between the self and its true home. . . . Exile is predicated on the existence of, love for, and bond with one's native place" ("The Mind of Winter," 49, 55).[19] In *Black Orpheus*, Sartre exploits the powerful, resonant symbolism of the Haitian poet's geographical displacement, celebrating an imagined or "mystic" geography of exile as it contributes to the inspired poetic expression of black identity as negritude. "He begins thus by exile; the exile of his body offers a striking example of the exile of his heart," Sartre observes.

He is most of the time in Europe, in the midst of its gray crowds; he dreams of Port-au-Prince, of Haiti. But this is not enough; in Port-au-Prince he was already in exile. The slavers have torn his fathers from Africa and have dispersed them. . . . We have one hemisphere with three concentric circles. At the periphery stretches the land of exile, colorless Europe. Next comes the dazzling circle of the Indies and of childhood, which dance the round in circling Africa. And then Africa, the last circle, navel of the world, pole of all black poetry; Africa, dazzling, incendiary, oily as the serpent's skin; Africa of the fire and the rain, torrid and suffocating, phantom Africa, vacillating as a flame, between being and non-being, more true than the "eternal boulevards and their legions of cops," but yet remote, disintegrating

Europe by its black invisible lines; Africa beyond reach, *imaginary* continent.[20]

In this passage, Sartre's "mystic geography" functions as a necessary, magnificent symbol of exile which represents an inner exile of the heart: negritude, the black soul, is "an Africa from which the Negro is exiled," surrounded by the sterile technology, the "cold buildings" of white culture (*BO*, 19). The hemisphere Sartre envisions, with dazzling Africa at its center, transforms the potentially mutilating exilic encounter with cultural difference and self-difference into an experience that is constitutive of identity: "[The Negro] must indeed breach the walls of the culture prison, and he must indeed, one day, return to Africa," he concludes. "Thus, with the apostles of negritude, indissolubly fused are the theme of the return to the native land and that of redescent into the bursting Hell of the black soul" (*BO*, 20–21).

Sartre's emphasis on the symbolism of geographical displacement promotes his own political, philosophical, and literary agenda in *Black Orpheus* in three respects. First, it provides Sartre with the opportunity to exhibit the powerful effects of this symbology, not only in the poetic production of black identity, but also on the workings and triumph of his own poetic imagination, the production of his own text. Second, Sartre's celebrated image of Africa as the pole of all black poetry paradoxically (but not surprisingly) functions to establish the significance and centrality of Europe as "the land of exile." And finally, Sartre's construction of an imaginary geography of exile provides the ground of his claim to have comprehended the meaning of black identity as negritude; an appropriative gesture which Fanon deplores in *Black Skin, White Masks*. Fanon insists that Sartre could not have heard a black cry, because there has as yet been no mutual recognition between blacks and whites: "I am speaking here, on the one hand, of alienated (duped) blacks, and, on the other, of no less alienated (duping and duped) whites," he writes.

Sartre begins *Orphée Noir* thus: "What then did you expect when you unbound the gag that had muted those black mouths? That they would chant your praises? Did you think that when those heads that our fathers had forcibly bowed down to the ground were raised again, you would find adoration in their eyes?" I do not know; but I say that he who looks into my eyes for anything but a perpetual question will have to lose his sight; neither recognition nor hate. And if I cry out, it will not be a black cry. No, from the point of view adopted here, there is no black problem. Or at any rate if there is one it concerns the whites only accidentally. It is a story that takes place in darkness, and the sun that is carried within me must shine into the smallest crannies. (*BS, WM*, 28–29)

Fanon's critique of Sartre's appropriation of negritude—an appropriative strategy that is inextricably bound up with Sartre's symbolic geography of exile—is registered in Fanon's own deliberate avoidance of concrete geographical detail in his attempt to grapple with the meaning of exile. Thus while, as we have seen, in *Souls* Du Bois' conceptualization of exile is often represented by processual images of travel—images that express Du Bois' ambivalence toward the landscape—in *Black Skin, White Masks* Fanon avoids any concrete references to landscape or geographical displacement.

Having repudiated Sartre's symbolism of geographical displacement, Fanon turns instead to the exilic effects of speech: for Fanon, exile consists in a verbal gesture, the attempt to enlarge difference by assuming the white mask of language, which the colonized subject is driven to enact. "I ascribe a basic importance to the phenomenon of language," Fanon writes (*BS,WM*, 17).

To speak means to be in a position to use a certain syntax, to grasp the morphology of this or that language, but it means above all to assume a culture, to support the weight of a civilization. . . .

Every colonized people . . . finds itself face to face with the language of the civilizing nation; that is, with the culture of the mother country. . . .

Every dialect is a way of thinking. . . . And the fact that the newly returned Negro adopts a language different from that of the group into which he was born is evidence of a dislocation, a separation. (*BS,WM*, 17, 18–19, 25)

In *Black Skin, White Masks*, Fanon persistently returns to this central significance of language, the Martinican's assumption of a white mask, for the experience of exile. On the one hand, he describes the exilic effects the white mask produces at "home": the "magic vault of distance" created by the native Martinican who, just before leaving for France, will acknowledge only those who hold the keys, the magic words *Paris, Marseille, Sorbonne, Pigalle* (*BS,WM*, 23); the fact that if a native returns from France and says "I am so happy to be back with you. Good Lord, it is hot in this country, I shall certainly not be able to endure it very long," his family and acquaintances will know that "a European has got off the ship" (*BS,WM*, 37); the experience of the returning Martinican, no longer understood by his "old mother . . . when he talks to her about his *duds*, the family's *crummy joint*, the *dump* . . . all of it, of course, tricked out with the appropriate accent" (*BS,WM*, 36–37). On the other hand, Fanon shows us that the Martinican who is driven to seek admittance into the sanctuary of white culture, will be exiled, barred from participation, immediately upon his arrival in France. "What I am asserting is that the European has a fixed concept of the Negro and there is nothing more exasperating than to be asked: 'How long have you been in France? You speak French so well,' " Fanon observes. "Nothing is more astonishing than to hear a black man express himself properly, for then in truth he is putting on the white world" (BS,WM, 35,36).

Fanon's engagement with Sartre in *Black Skin, White Masks* results in a distinctive framework for thinking about exile: for Fanon, exile is an "existential deviation" (BS,WM, 14) which white European culture imposes on the black man. Fanon presents us with his analysis and diagnosis of this form of exile at the very beginning of *Black Skin, White Masks* when he calls our attention to the experience of a black man who has been "uprooted, pursued, baffled, doomed to watch the dissolution of the truths that he has worked out for himself one after another" (BS,WM, 8). Fanon observes that this man, having embraced an essentialist concept of "the black soul" constructed by white civilization and European culture, will do one of two things. Either he will—even in his state of total imprisonment within the mythic, European concept of the black soul—naively believe that he has chosen his state of exile as an act of free will; or he will seek to belong to his people. "The educated Negro, slave of the spontaneous and cosmic Negro myth, feels at a given stage that his race no longer understands him," Fanon insists. Or that he no longer understands it.

Then he congratulates himself on this, and enlarging the difference, the incomprehension, the disharmony, he finds in them the meaning of his real humanity. Or more rarely he wants to belong to his people. And it is with rage in his mouth and abandon in his heart that he buries himself in the vast black abyss. We shall see that this attitude, so heroically absolute, renounces the present and the future in the name of the past. (BS,WM, 14)

At this point, one fact about Fanon's analysis of identity and exile in *Black Skin, White Masks* should be absolutely clear: namely, that the particular manifestation of exile he describes in this passage is one that Fanon *diagnoses* and does not in any way *prescribe*. Although the exile *believes* that his gesture of assuming the mask of white culture is an act of free will, Fanon insists at the very outset that this man is in fact an existential deviation, "slave of the spontaneous and cosmic Negro myth," which white civilization and European culture have imposed on him. This colonized subject is not free but rather, driven to assume the white mask: "On the basis of other studies and my own personal observations, *I want to try to show why the Negro adopts such a position*, peculiar to him, with respect to European languages," he writes. "Let me point out once more that the conclusions I have reached pertain to the French Antilles; at the same time, I am not unaware that the same behavior patterns obtain in every race that has been subjected to colonization" (BS,WM, 25, emphasis added).

Fanon's rhetoric of diagnosis, which emerges at crucial moments during the course of his analysis in *Black Skin, White Masks*, presents us with a pathology of exile: what his countless anecdotes and references to case studies disclose is that the exile's obsessive repudiation of blackness, his demand to be acknowledged as white, precisely exhibits his enslavement to a definition of himself which the white man has built. "After what has just been said, it will be understood that the first impulse of the black man is to say *no* to those who attempt to build a definition of him," he writes.

Since the Negro is appraised in terms of the extent of his assimilation, it is also understandable why the newcomer expresses himself only in French. It is because he wants to emphasize the rupture that has now occurred. He is incarnating a new type of man that he imposes on his associates and his family. . . .
The black man wants to be like the white man. For the black man there is only one destiny. And it is white.
Long ago the black man admitted the unarguable superiority of the white man, and all his efforts are aimed at achieving a white existence. (*BS,WM*, 228)

Fanon's diagnosis of what he regards as a historically determined condition of exile—an exile resulting from the social fact of visibility and blackness on the one hand and, on the other, the drive to assume the white mask of French language and culture—is central to his analysis of the antinomy that structures black identity, an antinomy that emerges out of the colonial environment and to which he directs our attention in *Black Skin, White Masks*. "The black man has two dimensions," he writes. "One with his fellows, the other with the white man. A Negro behaves differently with a white man and with another Negro. That this self-division is a direct result of colonialist subjugation is beyond question" (*BS,WM*, 17). But in recent postcolonial (and predominantly poststructuralist) criticism, the question remains: what possibilities for identity and self-representation does Fanon prescribe—what should the colonized person *do* in light of this poetics of exile, his enslavement to the essentializing artifacts of white culture, this unwilled inhabiting of language? A nagging doubt among critics as to whether or not Fanon's diagnosis offers the colonized a way out of his predicament has resulted in a prolonged, heated debate concerning the problematic significance of colonial discourse for Fanon's analysis of subject formation.[21]
It is not my intention to add to the literature in this debate. However, two aspects of Fanon's thinking about exile may be brought directly to bear on the agonizing question of whether colonial discourse is empowering

or debilitating to the colonized. First, Fanon's differences with Du Bois concerning the uses of democratic language as colonialist discourse underscore the salient point that whether an invocation of rights bears reference to anything beyond itself depends, as is the case whenever we resort to words, upon where and how these rights are invoked and by whom. Second, as Fanon repeatedly observes, there is a crucial distinction to be made between exile that results from the pathological, compulsive assumption of the white mask of discourse, and volitional manipulation of that mask as a means of struggle. Fanon's vision of exile as a freely chosen act of self-invention is finally brought forward in this moving, prescriptive reminder:

I should constantly remind myself that the real *leap* consists in introducing invention into existence.
   In the world through which I travel, I am endlessly creating myself. *BS,WM*, 229)[22]

The concept of freedom Fanon promotes in the concluding pages of *Black Skin, White Masks* is Sartrean—in contrast to Du Bois, Fanon does not conceive of this freedom as a civil right. "In other words, the black man should no longer be confronted by the dilemma, turn white or disappear; but he should be able to take cognizance of a possibility of existence," Fanon writes. "In still other words, if society makes difficulties for him because of his color . . . my objective, once his motivations have been brought into consciousness, will be to put in him a position to *choose* action (or passivity) with respect to the real source of the conflict—that is, toward the social structures" (*BS,WM*, 100).[23] Rather than articulating a meaning for freedom expressed as participation within preexisting social structures, the freedom Fanon prescribes is an existential, creative, demanding freedom of consciousness, upon which any possibility of willed action or passivity with respect to social structures is predicated.[24]

I have suggested that Fanon's poetics of exile is best understood in light of his response to the tradition in identitarian thought represented by Sartre's *Black Orpheus*. By contrast, Du Bois' poetics of exile in *Souls* results from his critique of an altogether different philosophical tradition, represented by the writings of Alexander Crummell. In "The English Language in Liberia," an address delivered in 1860 before the Liberian citizens of Maryland County, Liberia, Crummell insists that the language of the colonizer must be assumed by the colonized, arguing that English is the language of democracy and thus represents the sole means of articulating a recognizable political identity.[25] Exploring what he calls "the peculiar advantage which Anglo–Africans have gained by the loss of their mother tongue,"[26] Crummell argues that "the English language . . . is marked by these prominent peculiarities . . . (a) *It is a language of unusual force and power* . . . (b) [It] *is characteristically the language of freedom* . . . [and] (c) . . . *the English language is the enshrinement of those great charters of liberty which are essential elements of free governments, and the main guarantees of personal liberty* . . . " (*FA*, 22, 23, 25). Exhorting his audience to "endeavor to live up to the sentiments breathed forth in all the legal charters, the noble literature, the religious learning of this tongue," Crummell writes as follows:

Let us guard, even here, the right of FREE SPEECH. . . . Let us prize the principle of PERSONAL LIBERTY, as one of the richest jewels of our constitutional diadem. . . . Moreover, let us cultivate the principle of INDEPENDENCE, both as a nation and as individuals, and in our children. . . . (*FA*, 51–53)

Du Bois' persistent engagement with the liberal discourse of rights in his rendering of African–American exile in *Souls* reveals his sympathetic comprehension of Crummell's writings on identity and language. For example, Crummell's influence is visible in Du Bois' critique of Booker T. Washington, where Du Bois exhibits his intense preoccupation with the expressive possibilities of democratic language. For Du Bois, this critique of Washington's surrender of civil rights devolves upon the central question of language. Deploring Washington's use of what he calls "the speech of triumphant commercialism" (*Souls*, 241), Du Bois then goes on to invoke and recuperate what he describes as the forgotten language of the Founding Fathers, the sacrosanct discourse of rights. "So far as Mr. Washington does not rightly value the privilege and duty of voting . . .—so far as he, the South, or the Nation, does this,—we must unceasingly and firmly oppose them," Du Bois concludes. "By every civilized and peaceful method we must strive for the rights which the world accords to men, clinging unwaveringly to those great words which the sons of the Fathers would fain forget: 'We hold these truths to be self-evident: That all men are created equal; that they are endowed by their Creator with certain unalienable rights . . .' " (*Souls*, 252).

Du Bois' view of the relationship between exile, identity, and language— and, in particular, his practical acknowledgement of the necessity of a common democratic vocabulary of rights for the coherent articulation of individual and collective identity for African-Americans—raises a final point of comparison with Fanon. For both writers, the exilic symbology of the veil is foundational to the expression of their utopianism.

We have seen that in *Black Skin, White Masks*, Fanon describes the exilic effects produced by the white mask of language assumed by the returning Martinican. Like Fanon, in "Of the Coming of John," Du Bois depicts

John's exile when he speaks at the Baptist church and the audience fails altogether to comprehend his "unknown tongue": "A painful hush seized that crowded mass," Du Bois writes.

Little had they understood of what he said, for he spoke an unknown tongue, save the last word about baptism; that they knew, and they sat very still while the clock ticked. (*Souls*, 371)

Unlike Fanon, however, Du Bois' imaginative exploration of the relationship between language and exile in *Souls* has powerful biblical resonance. The passage alludes to the story in Exodus, when Moses returns to his people after speaking with God only to find that he can only be heard and understood by them when he covers his face with a veil. The religious and political significances of the veil converge in "Of the Meaning of Progress," when Du Bois explicitly figures the collective experience of exile for African-Americans as exile behind a veil that debars them from economic opportunity and access to rights. "I have called my tiny community a world, and so its isolation made it; and yet there was among us but a half-awakened common consciousness, sprung from common joy and grief, at burial, birth, or wedding; from a common hardship in poverty, poor land, and low wages; and, above all, from the sight of the Veil that hung between us and Opportunity," he recalls.

All this caused us to think some thoughts together; but those, when ripe for speech, were spoken in various languages. Those whose eyes twenty-five and more years before had seen "the glory of the coming of the Lord," saw in every present hindrance or help a dark fatalism bound to bring all things right in His own good time. The mass of those to whom slavery was a dim recollection of childhood found the world a puzzling thing. . . . There were, however, some . . . to whom War, Hell, and Slavery were but childhood tales. . . . Ill could they be content, born without and beyond the World. And their weak wings beat against their barriers,—barriers of caste, of youth, of life; at last, in dangerous moments, against everything that opposed even a whim. (*Souls*, 257–58)

Read in biblical terms, the passage alludes to the story of Babel, where the attempted construction of a city and a tower resulted in the confusion of languages (Genesis 11). In political terms, Du Bois follows Crummell and the political philosophy of John Stuart Mill by suggesting that coherent expression and recognition of political community entails community of language.[27] What Du Bois suggests is that differences in language create divisions within the community, thereby impeding the raised consciousness of a collective experience of exile. Using the veil as a symbol of exile— an insurmountable barrier to opportunity and rights—Du Bois opens the conceptual possibility of a distinctive, collective identity for African-Americans, at the same time that he points to democratic prospects for political coexistence.

The exilic symbology of the veil Du Bois imagines in *Souls* results in a model of ideal nationhood that mandates the coexistence of rights and race as contradictory but equally necessary modes of political representation. At the same time that Du Bois imagines a black community in isolation behind the veil, a community that stands in a dissenting position of withdrawal from the United States, he also insists that the truest meaning for progress entails the democratic ideal of universal access to the benefits of citizenship, of "fostering and developing the traits and talents of the Negro, not in opposition to or contempt for other races, but rather in large conformity to the greater ideals of the American Republic, in order that some day on American soil two world-races may give each to each those characteristics both so sadly lack" (*Souls*, 220). Du Bois symbolically constitutes and threatens the dissolution of this exilic space in his description of the volitional act of lifting the veil: "Leaving, then, the white world, I have stepped within the Veil, raising it that you may view faintly its deeper recesses," he writes. "And . . . need I add that I who speak here am bone of the bone and flesh of the flesh of them that live within the Veil?" (*Souls*, 209). Just as in *Black Skin, White Masks*, Fanon represents the utopian possibilities of exile as self representation, the willed act of manipulating the white mask as a means of struggle, so in this symbolic, deliberate gesture of lifting the veil of exile Du Bois creates new utopian and structural possibilities for group formation.

Du Bois' sustained, labored attention to the complexities of exile in *Souls* culminates in the utopian symbol of the lifted veil. For Fanon, too, the question of exile leads inevitably to his construction and analysis of a utopian symbol, the veiled Algerian woman in *A Dying Colonialism*. In this volume of essays, Fanon records the emergence of Algeria's sovereignty and identity by tracing the difficulties faced by the Algerian woman upon her entrance into the European city. Given the highly problematic nature of Fanon's rendering of female subjectivity in *Black Skin, White Masks*, his elaborate description of the Algerian woman's experience in *A Dying Colonialism* assumes a startling centrality for the expression of his utopianism. The veil worn by this woman is described by Fanon as a site of contestation between the occupying forces and Algerian men: the symbolic unveiling of a woman increased the occupier's aggressiveness and hopes because it suggested cultural dislocation and the destruction of what Fanon describes as "the people's originality":[28] "The young Algerian woman . . .—must overcome a multiplicity of inner resistances, of subjectively organized fears, of emotions," he observes.

She quickly has to invent new dimensions for her body, new means of muscular control. She has to create for herself an attitude of unveiled-woman-outside. . . . The Algerian woman who walks stark naked into the European city relearns her body, re-establishes it in a totally revolutionary fashion. This new dialectic of the body and of the world is primary in the case of one revolutionary woman.

To the colonist offensive against the veil, the colonized opposes the cult of the veil. . . . Removed and reassumed again and again, the veil has been manipulated, transformed into a technique of camouflage, into a means of struggle. (*ADC*, 59, 47, 61)

I began this discussion by suggesting that Du Bois' conceptualization of exile as entailing the deprivation of rights bears a striking similarity to the political stance of the civil disobedient. Although, for Du Bois, exile represents an impaired relationship to the state, this is nonetheless a relationship of political obligation: it is precisely the African-American exile's dissatisfaction and hence justification for resistance that is constitutive of his or her political identity. Viewed in these terms, Du Bois' thinking about exile is not only foundational to a distinctive tradition in African-American literature of exile; it also helps us to understand why and how this literature of exile is also a literature of protest.[29]

Although, as we have seen, Fanon celebrates the Algerian woman's symbolic action of lifting the veil as a means of resistance in *A Dying Colonialism*, he is best known for his dismissal of civil disobedience as a deceptive, self-interested ruse on the part of the colonialist bourgeoisie, a dismissal that fits well with his skepticism with regard to the referential capacities of rights discourse, and his subsequent repudiation of the premises of liberalism. "At the decisive moment, the colonialist bourgeoisie . . . comes into the field," he writes in *Wretched of the Earth*.

It introduces the new idea which is in proper parlance a creation of the colonial situation: non-violence. In its simplest form this non-violence signifies to the intellectual and economic elite of the colonized country that the bourgeoisie has the same interests as they and that it is therefore urgent and indispensible to come to terms for the public good. Non-violence is an attempt to settle the colonial problem around a green baize table, before any regrettable act has been performed or irreparable gesture made, before any blood has been shed. But if the masses, without waiting for the chairs to be arranged around the baize table, listen to their own voice and begin committing outrages and setting fire to the buildings, the elite and the nationalist bourgeois parties will be seen rushing to the colonialists to exclaim, "This is very serious! We do not know how it will end; we must find a solution—some sort of compromise." (*WE*, 61–62)

Writing in the wake of student uprisings, urban rioting, and the advent of Black Power, Hannah Arendt once observed that Fanon, as one the few authors of rank who glorified violence for violence's sake, was motivated by a distrust of language and a deep hatred of bourgeois society that led to a radical break with its moral standards.[30] Fanon's dismissal of the conceptual possibilities of civil disobedience as a framework for social cohesion, and as a tactical strategy for challenging unjust laws while upholding the possibility for political coexistence,[31] leads him in *Wretched of the Earth* to his famous and controversial justification of defensive violence.[32] "The practice of violence binds [the colonized people] together as a whole, since each individual forms a violent link in the great chain, a part of the great organism of violence which has surged upward in reaction to the settler's violence in the beginning" (93). The complex relationship between, on the one hand, the poetics and symbology of exile in the work of Fanon and Du Bois, and, on the other, the registration of political identity in acts of disobedience— whether civil or violent—is an important and little-understood subject that extends beyond the frame of the present analysis. But in light of violent events and debates in recent years, it is clear this matter ought to be attended to thoroughly and soon.

NOTES

1. Frantz Fanon, *Black Skin, White Masks,* trans. Charles Markmann (New York: Grove Press, 1965), 203. All future references are to *BS, WM* and will be cited parenthetically.

2. In an essay entitled "Worldliness-Without-World, Homelessness-As-Home: Toward a Definition of the Specular Border Intellectual," Abdul R. JanMohamed elucidates a concept of exile and intellectual activity associated with what he calls "the Specular Border Intellectual," represented by writers such as Edward Said, W. E. B. Du Bois, Richard Wright, and Zora Neale Hurston. For JanMohamed, this particular form of exile is experienced only by individuals who are equally familiar with two cultures and unwilling to be "at home" in either. "Caught between several cultures or groups, none of which are deemed sufficiently enabling or productive," he argues, "the specular intellectual subjects the cultures to analytic scrutiny rather than combining them; he or she utilizes his or her interstitial cultural space as a vantage point from which to define, implicitly or explicitly, other, utopian possibilities of group formation" (*Edward Said: A Critical Reader,* ed. Michael Sprinker [Oxford: Blackwell, 1992], 97). All future references are to "The Specular Border Intellectual" and will be cited parenthetically.

3. W. E. B. Du Bois, *The Souls of Black Folk, Three Negro Classics* (New York: Avon Books, 1965), 361. All future references are to *Souls* and will be cited parenthetically.

4. Although he warns us that "to think of exile as beneficial, as a spur to humanism or creativity, is to belittle its mutilations," Said also argues that the exile's "contrapuntal" awareness can be a source of power: "Exiles cross borders, break barriers of thought and experience," he writes. "Seeing 'the entire world as a foreign land' makes possible originality of vision." ("The Mind of Winter: Reflections on Life in Exile," *Harpers Magazine* [September 1984], 54–55. All future references are to "The Mind of Winter" and will be cited parenthetically.)

5. In his introduction to a recent collection of critical essays on the subject, David Bevan writes, "For exile, in its broadest sense, is not only a specific historical circumstance, it is also a constant of our common predicament. In this the evident particularity of political displacement may be merely a symptom or an image of some other form of estrangement: womanhood, the Third World, migrant labour, apartheid, colonisation and sundry further estates of marginality.

. . . Exile, viscerally, is different, otherness" (*Literature and Exile* [Amsterdam: Rodopi, 1990], 3).

6. Fanon makes reference to the psychoanalytic framework when he refers to the phenomenon of narcissism: "The only possibility of regaining one's balance is to face the whole problem. . . .: to make man admit that he is nothing, absolutely nothing—and that he must put an end to the narcissism on which he relies"; "I am Narcissus, and what I want to see in the eyes of others is a reflection that pleases me. . . . Me, nothing but me" (*BS, WM*, 22, 212). But his critique of psychoanalysis consists in his repudiation of Freud's emphasis on "the individual factor," and thus his attempt to account for social and economic realities: "The analysis that I am undertaking is psychological," he writes. "In spite of this it is apparent to me that the effective disalienation of the black man entails an immediate recognition of social and economic realities. . . . It will be seen that the black man's alienation is not an individual question. Beside phylogeny and ontogeny stands sociogeny. In one sense . . . , let us say that this is a question of a sociodiagnostic" (*BS, WM*, 10–11).

7. For an interesting account of Du Bois' treatment of "sympathy," see Robert Gooding-Williams, "Du Bois, Crummell, and the Sorrow of Slavery," paper presented at the annual meeting of the Organization of American Historians, Anaheim, April 1993.

8. "The former slave wants to *make himself recognized*," Fanon writes. "It is in the degree to which I go beyond my own immediate being that I apprehend the existence of the other as a natural and more than natural reality. If I close the circuit, if I prevent the accomplishment of movement in two directions, I keep the other within himself" (*BS, WM*, 217). In his discussion of love between white women and black men in *Black Skin, White Masks,* Fanon argues that he is presenting "a form of recognition that Hegel had not envisaged" (*BS, WM*, 63). For a discussion of Du Bois' Hegelianism, *see* Gooding-Williams, "Philosophy of History and Social Critique in *The Souls of Black Folk,*" *Social Science Information* (London, Newbury Park, Beverly Hills and New Dehli: Sage) 26, 1 (1987), 99–114.

9. Robert Gooding-Williams offers a useful analysis of Fanon's analysis of "the look" and indebtedness to the phenomenological tradition of European philosophical thought in "Look, A Negro!," *Reading Rodney King, Reading Urban Uprising,* ed. Robert Gooding-Williams (New York: Routledge, 1993), 164–165, 173–174.

10. Elaine Scarry, "The Railway Emergency Brake: The Use of Analogy in Legal and Political Argument," chapter 4 in *The Matter of Consent* (manuscript). Delivered at Law and Literature Seminar, Center for Literary and Cultural Studies, Harvard University, March 1991.

11. In *Johannesburg and Other Poems* (Chicago: Another Chicago Press, 1993), Sterling Plumpp reveals the striking capacity of blues language to frame and explicate the relationship between exile, the deprivation of rights, and the imaginative act of self invention. Consider, for example, these lines from the poem "Logged In My Eyes":

> . . . Empty
> road, blind road/where
> will you push my song?
> I see my father. Listen
> to my grand/mother moan
> her mother's chains/at
> the cross/roads. Don't
> know/where I live. Don't
> know why I travels this way. . . .
>
> You got no right. To
> bones of time. They
> tell me.
> Blues (74–75).

In poems such as "Sanders Bottoms," as in *Souls,* the powerful symbology of exile registers a complex ambivalence to the land:

Home/land the landless
'herited. Plots of the
future/down behind generations.
Heir property/locked in blood.
Land/nobody wants to know.
Winding acres of unsung blues.
Land/spirituals come up
in. Pasture of suffering/
home of yearning. Twisting
miles in my soul. Like rusted
wire/tangled round a sapling (32).

Paradoxically, at the same time that Plumpp's poetry represents a distinctive cultural form that works against the premises of integrationism, it also registers an engagement with the integrationist vocabulary of rights. Viewed in these terms, blues poetry, like the blues, comprise what Houston Baker has called "a mediational site where familiar antinomies are resolved (or dissolved) in the office of adequate understanding" (*Blues, Ideology, and Afro-American Literature: A Vernacular Theory* [Chicago: University of Chicago Press, 1984], 6).

12. In a set of lectures on the problem of consent, Elaine Scarry explored Locke's notion of free movement on a public highway. Drawing on narrative accounts by slaves detailing their escape on the Underground Railroad, and Justice Harlan's dissent in *Plessy v. Ferguson* (1896), Scarry traced the significance of this concept for the legal and social history of African Americans. In particular, Scarry examined Harlan's references to case law, which affirmed his vision of the railroad as a public, democratic space in which the enjoyment of civil rights is protected regardless of race. Scarry observed that over the course of his argument, Harlan compares the railroad to a public highway, to a voting booth, to a jury box, and to a legislative hall ("Problem of Consent," Harvard University, March 21–April 11, 1991).

13. Compare Houston Baker's analysis of the image of the blues singer at the railway junction in *Blues, Ideology, and Afro-American Literature:* "The railway juncture is marked by transience. Its inhabitants are always travelers—a multifarious assembly in transit. . . . Polymorphous and multidirectional, scenes of arrivals and departures, place between (ever *entre les deux*), the juncture is the way-station of the blues. . . . The singer's product, like the railway juncture itself (or a successful translator's original), constitutes a lively scene, a robust matrix, where endless antinomies are mediated and understanding and explanation find conditions of possibility" (7).

14. Robert B. Stepto, *From Behind the Veil: A Study of Afro-American Narrative* (Urbana: University of Illinois Press, 1991), 75.

15. Stepto explores a connection between Du Bois' description of the Jim Crow Car and Victor Turner's analysis of "communitas" and extra-structural relationships, suggesting that the railroad coach is analogous to Melville's whaling vessel in *Moby Dick:* "each is mobile in a nearby cosmic geography, each has a leader, a captain, an articulator as self-designated hero, but each has the egalitarian spirit of individuals jointly undergoing ritual transition as well," he observes. "Yet there is this considerable problem: is the Jim Crow car outside structure and, hence, an anti-structure? Can it ever be? The answer seems to be a negative one. . . . One expects, then, a spatial image of destination not simply in the interior of the Black Belt (indeed, we receive this many times) but more profoundly in *communitas* itself. Unfortunately, such an image is not forthcoming" (*From Behind the Veil*, 75).

16. In *Black Skin, White Masks*, Fanon observes that "what is often called the black soul is a white man's artifact" (*BS, WM*, 14).

17. Frantz Fanon, *The Wretched of the Earth,* trans. Constance Farrington (New York: Grove Press, 1963). All future references are to *WE* and will be cited parenthetically.

18. Irene Gendzier explores Fanon's interest in Sartre, and Sartre's doubts about the concept of negritude in *Frantz Fanon: A Critical Study* (New York: Pantheon Books, 1973), 22–44. For a discussion of Sartre's *Black Orpheus* see Abiola Irele, "A Defence of Negritude: A Propos of *Black Orpheus* by Jean Paul Sartre," *Transition* Vol. 3, No. 13 (March–April, 1964), 9–11.

19. As JanMohamed has observed, "the notion of exile always emphasizes the absence of 'home,' of the cultural matrix that formed the individual subject, it implies an involuntary or enforced rupture between the collective subject of the original culture and the individual subject" ("The Specular Border Intellectual," 101).

20. Jean Paul Sartre, *Black Orpheus,* trans. S. W. Allen (Paris: Presence Africaine, 1963), 18–19. All future references are to *BO* and will be cited parenthetically.

21. Henry Louis Gates, Jr. lays the groundwork for contextualized readings of Fanon in "Critical Fanonism," an essay in which he lucidly articulates the double bind faced by critics who enter this debate concerning the role of colonial discourse in Fanon's definition of the relationship between colonizer and colonized. "You can empower discursively the native, and open yourself to charges of downplaying the epistemic (and literal) violence of colonialism; or play up the absolute nature of colonial domination, and be open to charges of negating the subjectivity and agency of the colonized, thus textually replicating the repressive operations of colonialism," Gates writes. "In agency, so it seems, begins responsibility" (*Critical Inquiry* 17 [Spring 1991], 462). See also Homi K. Bhabha, "The Other Question: Difference, Discrimination and the Discourse of Colonialism," *Literature, Politics, and Theory,* eds. Francis Barker, Peter Hulme, Margaret Iverson, Diana Loxley (London: Methuen, 1986), 148–172; and Abdul R. JanMohamed, "The Economy of Manichean Allegory: The Function of Racial Difference in Colonialist Literature," *"Race," Writing, and Difference,* ed. Henry Louis Gates (Chicago: University of Chicago Press, 1985), 78–106.

22. In *To Wake the Nations: Race in the Making of American Culture* (Cambridge: Harvard University Press, 1993), Eric Sundquist has recently argued that "Douglass was realistic about the need to appropriate the tools of the master" and that in contrast to Fanon, Douglass's act of literacy demonstrates that "the acquisition of the 'colonizer's' language need not be simply a new form of enslavement" (105). Sundquist's reading of Fanon fails, I think, to account for the prescriptive dimension of Fanon's project I emphasize in this discussion. Moreover, Sundquist's insistence that Fanon's analysis of language and subject formation in the colonial context "are suggestive but only marginally applicable to African Americans" (637) does not adequately explain why Fanon's powerfully articulated distrust of the democratic vocabulary of rights had, and continues to have, such a widespread appeal for black Americans involved in the freedom struggle.

23. In his essay "Cartesian Freedom," Sartre explores Descartes' notion of freedom as establishing a connection between what Sartre calls the "spirit of science and the spirit of democracy" (*Literary and Philosophical Essays,* trans. Annette Michelson [New York: Criterion Books, 1955], 172). Although in this essay Sartre clearly regards himself as having lived by Cartesian freedom, he also resists Descartes' attribution of creative freedom to God and not to man: "It took two centuries of crisis—a crisis of Faith and a crisis of Science—for man to regain the creative freedom that Descartes placed in God, and for anyone finally to suspect the following truth, which is an essential basis of humanism: man is the being as a result of whose appearance a world exists," he writes. "But we shall not reproach Descartes with having given to God that which reverts to us in our own right. Rather, we shall admire him for having, in a dictatorial age, laid the groundwork of democracy, for having followed to the very end the demands of the idea of *autonomy* and for having understood . . . that the sole foundation of being is freedom" (184).

24. Compare Orlando Patterson's description of existential rebellion as a medium of moral

transformation for Black Americans: "in the same way that a slave who has conformed all his life suddenly says 'no,' for absolutely no other reason than the purely moral fact that sooner or later an inherent sense of dignity demands to be released, so it is that some members of modern black communities sometimes, out of sheer need to exist in dignity and as human beings, forcefully transform themselves into morally responsible creatures" ("The Moral Crisis of the Black American," *The Public Interest* 32 [Summer 1973], 63–64).

25. As Anthony Appiah has observed, "Now, over a century later, more than half of the population of black Africa lives in countries where English is an official language. . . . Perhaps the Reverend Crummell would have been pleased with this news, but he would have little cause to be sanguine. For—with few exceptions outside the Arabic-speaking countries of North Africa—the language of government is the first language of a very few and is securely possessed by only a small proportion of the population; in most of the anglophone states even the educated elites learned at least one of the hundreds of indigenous languages as well as—and almost always before—English (*In My Father's House: Africa in the Philosophy of Culture* [New York: Oxford University Press, 1992], 3).

26. Alexander Crummell, *Future of Africa* (New York: Negro Universities Press, 1969), 21. All future references are to *FA* and will be cited parenthetically.

27. In his *Considerations on Representative Government* (Buffalo: Prometheus Books, 1993), in a chapter entitled "Of Nationality as Connected With Representative Government," Mill argues that the "feeling of nationality" emerges only where there is community of language. "The question of government ought to be decided by the governed," he writes. "Among the people without fellow-feeling, especially if they read and speak different languages, the united public opinion necessary to the working of representative government can not exist" (310).

28. Frantz Fanon, *A Dying Colonialism*, trans. Haakon Chevalier (New York: Grove Press, 1965), 37. All future references are to *ADC* and will be cited parenthetically.

29. I am thinking of Alice Walker's description of her response to Dr. King's disobedience, and her development of a meaning for exile that is inextricably bound up with the concept of citizenship, disobedience, and the deprivation of rights. "At the moment I saw his resistance I knew I would never be able to live in this country without resisting everything that sought to disinherit me, and I would never be forced away from the land of my birth without a fight" she recalls:

He gave us back our homeland. . . . He gave us continuity of place, without which community is ephemeral. . . . And when he spoke of 'letting freedom ring' across 'the green hills of Alabama and the red hills of Georgia' I saw again what he was always uniquely able to make me see: that I, in fact, had claim to the land of my birth (*In Search of Our Mothers' Gardens: Womanist Prose* [San Diego: Harcourt Brace Jovanovich, 1983], 144, 160).

30. "To tear the mask of hypocrisy from the face of the enemy, to unmask him and the devious machinations and manipulations that permit him to rule without using violent means . . .—these are still among the strongest motives in today's violence on the campuses and in the streets," Arendt writes. "And this violence again is not irrational. . . . Words can be relied on only if one is sure that their function is to reveal and not to conceal" (*Crises of the Republic* [San Diego: Harcourt Brace Jovanovich, 1969], 65–66).

31. In Thoreau's "Resistance to Civil Government," civil disobedience represents a rhetorical means of establishing group unity through symbolic action and the appeal to conscience. More recently, for Gandhi and King, civil disobedience as nonviolent resistance has functioned as a tactical strategy for challenging unjust laws and political practices while upholding the utopian ideal of democratic political coexistence, what King called "true brotherhood, true integration, true person-to-person relationships" (*A Testament of Hope: The Essential Writings and Speeches of Martin Luther King, Jr.,* ed. James Washington, [San Francisco: HarperCollins, 1986), 51).

32. Edward Said has recently observed that "[Fanon's] theory of violence is not meant to

answer the appeals of a native chafing under the paternalistic surveillance of a European policeman and, in a sense, preferring the services of a native officer in his place. On the contrary, it first represents colonialism as a totalizing system nourished in the same way—Fanon's implicit analogy is devastating—that human behavior is informed by unconscious desires. In a second, quasi-Hegelian move, a Manichean opposite appears, the insurrectionary native, tired of the logic that reduces him, the geography that segregates him, the ontology that dehumanizes him, the epistemology that strips him down to an unregenerate essence. . . . The struggle must be lifted to a new level of contest, a synthesis represented by a war of liberation, for which an entirely new post-nationalist theoretical culture is required" (*Culture and Imperialism* [New York: Alfred A. Knopf, 1993], 267–268).

4.

Disco Dancing in Bulgaria

SCOTT L. MALCOMSON

The population of rural Turks in Bulgaria has been divided more or less between the Deli Orman and Dobrudja regions in the north and the Rhodope Mountains in the south. The Rhodopes form most of Bulgaria's southern border with Greece and Turkey.

The village of Yeni Maġalì lies at the end of a road, near the crest of the Rhodopes. On a clear day you can stand in Yeni Maġalì and look down the valley to see the plain of the Maritsa. But most days, even in midsummer, Yeni Maġalì is shrouded in fog. It's always green, and a little damp, and cool.

Except for the disco, the only one for miles, which is always smoky and hot. The disco—known as "The Disco"—occupies the ground floor of a building just behind and downhill from the mosque. As Ergin walks you down to the entrance one spring evening in 1992 he notes the oddness and shrugs, "Well, we *are* in Europe." You enter the disco and greet Necmi. A big, clean-shaven man, Necmi was the best friend of Mehmet, who built this disco in 1984. (Mehmet later emigrated to New Jersey.) Ergin, Mehmet, and Necmi are related, as are most residents of Yeni Maġalì with the exception of a few Gypsies, three or four ethnic Bulgarians, and some genetic mavericks. "Yeni Maġalì was started by the Seyh family from Konya," Ergin says. Konya's now part of Turkey. "They were Oġuz Turks. Later the Şerif family came, possibly as Ottoman administrators. Almost everybody here is either a Şeyh or a Şerif." Ergin is a semi-employed sculptor. Short and powerful, he wears a black leather jacket, his strong features set off by flowing black hair. Like most everyone you have occasion to meet in Yeni Maġalì, he likes to drink and dance. Two to three hundred people will pass through the disco each night, weekday or weekend, from nearby villages or hamlets as well as Yeni Maġalì itself. Young and old, men and women, married and unmarried, they will come and drink beer, wine, vodka, raki; they will dance to American and European rock, Turkish *arabesk*, plaintive Kurdish songs, Greek *bouzouki*. They will drink anything and dance to anything, with whomever they like and even people they don't like, for Yeni Maǵalì is a small village and people have to get along.

There used to be more young people here, but now many have left to seek work outside Bulgaria. "A lot of the young people work in Germany, Switzerland, and Sweden," Necmi says over a bottle of sweet wine. The sun just set; dancing hasn't yet begun. "Some go to work in Turkey, but not too many, because Turkey is a Muslim country and they aren't comfortable there—Turkey isn't as European as here. Also, young people coming from a village find it hard in the cities." Ergin believes Turkey is not really home to Bulgarian Turks. "I feel that we are Europeans. We'll be joining Europe. It's true that we came from Asia, but that was a long time ago. We've been here for quite a while; we're Europeans. Look around you at this disco: we have a very modern life. This place used to be Oriental in design, before it became a disco. When Mehmet decided to build the disco, at the time of the name-change policy, he made it like this." Ergin indicates the walls with a sweep of his hand. They are nearly barren, certainly modern.

Mehmet built the disco in 1984 because local Bulgarian party authorities had insulted him, saying that as a Turk he was incapable of achieving anything. They had laughed at his intention—he headed the young-communist league—to build a disco. So he and Necmi built it, in this room beneath which lies the oldest cemetery in Yeni Maǵalì, a cemetery for (so Ergin says) the Yörük Turks, a formerly, famously nomadic group that guarded the Rhodope passes in Ottoman times.

Time to dance: Ergin brings you onto the floor. Raise your hands—this is how we do it—making gestures delicate now, then assured, or languid, so that one dance is nearly two, your hands with their own pattern, speaking to your feet, who speak back. Ergin will shout above the music: "Listen! We don't have any racial problems here! We'll dance to anything!" He'll laugh, you'll laugh, you'll close your eyes, inhale the music and listen to your heart. When the music is sad you may remember that in the late 1980s soldiers would have been sitting a few feet away, with rifles, making sure that no Turkish music was playing and that when people danced they didn't raise their hands in the Turkish manner but rather held them at their sides as if bound. Mehmet, what a reply you gave to their insults! For a time, back then, people danced like tin soldiers. Now they raise their hands and shout, laugh, make silly faces, as do you on a cool night in Mehmet's hot and smoky disco.

" 'The doer,' " Nietzsche wrote, "is merely a fiction added to the deed." From an ethnic Turkish perspective in Bulgaria, the doers have been ethnic

Bulgarians, at least since Bulgaria gained autonomy from the Ottoman Empire in 1878. From that time onward Bulgarians would try various means to purify their nation of Ottoman and Muslim institutions, of Muslims proper, and of Greeks. The Greeks posed a lesser problem; they were dispatched by pogroms, deportations, population exchanges with Greece, and discriminatory laws. In 1884 there were over 50,000 Greeks in Bulgaria. By 1934, the number had dropped beneath 10,000. The ethnic Turkish population in 1884 was over 700,000, nearly a quarter of the Bulgarian total. The Ottomans offered land to immigrants from the former province, and out-migration kept a steady pace. But hundreds of thousands of ethnic Turks remained, offering a challenge to the Bulgarians' perilous sense of Bulgarianness.

Bulgarian intellectuals worked hard to purge their Slavic language of Turkish elements. Thousands of Turkish place-names were replaced by Bulgarian ones. Mosques were on occasion destroyed, and Ottoman gravestones used as building material.

But given the steady turmoil and unflagging nationalism throughout Europe in the period 1878–1945, life could have been far worse for the ethnic Turks of Bulgaria than it was. No Bulgarian regime was strong enough to afford alienating either the Muslim minority or the Ottoman (later Turkish) government next door. Even the postwar communist state, tempered by internationalism and rather lacking in popular support, acted, on the whole, cautiously with regard to its Muslim subjects. Yet, by the 1960s, the government under Todor Zhivkov had seen the utility of chauvinistic nationalism. At the same time that Nicolae Ceauşescu elaborated his own nationalist program, and for some similar reasons, Zhivkov began a policy, tentative at first, of ethnic-religious purification. (Zhivkov and Ceauşescu, by the way, often went hunting together.) Initial efforts were directed in particular against the Pomak people, who were especially problematic for Bulgarianness because they were ethnically Bulgarian while of the Muslim faith. "There will be a struggle," Nikolai Vranchev had written with unwarranted confidence in 1948, "between ignorance and deception, on the one hand, and knowledge and truth on the other. The bearers of the former are the old Bulgarian Muslims [the Pomaks], and the bearers of the latter are members of the younger generation. Someday the older generation will pass away and take their ignorance with them. The young will remain and consolidate the new system with enlightenment and culture. And then there will not be even a memory of the Bulgarian Muslim problem that troubles us today."

Beginning in the 1960s, the Zhivkov government forced Pomaks to change their names to Bulgarian ones. Their mosques and Muslim schools were closed, Muslim rituals forbidden, and those Pomaks who resisted were imprisoned. As the official *Sofia News* explained in 1985, "The 1960s witnessed the first big wave of resurging national self-consciousness among

Muslim Bulgarians, which found expression in the renunciation by tens of thousands of people of the once assumed personal names of Arabic and Turkish origin." The official argument was that the Pomaks had been forcibly converted to Islam, a belief for which there is no scholarly base despite reams of pseudo-scholarship published in Bulgaria at the time. A *Sofia News* writer expressed the government line: "The forcibly converted part of the population has become aware of the historical truth about their national identity and has been regaining national self-consciousness in the whole course of a century after Bulgarian liberation in 1878." In this way the government sought to make the Pomaks what they had actually always been.

The principle applied to the Pomaks was then transferred to the Turks and Gypsies, or at least those Gypsies, a majority, who were Muslim. In 1971, the tenth party congress already emphasized that citizens "of different national origins will come ever closer together"; the party spoke of *priobshtavane* ("homogeneity") and *edinna bulgarska natsiya* ("a unified Bulgarian nation"). The government and its scholars argued that all of the non-ethnic Bulgarians in Bulgaria were in fact ethnic Bulgarians deluded long ago by the Ottomans and (temporarily) made unaware of their true nature. "All our countrymen who reverted to their Bulgarian names are Bulgarians," Minister of Internal Affairs Dimitur Stojanov declared in 1985. "They are the bone of the bone and the flesh of the flesh of the Bulgarian nation; although the Bulgarian national consciousness of some of them might still be blurred, they are of the same flesh and blood; they are children of the Bulgarian nation; they were forcibly torn away and now they are coming back home. There are no Turks in Bulgaria."

To make sure of this, the Bulgarian government closed Turkish-language newspapers and other media, forbade various Muslim rites, even in some cases forbade the use of Turkish. Ottoman funeral sites were bulldozed, mosques destroyed. The government, sometimes at gunpoint, made everyone change their Turkish or Muslim names to Bulgarian names. For years, someone named Muhammad would walk around being called Hristo. On passports, government forms, identity cards—in every conceivable place where a Turk's or Muslim's name might be written down, that name had to be changed to a new one. People who opposed this renaming policy were beaten, imprisoned, or even killed. In 1989, some 320,000 Turks fled to Turkey. The theory was that these people were going "back" to Turkey, though of course most had never been there and many of their families had lived in Bulgaria for centuries.

At the end of 1989, Zhivkov was ousted by some of his old comrades, and soon the anti-Turk policy was rescinded. Perhaps a majority of the so-called Turks who had fled to their alleged homeland, Turkey, returned to Bulgaria.

Aydin Abas is a young man from Yeni Maǵalì, now a student of architectural engineering in Sofia. He has a mustache, a wrinkled, expressive forehead, a lively face with the preoccupied look of youthful seriousness. He says: "As a Turk, life for me in Sofia is a little rough. There aren't many Turks there, and very few in the university. From my village, only four people are in university.

"It's wonderful to go back to the village because there I'm surrounded by Turks. You can go there and be what you are. Everybody is at least your cousin.

"Life in Turkey is much different from here. Here—you've seen what it's like, very free, with men and women in the disco together, no problems. In Turkey that isn't the case. It's an Oriental society, very Muslim. That's not what we're used to. We're more European."

A friend of yours once said something similar. He coined a term for Muslims in Bulgaria: *Avrupamusulmanlar,* Euromuslims.

Aydin continues: "Besides, in Turkey you have to work constantly, and if you don't, you're finished. The government won't give you a thing. In Turkey, if you don't fight to live, you could die."

So now ethnic Turks in Bulgaria have to figure out who they are, the question having been raised so forcibly by their Bulgarian neighbors. Although the government no longer oppresses Turks or Muslims, this question of identity has not necessarily become easier. It isn't as if some old, pre-oppression identity is waiting there to be picked up like a favorite pair of comfortable shoes. Of the many identities probably available in Ottoman Bulgaria, ethnic Turkishness could not have been high on the list if it existed at all. In written sources, the notion of ethnic Turkishness originated with European enthusiasts in the mid-nineteenth century. It is highly unlikely that any ethnic Turk in Bulgaria prior to Bulgarian independence ever based his or her identity on ethnic Turkishness, or even gave it much thought.

With Ergin, Ahmet, and Cevat you hike upward into the summer pastures above Yeni Maǵalì, moist dales or grassy upland humps edged by pine, fir, beech. When it rains you dip into the forest or run for shelter in one of the wooden huts used by shepherds. Soon the huts and pastures will be occupied, the rains will clear, the sun will shine. It is May 24. You walk across a wide bowl with a view of Yeni Maǵalì and the valley below. May 24 is "Cyril and Methodius Day," a national holiday, an opportunity to celebrate the two Greeks who brought Orthodox Christianity north to the Slavs. Cyril and Methodius wished to preach in the vernacular, so they translated the Bible into Bulgarian, creating along the way an alphabet—Cyrillic. Proud Bulgarians tend to believe that Bulgarian, as the first major Slavic language to receive the new alphabet, is more pure or otherwise better than other

Slavic languages. So Cyril and Methodius Day is an occasion for patriotic expression.

In this wide bowl with its arresting view Turks, Gypsies, Pomaks, and Bulgarians from Yeni Maǵalì and surroundings used to assemble every May 24 to celebrate Cyril and Methodius Day with drinking, singing, dancing, and speeches. The school in Yeni Maǵalì was named Cyril and Methodius School. "They had the celebration here," Ahmet says, "to mark the togetherness of Bulgarians and Turks." They had it here until 1983, when the authorities began to force Turkish parents to give their newborns Bulgarian names. "Since then we haven't gathered here. And we won't gather here now."

Up and up into the Rhodopes, into the mist, the four of you smelling of damp wool and linen, sweat, and tobacco, your hair and faces moist. At a high clearing you notice that the earth is terraced, with rows of mounds. Above you is a ruined fortification. It was built by the Romans as a lookout; the mounds are ancient graves, the terraces an outwork for defense. Cevat and Ergin crouch behind one and act as if they're holding pikes, bracing for an assault by unknown enemies.

Down again on slippery ground toward the village. You pass by fields, once farmed cooperatively but now broken up into individual plots too small for mechanized farming. A man maneuvers a horse pulling a plow. "You see," Ergin says, "it's like feudalism all over again!" Now that communism has fallen, Bulgarian Turks, indeed all Bulgarians, are having to adjust to a new identity as backward poor people in a new world where money means everything. Ergin, at least, is approaching this identitarian challenge with a sense of humor. Others, of course, are not, and many are finding it difficult to adjust to their new identity as big losers on the stage of world history. Also, grasping the idea that poverty is an identity rather than a circumstance has proved difficult for many people.

You pile into a car with hopes of reaching Velingrad to celebrate Cyril and Methodius Day. But first you stop by Batak, a remote village and the site of a famous massacre in 1876. Several thousand Bulgarian villagers were slaughtered by *başibozuklar* ("broken-heads," irregular troops with faint loyalty to the Ottoman Empire) led by Ahmed aǵa Barutanlijata, a Pomak. *Başibozuklar* in this region included Turks, Circassian refugees forced from their Causasus homes by Russia and resettled by the Ottomans, Crimean Tatars resettled here for similar reasons, Muslim Gypsies, and Pomaks, plundering on their own account and sometimes taking orders from the Ottoman authorities. In 1876, Bulgarian revolutionary nationalists, encouraged by the Russians and addled by their own enthusiasm, chose this area for their first uprising. It failed. Particularly distressing was the attitude of the Pomaks, who failed to seize upon their own ethnic Bulgarianness and join the revolution. Instead, Pomak leaders opposed the Bulgarians and set up their own short-lived "Pomak Republic." (History can take odd turns. Initial concern about Pomak intentions had appeared among Russian diplomats ten years before. Misled by the phonetic similarity between *Pomak* and *Poljak*—"Pole"—and worried that Polish nationalist propaganda might have some effect on the Pomaks, they began to meddle in Pomak affairs. This surely constituted a low point in Tsarist diplomacy.) At any rate, the massacres at Batak were quickly embroidered upon and used by European politicians to justify anti-Ottoman policies; they are still used today as shorthand to represent the special malevolence of "the Turk."

You leave Batak with your Turkish friends and drive to Velingrad, a mostly Bulgarian town with a large Pomak minority. In the last years of Zhivkov, Bulgarian nationalists held angry rallies at Batak and Velingrad, dwelling on memories of the massacres and the abortive uprising of 1876. You take four chairs at a cafe on the town square. A reviewing stand has been set up, with chairs for dignitaries and a mixed podium. A crowd gathers; at its edge stand groups of Pomaks, the women wearing knit leggings under knee-skirts or dresses, over these a sweater or jacket and a brightly colored scarf. "These Pomak outfits were forbidden under Zhivkov," Ergin says. "Buses wouldn't stop for you if you wore these clothes. Until fifteen years ago, we too wore more traditional clothes. But not now. The Pomaks are less European than we are."

Most of the gathering crowd appears to be Bulgarian. The mike is tested, a speech given. Tall young girls in majorette outfits appear. The dignitaries on stage rise and sing the Cyril and Methodius song. No one sings along. A band plays Bach's "Jesu, Joy of Man's Desiring" and the majorettes perform a saucy choreography, like deeply subdued Rockettes; each has a baton. "You see," Ergin says, "Rhodope women are very beautiful because we're all mixed together. And the air is clean and rich in oxygen." The young women leave, then reappear in "Spanish" outfits—black skirts, red blouses with short, puffy sleeves, artificial red flowers in their hair. And batons. They dance to "Frère Jacques" and the theme from *Can-can,* with interludes of military gesturing and some truly baffling, though languid, movements, the music slipping into Latin lounge-tunes.

Thus you celebrate Cyril and Methodius Day in the Bulgarian and Pomak town of Velingrad.

" 'The doer' is merely a fiction added to the deed." Perhaps that depends on the doer. Perhaps that depends on the deed. Perhaps *fiction* is an overused word when applied to doers and deeds. Not wrong, necessarily, but nevertheless a little light.

You are lounging with Ergin and some other friends at the disco in Yeni Maġalì when you notice at the next table a broad-shouldered man, unusually tall, speaking in Bulgarian with some other men. Except for him, they all have a rough, somewhat thuggish appearance. Ergin says hello to him in Bulgarian, which is unusual, so you ask in Turkish: Who is that man?

"He's a mathematics teacher at the Cyril and Methodius School. He's been teaching here for eleven years, with two years spent in Algeria. He still doesn't speak any Turkish, though he does speak French. After eleven years, he doesn't speak Turkish."

You're introduced to the man, named Hristo, and exchange pleasantries in French.

Ergin says: "This man is not a person who can be trusted. He is a sly fox. During the Zhivkov period, he was a nationalist. He was like a Nazi. He didn't seem to dislike the idea of Turks as slaves. I remember talking to him about the name-changing and he agreed that such a policy shouldn't come from above. He said instead that the ethnic Bulgarians should have a referendum on what should be done with the Turks as far as name-changing went. *They* should have a referendum! Is that democracy, where other people get to vote on what *you* should be? On who you are?"

You turn to Ahmet, a gentle man with a sense of humor of a person older than him. You ask Ahmet: How can you have a man like this here? And he replies, "Well, it's complicated. He—the few people who really believed in the Zhivkov policy are still here, but they have been . . . isolated. Do you understand?" He smiles. "His wife is the tall, good-looking woman you saw last night. Do you remember? You may have noticed that she is interested in other men." You had noticed.

You invite Hristo outside for a chat. "I was in Algeria, in Annaba, in '85–'86," he says. "At that time, you know, there was a war of words back here in Bulgaria. When I got back here I thought, 'This is politics, but I am a mathematics teacher. Mathematics is not political.' " Hristo gives a weak smile. "In 1989, many of my Turkish friends went to Turkey. I visited them there once. There aren't many people left here now, so life isn't as happy as it used to be. But I have a big lovely house in Plovdiv—my daughter goes to school there—and an apartment here, where my wife and other daughter live."

Back inside, Ahmet asks what Hristo said. "He said his friends all went to Turkey and mathematics isn't political." Ahmet laughs for some time and you raise your glasses with the toast, "Mathematics isn't political."

Hristo joins us. Ahmet and Ergin both joke with him, raising glasses, slapping backs. A butcher called "the Arab" tells dumb jokes and makes faces. Everybody is very drunk. We laugh. Hristo buys everyone more wine. And as we laugh you whisper in Ahmet's ear: "Ahmet, I still don't understand. This man is a nationalist. He doesn't like Turks. Turks don't like him. So why is he here? Did you ever consider killing him? Why are we all sitting here like friends?"

Ahmet says: "This is not like friends. This is drinking-friends. We cannot kill him because then we would have to leave the village. He can't leave either, because his wife and job are here. So—look at him. Does he really look alive to you? He is not a happy man."

Ahmet has been smiling all this time, while Hristo keeps raising his glass to you, saying "à votre santé!" He suddenly appears to be the loneliest man in the world, and unable to grasp his loneliness, which means that it will never end.

Ahmet has been watching your face and now he looks at you calmly. "Now do you understand?"

One afternoon you sit at Ergin's home with him, his mother, Ahmet, and various female relatives ranging from infants to Ergin's grandmother. You loll around watching a TV station beamed from Turkey and filled with images of prosperity. What, you ask, is it like seeing all these other ways of life on TV?

"We see how rich places like American and Germany are," Ahmet says pleasantly, "and how poor we are in Bulgaria."

Do you think you had a happier life before you started seeing all this prosperity on television?

"No! No!" Ahmet says, and everyone laughs.

"We're happy here," Ergin's mother adds, smiling. "We just don't have any money." You recall what she'd said on another occasion: "It's a terrible thing to have democracy and no money."

Ergin's ancient grandmother leans forward with a knowing expression. "True, we don't have any money," she says. "But we *do* have the disco. And we can dance."

You are standing on a street with Ahmet in the bright light of morning. He is trying to explain what has happened. Once, his ancestors were here under the Ottoman Empire. Then the Ottomans left, Bulgaria was founded, and his family became Bulgarians. Later the Bulgarian government tried to take away much of what made him what he is and transform him into a true Bulgarian. Then communism fell, Bulgaria sought to become part of Europe, and he and his family got their old names back.

But now everyone wants to leave. They want to leave so badly that they no longer really occupy the ground they stand on, because the future lies elsewhere, in Europe and North America, and no one would really want to live in exile from the future. Indeed, in terms of imagination—which has so much to do with identity, and citizenship—one can only live in the future. When the future lies elsewhere, one can't really live. And Ahmet says, "So— it's a curious thing—I feel that we have become exiles in our own country. Time has gone elsewhere, it has taken the land from beneath our feet. So, without moving at all, we have become exiles."

PART II
BLURRING BOUNDARIES:
AUTOBIOGRAPHY AND CRITICISM

5.

Our Classes, Ourselves: Maternal Legacies and Cultural Criticism

NANCY K. MILLER

I begin with the death of a mother: the first, Carolyn Steedman's in *Landscape for a Good Woman*, the second, Annie Ernaux's in *A Woman's Story*.[1]

She died like this. I didn't witness it. My niece told me this. She'd moved everything down into the kitchen: a single bed, the television, the calor-gas heater. She said it was to save fuel. The rest of the house was dark and shrouded. . . . She had cancer, had gone back to Food Reform, talked to me about curing it when I paid my first visit in nine years, two weeks before her death: my last visit. . . . She complained of pains, but wouldn't take the morphine tablets. It was pains everywhere, not in the lungs where the cancer was. It wasn't the cancer that killed: a blood clot travelled from her leg and stopped her heart. Afterwards, the doctor said she'd been out of touch with reality. . . . (1)

Toward the end of this preface to her narrative, which she entitles, "Death of a Good Woman," Steedman goes on to invoke Simone de Beauvoir's memoir, *A Very Easy Death*, framing her reference with these words:

Simone de Beauvoir wrote of her mother's death, said that in spite of the pain it was an easy one: an upper-class death. Outside, for the poor, dying is a different matter.

She then quotes Beauvoir directly:

And then in the public wards when the last hour is coming near, they put a screen round a dying man's bed: he has seen this screen round other beds that were empty the next day: he knows. I pictured Maman, blinded for hours by the black sun that no one can look at directly: the horror of her staring eyes with their dilated pupils.

Directly after this reference, Steedman concludes the preface to her narrative, with a brief paragraph, describing the moment of death:

Like this: she flung up her left arm over her head, pulled her knees up, looked out with an extraordinary surprise. She lived alone, she died alone: a working-class life, a working-class death. (1–2)

The following passages appear at the very beginning and end of Ernaux's memoir, which is also the story of a working-class mother's life and death:

My mother died on Monday April 7 in the old people's home attached to the hospital at Pontoise, where I had installed her two years previously. The nurse said over the phone: "Your mother passed away this morning, after breakfast." It was around ten o'clock. . . . (1)

She died eight days before Simone de Beauvoir.

She preferred giving to everybody, rather than taking from them. Isn't writing also a way of giving. . . .

It was only when my mother—born in an oppressed world from which she wanted to escape—became history that I started to feel less alone and out of place in a world ruled by words and ideas, the world where she had wanted me to live.

I shall never hear the sound of her voice again. It was her voice, together with her words, her hands, and her way of moving and laughing, which linked the woman I am to the child I once was. The last bond between me and the world I come from has been severed. (91–92)

Steedman's *Landscape for a Good Woman: A Story of Two Lives* and Ernaux's *A Woman's Story* (*Une Femme*) are contemporaneous accounts of a mother's death. (Steedman's was published in 1986, Ernaux's written betweeen 1986 and 1987, published in 1987.) At least this is their point of departure. For both writers the mother's death becomes, to differing degrees, the occasion for a reflection about mothers and daughters, women and class, and more specifically about the ways in which working-class identity shapes the stories of female development in postwar England and France. Like Beauvoir's monumental accomplishment in *A Very Easy Death* (1964) both are acts of cultural criticism which emerge from an autobiographical space. These are narratives inseparable from a problem of definition, which is both a matter of genre and interpretation—a "cross [*jointure*] between family history and sociology, reality and fiction" (13) as Ernaux puts it; about "lives," Steedman writes, "lived out on the borderlands . . . for which the central interpretative devices of the culture don't quite work" (5).

Steedman's stated aim is to challenge two powerful bodies of thought: "the tradition of cultural criticism [in England]" which has no place for her mother in its "iconography of working-class motherhood" (6) and feminist "theories of patriarchy" (7) which ignore the class-consciousness of working-class children. By placing a biographical and autobiographical story at the center of her book, Steedman seeks to "*reverse* a central question within feminism and psychoanalysis about the desire to mother in little girls and replace it with a consideration of *women who, by refusing to mother have refused to reproduce themselves or the circumstances of their exile*" (7; emphasis added). The story is told in its "difference and particularity," but told also for the effects of its representativity: "so that people in exile, the inhabitants of the long streets, may start to use the autobiographical 'I,' and tell the stories of their life" (16).[2] Like Steedman, Ernaux sees identity as a process and autobiographical writing as a performance embedded in the social, but for her the task of testimony is more narrowly focused on the representation—we might even say the reproduction—of maternal experience:

This book can be seen as a literary venture to the extent that its purpose is to find out the truth about my mother, *a truth that can be conveyed only by words.* (Neither photographs, nor my own memories, nor even the reminiscences of my family can bring me this truth.) And yet, in a sense, I would like to remain a cut below literature. (tm,13)

If we take seriously Beauvoir's achievement in making the maternal body—its wounds, demands and desires—give voice to a culture's life and death narratives, what we can read here are further experiments in the construction of an autobiographical cultural authority. In all three instances embodiment is inseparable from the constraints and repercussions of materially located stories, but we also get to see the ways in which figuration of the embodiment depends on the work, distortions, and gaps of individual memory.

Steedman argues that life stories like hers have not been told largely because they tend not to be heard; their specificity is tuned out because *as stories* they issue from a "structure of feeling" unavailable to middle-class readers, who by definition are assigned to a position of cultural centrality and domination. She writes:

I read the collection *Fathers: Reflections by Daughters* or Ann Oakley's *Taking It Like a Woman* and feel the painful and familiar sense of exclusion from these autobiographies of middle-class little-girlhood and womanhood, envy of those who belong, who can, like Ann Oakley, use the outlines of conventional romantic fiction to tell a life story. And women like this, friends, say: but it was like that for me too, my childhood was like yours; my father was like that, my mother didn't want me. What they cannot bear, I think, is that there exists a poverty and marginality of experience to which they have no access, structures of feeling that they have not lived within (and would not want to live within: for these are the structures of deprivation). They are caught in a terrible exclusion, an exclusion from the experience of others that measures out their own central relationship to the culture. (17)

Steedman's mapping of this double exclusion is at the heart of her autobiographical project. On the one hand, you don't know us because you are the center from which, against which the borders are defined, and you don't know it. On the other, I know you but am not of you. The storyteller positions herself as irretrievably separate and set off from this audience; yet her tale is *also addressed* to other women, "friends" who think they speak the same language. Those readers must in turn confront Steedman's accusation of their failures to perceive the divide.

Having lived a "middle-class little-girlhood" I find myself in a predicament. I have just this projected reaction to Steedman's narrative. Like Steedman I tend to define myself in my life against the desire, as she puts it, to reproduce and its enactment as mothering, which she poses as the ground of *her mother's* and hence her own *difference:* their "sense of exclusion, of being cut off from what others enjoy" (18). But for me to insist *autobiographically* as a reader on resemblance—I felt cut off too, I didn't want to mother and my mother didn't either—would only seem to prove her point about middle-class mentalities: I can't see that however similar those feelings may seem to me, the structures of our experiences are fundamentally different. At the same time, I find myself protesting in turn against the assumption that simply by virtue of being middle-class—like Oakley—I automatically identify with the story of that life. My middle-class "womanhood" in no way resembles Oakley's; I identify not at all with the woman who defines herself as much by her children as by her writing.[3] I read *Taking It Like a Woman* resisting all the way, the account of Oakley's many desired pregnancies (five) and several children (three) whose needs and bodies figure significantly in her narrative.

Landscape for a Good Woman is powerful for me despite the differences in our original class assignments because of the ways in which it renders the maternal legacy that makes the daughter *not a mother.* Thus, reading as a middle-class girl now grown up, I meet Steedman autobiographically in a gesture of *counter-identification* (or as Eve Sedgwick puts it in "Axiomatic," "identifying with"): I read *with* her—reader to writer, writer to writer—when I read "as a woman" who also lacked the desire to mother.[4] And in that occasion of a possible encounter—"the autobiographical moment" de Man described as "an alignment between the two subjects involved in the process of reading" (921)—I reread, which is also to say, rewrite my history with hers.[5]

Between the two passages of "Death of a Good Woman" excerpted above to frame this discussion, Steedman recalls an episode from her childhood in which a social worker, shortly after the birth of Steedman's baby sister, comes to inspect her mother's house and declares, " 'This house isn't fit for a baby' " (2).[6] Steedman describes her mother's reaction to the violence of that judgment, her tears of rage and bitter courage, and then adds:

And I? I will do everything and anything until the end of my days to stop anyone ever talking to me like that woman talked to my mother. It is in this place, this bare, curtainless bedroom that lies my secret and shameful defiance. I read a woman's book, meet such a woman at a party (a woman now, like me) and think quite deliberately as we talk: we are divided: a hundred years ago I'd have been cleaning your shoes. I know this and you don't. (2)

As a four-year-old little girl, Steedman bonds with her mother against the social worker: "We both watched the dumpy retreating figure of the health visitor through the curtainless windows" (2). The social violence of that scene in memory shapes the daughter's pattern of future identifications with women: with the mother, against all others. In the present of writing, the time of the memoir, the health visitor has been reconfigured as a published intellectual, or academic: a woman whose book Steedman will have read. A woman she puts into parenthesis, "now, like me." A woman, now *like me*. And I? Do I take up my position—like her now, not like her then? Or do I try to read across the divide otherwise through an identification with maternal rejection that flits through the particular zones of class boundaries unevenly; now you see it, now you don't. Although Steedman's theoretical project is to elaborate (which she brilliantly does) a *working-class* self-portrait, "a drama of *class*" (22), what I think this literary encounter can show are the twinned limits of class-based identifications: mine *and* hers, our predictable emotional blind spots, but also our unexpected intimacies.[7] In that sense, my response pulls two ways at once in the two times of autobiography. "We are divided": on the one hand, as a daughter of the American postwar professional middle class, I would add even more specifically, New York Jewish professional middle class of the fifties.[8] And on the other, as a middle-aged feminist intellectual—"a woman now, like me"—

who perhaps (also?) took Simone de Beauvoir too seriously, or at least too uncritically.[9] If we talked at a party, would this give us something to say to each other?

Steedman's central question turns on the attempt to understand "*how* the wish not to have a child might come to be produced in a little girl, or in a grown woman" (85–86) and "what the refusal of a baby or a child is actually a refusal *of*" (84). She distinguishes in this between the "refusal to reproduce oneself . . . to perpetrate what one is . . . the way one understands oneself to be in the social world" and the refusal to be a mother.[10] "Some women of the recent past," she writes, "have been mothers," but not according to the official rules. She also emphasizes the kind of revolt that occurs *within* motherhood in a culture where "either socially or physiologically" women could not bodily refuse to bear children (84); this is how she understands her mother's performance. In both her mother's case and her own what's at stake is a rejection of the dominant social script. Despite the class differences between our mothers, and despite the lack of detail about *how* she came not to have a child, what attracted me to Steedman's story and what makes it (I guess I would have to say) thrilling to me—given the maternalism in and outside of contemporary feminism—is the conjunction of those intertwined repudiations, and in particular her defiant self-identification as a woman who has not had a child.[11]

Now I cannot, like Steedman, claim that I have *refused* to reproduce, since at various times in my life I flirted with the possibility and tried to conceive a child—strenuously, for three miserable years—at the borderlines of my fertility and failed a decade ago; rather, by virtue of a tenacious ambivalence and treacherous propensity for deferral I have not, and probably never really wanted to in the first place. For me, as for many women of my generation in the United States who modeled our identities on Beauvoir's famous split—intellectual accomplishment *or* babies—it might be more accurate to say that, like Steedman, we refused to reproduce *as women*, as though anatomy were our destiny instead of history, on schedule as though we had no say; only some of us then changed our minds (or thought we did in a frenzy of belatedness) and it turned out that for some of us "nature" (or maybe it really was history) would have the last word after all.[12] There's a poignant irony in the coexistence at the end of the twentieth century of a massive infertility that has given rise to dizzying adventures in reproductive techniques, and the ongoing challenges to women's reproductive rights. Choosing motherhood or refusing it have proven to be more complex than seventies feminists had imagined.

Our Bodies, Ourselves, the title of one of the most important collective projects to emerge out of seventies feminism, nicely glosses the conviction of that moment: the comma, rather than the copula—our bodies *are* our selves—meant that we would decide on what relation of apposition best described the relation between our bodies and our selves. We were not *just* our bodies, but we authorized ourselves to have the decisive role in deciphering their meaning and adjudicating their circulation in the world. (The update of the volume, by the way, for women over thirty-five is called *Ourselves, Growing Older*. I guess without bodies. Which might actually be an improvement.) Whatever our respective singular and collective intents about reproduction, however, the effects—wished for or not—are shared; for to be a "non-procreative adult" (63) as Sedgwick puts it, winds up being a marker of social difference more important, I'd like to argue, to a cultural critique of marginalities and dominations than one might think. I'm very taken with Michael Warner's definition of "repro-narrativity" as "the notion that our lives are somehow made more meaningful by being embedded in a narrative of generational succession" (7). What we might think of as "compulsory repro-narrativity" has everything to do with the radicality of Steedman's formal and theoretical project: what it refuses.[13]

When I was a little girl I had a doll house which I loved with an intensity perhaps peculiar to urban children whose experience of space is an apartment and a shared bedroom. The doll house was a present on the only Christmas my sister and I succeeded in getting our guilty assimilationist parents to celebrate (no tree, of course, but stockings hanging from the mantelpiece of the non-working fireplace); after that we returned to the more parsimonious installments of Hanukkah. I played for hours on end with my white-frame house and enlisted my mother's labor in the requirements of my scenarios for its inhabitants. She made dolls' clothes—tiny, knitted red snowsuits for my five (!) children. There was also a miniature tea set. I'm not sure I actually knew anyone who lived in a house (not to mention with five children) but it didn't seem strange at the time. Most of my playtime was spent either rearranging the furniture (which I still do), or coming up with names: Cheryl, Beryl, and Meryl. I can't explain the rhyme. Maybe they were triplets. I don't remember actually doing anything with the girls, but I have always been able to remember those three names; maybe the other two were boys. In any event, this failure of imagination—the children's reality was limited to the rooms they would occupy—may have something to do with my subsequent failure actually to conceive.

Recently I revealed the existence of my imaginary children to a colleague with whom I had also been plotting about job negotiations. He said, so when you discuss salary, tell them all the kids are in college now, and you need more money. I laughed because I was amused by the way he reshaped the material, but also because it reminded me how abstract (oddly, the word I want here is conceptual) the idea of children or motherhood had always been for me: in my fantasy, they never left their rooms; they certainly never grew up to go to college . . .

In much the same spirit, Steedman recalls the stationary existence of her two imaginary children, Joan and Maureen, who lived in the flat with her in their blue and green gingham dresses: "I don't know what I did with them when I conjured them up," she writes, "but they were there, behind the mangle all through the summer and winter of 1950–51, as my mother carried my yet-to-be-born baby sister" (91). Following Winnicott, Steedman takes the existence of these "fantasy children" (95) as proof that she had received "good enough" mothering when she was a small child.[14] Why then did she not go on (as her sister did) ultimately to wish for real children of her own?[15]

Here, close to the center of the book, toward the conclusion of the chapter called "Reproduction and Refusal," is a tantalizing opacity. Steedman seems to tie the wish for a child to a mimetic relation between the mother's body and the daughter's body; she thus begins by explaining the difficulty she had accepting her mother's adult female body as her destiny:[16] "My refusal of my mother's body was, I think, a recognition of the problem that my own physical presence represented to her; at the same time it was a refusal of the inexorable nature of that difficulty, that it would go on like that, that I would become her, and come to reproduce the circumstances of our straitened unsatisfying life" (95). She then moves on, with no articulated transition, from this class-bound maternal economics to a more general psychological view: "Part of the desire to reproduce oneself as a body, as an entity in the real world, lies in conscious memory of someone approving that body" (95). And again her mother—in memory—fails her. But she moves on to make the wider point of maternal "coldness towards daughters," which draws its power from its conjunction with the daughters' assessment of "the attitude of the social world towards them." In this moment of a double "exclusion"—always a key word for Steedman—the failure of "self-love," which she places "at the root of the wish for a child" (96), takes on its fullest meaning and leads to the refusal to "reproduce."

Now what's tricky in this characteristic moment is the oscillation operating in Steedman's arguments between an economic (class-based) and a (gender-based) psychoanalytic explanation. (These don't have to be incompatible positions—elsewhere in her writing Steedman refers to herself as a "good Freudian"—but they tend to be competitively polarized here.)[17] On the one hand she garners support for her views from working-class autobiographies; on the other, she acknowledges that daughters' "exile" from maternal attention is recorded "of course" in not exclusively working-class "literary and autobiographical sources" (95), including fairy tales like "The Little Mermaid" and "The Snow Queen," which are foundational in her accounts of childhood fantasies. Nonetheless, throughout the memoir when Steedman seeks to analyze maternal rejection—" 'If it wasn't for you two,' my mother told us, 'I could be off somewhere else' " (39); " 'Never have children dear, they ruin your life' " (85)—she insists on the working-class base of this (her) not-wantedness and in turn on its essential difference from a middle-class, Chodorowian repertoire of relatedness.[18]

Steedman's concomitant insistence on her father's distance from the phallus—having a "father who wasn't a patriarch" (16)—is central to her refusal of what she takes to be a monolithic psychoanalytic discourse that doesn't speak to the experience of working-class girls and women; in particular the desire not to reproduce one's circumstances. But if it is possible to bracket paternal authority (The Name of the Father), at least as the culture's dominant representation of hierarchies of violence, it's less easy to dispose of its familiar symbolics, even when displaced onto the fantasy power regime of the Good Mother.[19]

A father like mine dictated each day's existence; our lives would have been quite different had he not been there. But he didn't *matter*, and his singular unimportance needs explaining. His not mattering has an effect like this: I don't quite believe in male power; somehow the iron of patriarchy didn't enter my soul. I accept the idea of male power intellectually, of course (and I will eat my words the day I am raped, or the knife is slipped between my ribs; though I know that will not be the case: in the dreams it is a woman who holds the knife, and only a woman can kill). (19)

How are we to understand this linking of a knife between the ribs with rape in a parenthesis that comes to comment on the failure of patriarchy to penetrate (the iron of a sword?) one's soul?[20] Who is the woman wielding the knife?

Later in the narrative, Steedman describes a fantasy in which as a seven-year-old reader of fairy tales, she imagines her parents sitting naked, cutting each other "making thin surface wounds like lines drawn with a sharp red pencil, from which the blood poured." And she comments, "She was the most cut, but I knew it was she who did the cutting. I couldn't always see the knife in my father's hand" (54). Despite the contradictory "evidence" of the fantasy, the daughter maintains her belief in the murderous power of the mother she seems to eulogize: "Death of a Good Woman."[21]

Playing the gender card against class, and the class card against gender, Steedman set out to challenge both male Marxist readings of autobiography in which "working-class boys . . . grow up to write about their mother's flinty courage" (17)—and a mythified, motherist, largely American feminist theory which takes the Persephone/Demeter story as its foundational myth (86–88). In her refusal of that story as *not true*, Steedman emphasizes its failure to account for "non-mothering" and the "economic circumstances and . . . social understanding" in which it occurs. I want to give both pieces of that intervention their due, but at the same time I want to try and unhook the motherism under assault by Steedman—the assumed wish for a child—as well as maternal coldness from their specific class assignments. This is not to say that there aren't important local and institutionalized class and racialized differences at work in the structures of maternal experience; rather that not-wantedness and relatedness are *not only* a matter of class and material deprivation (as Steedman herself sometimes seems to know). What Steedman's insistence on the detail of maternal experience *as material*—her mother's longing for a New Look coat—can lead us to do, however, is to crosshatch maternal subjectivity with the full spectrum of class activity. For every class context there's a range of responses inside the mother/daughter/ mother/not mother narrative. The consequences (in life, as well as in feminist theory) of the identification/repudiation model we see at work in *Landscape* do not unfold against a unified horizon, even within a national working-class identity.[22] If as Adrienne Rich famously declared in *Of Woman Born*, "the cathexis between mother and daughter—essential, distorted, misused— is the great unwritten story" (225), it is not one story either.

It's in this sense that I want to turn now to *A Woman's Story*; for if like Steedman's case study, Ernaux's memoir is the story of two lives, it evokes a very different emotional landscape in which to place them. Ernaux weaves the trajectory of her mother's life with her own in a double and overlapping chronology: her mother's movement out of the peasantry into the life of small shopkeepers; her own, encouraged by her mother, out of that world into a professional class. The end of the mother's life is shaped by the hideous drama of Alzheimer's disease; the daughter's midlife entails a coming to terms with that illness, the death of both her parents, and the confirmation of her new class identity.

In Ernaux's memoir the violence of the mother/daughter plot is located in the familial dramas of adolescence; the mother's disgust at her daughter's developing female body becomes explicit in outbursts of rage over clothes: " 'You're not going out like *that*!' " "We both knew," Ernaux writes, "what to expect from each other: she knew I longed to seduce the boys, I knew she was terrified I would 'have an accident,' in other words, that I would start to sleep around and get pregnant." The daughter's evaluation of this struggle takes the succinct form of a remembered guilty wish: "Sometimes I imagined her death would have meant nothing to me" (50).

Although she does not, like Steedman, include references to psychoanalytic and feminist theory within her narrative, Ernaux seems to work out of the Kleinian categories that inform Steedman's reflection: the "good" and "bad" mother, violence and reparation. Writing within the year immediately after her mother's death, Ernaux talks about the difficulty of getting her mother straight.[23]

To get away from these oscillating views, which come from my earliest childhood, I try to describe and explain her life as if I were writing about someone else's mother and a daughter who wasn't me. Still, though I try to write as neutrally as as possible, certain expressions, such as "If you ever have an accident . . . " [s'il t'arrive un malheur] can never be neutral for me, while others, for instance, "the denial of one's own body and sexuality," remain totally abstract. When I remember these expressions, I experience the same feeling of depression I had when I was sixteen, and fleetingly, I confuse the woman who influenced me most with an African mother pinning her daughter's arms behind her back while the village midwife slices off the girl's clitoris. (tm, 50–51)

While the reference to clitoridectomy is a relative commonplace in certain kinds of feminist discourse (Steedman's, for instance), it's quite startling in this writerly rememoration.[24] Ernaux, whose mother's fear that her daughter's pregnancy would keep her from the bright and open future she wishes for her, seems to conjure the maternal assault on the clitoris as a local struggle, not global (its displacement onto an African mother notwithstanding).

In the memoir, this violent moment is followed by a passage in which Ernaux returns to the past and evokes her crisis of separation, her social disidentification from the mother, which is the dominant and guiding thread of this story. It begins: "I stopped trying to copy her" (51).[25] In the blank between the paragraphs lies the unsaid logic connecting maternal violence, sexual pleasure, and the terms of the daughter's autonomy: "Until I married, I still belonged to her, even when we were living apart" (57).[26] The price of that separation is the recognition of a double split: the daughter both is still and is no longer like the mother; the daughter both is and isn't like herself. The divide is double: separating mother and daughter, disjoining the autobiographical subject from her childhood self.

Ernaux's rage against her mother is located in the body, and this body ties (without permanently binding) her to class.

I was ashamed of her brusque manners and speech, especially when I realized how alike we were. I blamed her for being someone who I, by moving into new circles, no longer wanted to be. I discovered that there was a world of difference between wanting to be educated and actually acquiring that knowledge. (51)

The growing abyss separating the child from the parent produced by education and the acquisition of new knowledge that compounds the difference is a commonplace of contemporary American autobiographical writing in which the child moves into another world by virtue of the education the parent—generally uneducated—has wanted the child to have. But here that passage is figured—at least through juxtaposition—by the confusion of images that results in the doubling of intellectual distance by sexual violence. And as in Steedman's memoir, the violence to the daughter comes from the weapon in the mother's hand. Ernaux, however, does nothing directly with this image which cuts the book close to its center; within the next two pages, the daughter leaves home to go to "boarding school," and her departure is preceded by a summary of the mother's view of her daughter in social terms: "Sometimes she saw her own daughter as a class enemy" (tm, 53). What the mother seems to want to cut off, then, in her language—"If you ever have an accident"—is the possibility of a betrayal woven of sex and class.[27] On the one hand she fears that the daughter's adolescent rebellion, with its bourgeois overtones of scorn for social convention, will subvert the education plot, the *Bildung* out of the working class into the middle class. On the other, she demands class loyalty: recognition by the daughter of the mother's values, authority, and vision.

As the daughter who is leaving the mother behind, Ernaux also fears the inexorability of class betrayal, precisely through an education that gives her access to new language, new powers of interpretation, and new models of self-conscious behavior. The last third of the memoir, which is marked by the death of Ernaux's father, describes the attempt of the two women to live together in the daughter's house. The experiment of their life together reveals the complicated ways in which class alignments can shift within a family over the time of its own history. At her daughter's house, the mother feels out of place: "I don't think I belong here" (64). This is not cast, as it might be in an American context, as a psychological problem. For Ernaux it's a social one in which her mother looks for work to do in the house to help out, in order, she says jokingly, to pay her way:

It took me a long time to realize that the feeling of unease my mother experienced in my own house was no different from what I had felt as a teenager when I was introduced to people a "cut above us" . . . I also realized that in pretending to act like the hired help, she instinctively translated the real cultural domination of her children's reading *Le Monde* or listening to Bach into an imaginary economic domination of boss to worker: her form of revolt. (tm, 78)

In Ernaux's account, despite her identification with her mother's body/story/ desires, class differences come to structure the mother/daughter relation within the family and under the same roof.

The story of what those differences finally mean is inseparable in Ernaux's narrative from the memoir project itself; we could even say that those shifting class divides are Ernaux's subject: to memorialize her mother is to map the passage from the "dominated world" into which her mother was born to the "dominant world" of words (tm, 92).[28] It is in this mapping that we read most clearly the dissonance between Steedman's vision of maternal legacy and Ernaux's. Steedman takes up these issues within (at least between) the lines of her history as well, but she differs from Ernaux in two crucial areas: on the one hand, the stakes of separation; and on the other, in her reluctance (if not her failure) to acknowledge class change within herself, in her own life in the "dominant world" of words as an academic and writer. Steedman's attempt to separate from her mother displays an almost ontological resentment radically unlike Ernaux's essentially adolescent rites of passage: "There exists a letter that I wrote to a friend one vacation from Sussex . . . in which I described my sitting in the evenings with my mother, refusing to go out, holding tight to my guilt and duty, knowing that I *was* her, and that I must keep her company" (19). Despite this over-identification which would seem to freeze the daughter into immobility, like Ernaux, Steedman has in fact moved on: she has become a social historian, and it is in part, at least, as a historian that she researched the materials of *Landscape*. The University of Sussex, to which she had gone as a student in 1965, is the scene of another vantage point from which she can view her mother's story; even if, as she claims, the cultural narratives available to the women of her generation and class do not feature their scenarios. "And should I have met a woman like me (there must have been some . . .) we could not have talked of escape except within a literary framework . . . ignorant of the material stepping-stones of our escape: clothes, shoes, make-up" (15). In this sense, *Landscape* sets itself the task of producing that missing text: supplying a women's working-class cultural criticism through the autobiography of her childhood as it can be reconstructed through the biography of her mother's.

Steedman acknowledges directly the effects of the process she names as "embourgeoisement and state education" (20), the passage into the "dominant world" Ernaux poignantly invokes, only when she refers to her professional identity as a historian. Beyond that, as readers we come up against a silence, which, following Raymond Williams, Steedman describes negatively as the "cancellation of a writer's present" for the writer who has left (and not left) the working class (20). This silence has everything to do with the elusive quality of her narrative.[29] How can we understand the ways in which the childhood stories continue to be lived in the writing present if the adult story of conflict and desire is completely suppressed?

For instance, as we learned in the passage with which we began, when Steedman goes to visit her dying mother, this is the first time they have seen each other in *nine years*, except, she specifies later in passing, at her father's funeral. This break is not explained—another one of many important silences that underpin (or undermine) the narrative—and the reader is left to conjecture about what's happened.[30] Steedman alludes to their separation obliquely: her father, she writes, "was genuinely shocked when, at twenty-seven, I wrote to my mother and said that I didn't want to see her for a while because she upset me so much" (60). Why? What has happened between them?

If Steedman refuses to supply a motive for their separation, she says only this about their final scene: "An hour later I came away believing that I admired a woman who could, in these circumstances and in some pain, treat me as if I had just stepped round the corner for a packet of tea." This was, Steedman remarks in a tone that is eerily jubilant, the way things had aways been: "We were truly illegitimate, outside any law of recognition: the mirror broken, a lump of ice for a heart" (142). Without the mirroring of Winnicottian mothering that allows the daughter to want to reproduce, any form of continuity and social exchange seems permanently damaged. Or is it the other way round? Perhaps we should interpret the daughter's admiration for her mother's indifference as confirmation of their ultimate bond: not their identity, but the daughter's will to identification.[31]

In the late seventies, my sister, who at the beginning of the sixties had set out to declass herself through her relations and activities and to separate herself from our middle-class parents, decided to quit her job as a day care worker and try to earn her living as a potter.[32] What stood between this desire and her ability to put it into practice was the price of a kiln, a basic element of a potter's studio. My mother offered to stake her for the equipment, and by way, she thought, of encouragement, added jokingly: "Don't worry, if it doesn't work out I can take it as a business loss on my taxes." A few days later, she received a note from my sister in which she announced that in view of our mother's lack of confidence in her ability to make a go of it—she always "rained on her parade"—she would not be seeing her for a while. And she didn't. Almost five years later my sister reluctantly came to see our mother, who was rapidly dying of cancer. Our mother, who in response had written my sister out of her will, like Steedman's, betrayed neither anger nor surprise when her daughter showed up, but the wounds remained open on both sides.

This kind of violence between mother and daughter, which attests to the shattering of the mirror, crosses class identities as it shatters any comfortable motherism. There's a particular rage, I think, *in and between* mothers and daughters that comes precisely from women's inability to *choose* motherhood, in the sense that they/we cannot possibly know *what* they/we are choosing. And of course, in not choosing it to know *what* has been refused.[33]

Ernaux's memoir wants to tell the other side of Steedman's story; at least it describes a more conventional way for a daughter to experience her mother's illness and death, and more generally produces a Chodorowian instance of gender modeling and identification.[34] If Steedman's account is fueled by "matrophobia," the fear "of *becoming one's mother*,"[35] Ernaux's is punctuated by "matrophilia," the desire to become her mother (or at least one with her), despite, or even through, the displacement a university education entails, and her transformation into a writer. "Throughout the ten months I was writing this book," Ernaux reveals toward the end of her memoir, "I dreamed of her almost every night. Once I was lying in the middle of a stream, caught between two currents. From my genitals [de mon sexe], smooth again like a young girl's, from between my thighs, long tapering plants floated limply. The body they came from was not only mine, it was also my mother's" (89–90). The book called *Une Femme* is an act of emotional reconnection that passes through two bodies joined in resemblance.

Nonetheless, the book depends on their separateness: "I believe I am writing about my mother because it is my turn to bring her into the world" (32). The memoir of the dead other is both for oneself and for others: "over the past few days," Ernaux explains in the writing notes that shape the memoir, "I have found it more and more difficult to write, possibly because I would like never to reach this point. And yet I know I shall have no peace of mind until I find the words which will reunite the demented woman she had become with the strong, radiant woman she once was" (76). But this reparation is not only for her: when her mother starts talking to imaginary people, Ernaux first puts her hands over her ears not to hear. Then, "to make the thought bearable," she describes what's happening on a scrap of paper: "Maman's talking to herself." Finally, she explains toward the memoir's close, "I'm writing those same words now, but for other people, so that they can understand" (tm, 80).[36] Can they?

In the frame to *Landscape*, the two-page prelude entitled "Death of a Good Woman," Steedman, we saw, enlists Beauvoir's internal gloss on her mother's final suffering. "Simone de Beauvoir wrote of her mother's death, said that in spite of the pain it was a easy one: an upper-class death. Outside, for the poor, dying is a different matter" (2). Because she is so determined to maintain the difference class always makes, however, Steedman cuts out the heart of Beauvoir's irony. She omits the original appearance of the phrase, which occurs in Beauvoir's description of the actual moment of agony:

Maman had almost lost consciousness. Suddenly she cried, "I can't breathe!" Her mouth opened, her eyes stared wide, huge in that wasted, ravaged face: with a spasm she entered into coma. . . .

Already she was no longer there—her heart was beating and she breathed, sitting there with glassy eyes that saw nothing. And then it was over. "The doctors said she would go out like a candle: it wasn't like that at all," said my sister, sobbing.

"But, Madame," replied the nurse, "I assure you it was a very easy death." (88) [37]

Beauvoir's commitment to demystifying human experience, to seeing identity as the effect of a construction, compels her to refuse the clichés of death— "there is no such thing as a natural death"—just as she famously refused them of life: "one is not born, rather one becomes a woman." Although Beauvoir's vision therefore necessarily includes self-consciousness about the socially situated nature of experience, her project in this memoir is not uniquely focused on that aspect of a failing body's reality. Rather, she scrupulously charts the tension between the living's caretaking and the dying's suffering: "Without our obstinate watchfulness she would have suffered far more. For indeed, comparatively speaking, her death was an easy one" (94). But "comparatively speaking" does not erase the death work of the body as a "defenceless thing," which gives Beauvoir, we might say, her material, and her text. The memoir graphs this body in pain, a body located, even rooted in class distinctions (and Beauvoir is merciless in her critique of hospital hierarchy, on the one hand, and her mother's snobbery on the other); and yet in the end, what we retain are less the ways in which class markers divide bodies—the screen that blocks the gaze of the dying poor— than the ways in which bodies demand our attention despite the protection or vulnerabilities of class.[38] Steedman's misreading of Beauvoir is critically productive, however, for it gives us another metaphor with which to figure the blindness of her insight as a writer: is not class the screen, the "good mother" screen that stands between a daughter and the rage at work in her own project?[39] In the same way, despite the announced transparency of the "curtainless bedroom" (2) in which the origins of this story are said to be located, screening her own class displacements from view, Steedman refuses all allies.[40]

Let us return now to two images I think we can take as emblems of what's at stake in both these daughters' memoirs, indebted in their different ways to Beauvoir's: Ernaux's of her mother "confused" with the African mother whose constraint enables the daughter's clitoridectomy; Steedman's of patriarchy's force as the woman with the knife. But what do they tell us?

To the extent that the maternal memoirs tell the story of a daughter's emergence out of her class culture and by the act of writing itself mark her difference from that place, perhaps we should understand the threatened knife cut not only as a metaphor for the mother's resistance to the daughter's autonomy but also for the daughter's rage to be free, her need to leave the mother behind. I want to suggest that the violence is mutual, and these images its signature. This is not to say that the rupture is always fatal, although it seems to have been for Steedman. Here we can speculate that it was only by breaking class patterns of attachment and violently tearing the bonds that tied mother and daughter to each other that she could move into the writer's space. By making herself into a case study, however, we might argue that she did reproduce herself, especially if we understand, as Barbara Johnson suggests, that the "autobiographical desire par excellence" is "the desire for resemblance, the desire to create a being like oneself" (146).[41]

Is this the necessary path of a daughter's authority? There is no single answer, but I think that these violent embodiments of mother/daughter engagement supply powerful allegories for contemporary autobiographical writing by women who wish to perform a cultural analysis.[42] Like *Landscape* and *A Woman's Story* their texts will be marked by a double specificity: this will entail the representation of both the local material culture in which all childhood scenarios are rooted, and of the heavily freighted passage which characterizes a daughter's negotiation with maternal power, which will include betrayal and mutilation, hatred, and sometimes love.[43] This may mean that to some the testimony will not seem to bear the weight of (universal) authority because it feels too particular, too close to the maternal body, too monstrous. That, of course, is also its challenge.

In closing I recur to *A Very Easy Death* for another, more ambiguous image of these legacies. In her final, delirious moments, Françoise de Beauvoir speaks incoherently: " 'I should have liked to have the time to bring out my book. . . . She must be allowed to breastfeed whomever she likes' " (tm, 88).[44] I want to suggest that Beauvoir's text becomes that source of nurturance, severed, so to speak, from its metaphor of maternal nourishment.[45] What I'm sketching here is the position of giving separated from a natural body and recast in a writer's repertoire. Beauvoir had the time to bring out her book. We've had the time to read it. But what kind of readers are we? And what kind of daughters?[46] The figure Ernaux assigns herself in this project is that of "archivist" (16); it is to her that falls the task of recording the end of a certain tradition: of "household tips which lessened the strain of poverty," of a certain maternal lore which was passed on from mother to daughter. But there is also another task besides ending a tradition. By virtue of changing classes, Ernaux transforms its household materials. "Isn't writing," she asks toward the end of her memoir, "also a way of giving" (91).

These memoirs (and I include Beauvoir's) embody a daughter's knowledge about women and class: lived and retrospective, of it and at a distance from it. But not only. Or rather they show how talking about class *also* allows us to talk about that which is both most us and what escapes us, since it is where we come from, and not necessarily, in these instances, where we remain—what Steedman calls elsewhere "the lost past within each of us."[47] It is only because we have left those childhood places—the place we were made to occupy—that we can write of it; writing this past is implicitly to acknowledge our own self-division, the nostalgia *for*, inseparable *from*, the loathing of identity as a cultural fact. This knowledge, therefore, is a source of loneliness—we are cut off from the origin stories, the bond is broken— and at the same time a possible reconnection: since the memoir is a form of testimony that posits an addressee, we get to retell these stories so that our version of "pastness" gets to be heard. This also takes us, however fleetingly, out of the very family history has allotted us.

The inevitable price of writing *out* of the family is that it stays *in* the family, but because autobiography always operates in the tension between the writer's published family plot and the reader's private one, readers are likely to respond with a story of their own, like hers and also different, with other hearts of darkness, and other screens.[48]

Cultural criticism cannot do without these stories. What remains to be seen is what it can do with them.

Coda, in which I add an autobiographical death to the list.

Like Annie Ernaux's, my mother died on April 7. It was ten years ago. She had been in a coma for several weeks and finally her heart ceased beating. She died of lung cancer that had spread to her bones, throughout her body. The odd thing was that after a while she didn't seem to be in pain and had stopped taking all medication. The night she died we all went as usual to the Seder at her sister's house. No one cried or even said anything; it was as though nothing had happened, and I suppose in a way nothing had: she had already left us behind with her body; the doctor said she'd been out of touch with reality. The next day my father and I, like co-conspirators, trudged through the snow, unexpected so late in a New York spring, to the vault where I retrieved the jewelry she had left me in her will. No more than Steedman's, my mother did not die alone; she had a middle-class death, which resembled her life. At the funeral, the rabbi, counting the house, said it was a really good turnout, especially considering the weather.

NOTES

This essay is part of a work in progress on contemporary memoirs whose working title is "Legacies of the Other." When replaced in that context, the essay will include an American postwar example from a fifties generation, probably Vivian Gornick's *Fierce Attachments.* Gornick's memoir is structured around the daughter's relationship to the mother, but the mother—at the time of writing—is alive and well, and so the symmetry her text presents with Steedman's and Ernaux's isn't perfect. Still, it gives me a working-class childhood, a feminist, intellectual daughter, and a Jewish mother-daughter struggle at the heart of the project. When I say me, I mean both my role as the author of this book and as an autobiographical critic within it; I'm looking for a text against which to read my story, which I do briefly in these pages. Gornick's comes close, with the difference that class makes between us.

I also want to indicate a second sense of incompletion. If I were to flesh out the argument over cultural criticism (as opposed to an autobiographical reading of autobiography), I would have to take on, for the American context at least, the ways in which race structures the mother-daughter connection. This difference would necessarily change the tone of generalization as well as its range. Here, for instance, Maxine Hong Kingston's *The Woman Warrior* would enter the discussion (though like Gornick's, the mother is alive) as a postwar reflection. Audre Lorde's *Zami* is the only black-authored autobiography I know of that would come close to this paradigm (though Lorde is at least ten years older than these authors, and hence older during her fifties in New York), but the mother is not the central focus, nor the mother-daughter relation, rather the power of women: "To whom do I owe the power behind my voice, what strength I have become, yeasting up like the sudden blood from under the bruised skin's blister?" These lines open *Zami*; they are followed by a reply: "My father leaves his psychic print upon me, silent, intense, and unforgiving. But his is a distant lightning. Images of women flaming like torches adorn and define the borders of my journey, stand like dykes between me and the chaos. It is the images of women, kind and cruel, that lead me home" (*Zami, A New Spelling of My Name: A Biomythography*, The Crossing Press, 1982). In other words, I see this essay as the beginning of a discussion, rather than as its endpoint.

1. *Landscape for a Good Woman: A Story of Two Lives.* (London: Virago, 1986; rpt. Rutgers University Press, 1987); *A Woman's Story*. Trans. Tanya Leslie. (New York: Four Walls Eight Windows, 1991). *Une Femme.* (Paris: Gallimard, 1987). References to these works will be included in the body of the text. I have occasionally made changes in Leslie's translation and have indicated this by the abbreviation "tm."

2. Jill Johnston ends her reflection on the new "plebeian autobiography" with this quote from Steedman. "Fictions of the Self in the Making." *New York Times Book Review* (April 25, 1993), 33. Johnston clearly sees the possibility of producing social change through the practice of writing autobiography that I see at work in these texts: "As we write ourselves into existence, the class, race and sexual political structures of society inevitably change. The notion of who has rights, whose voice can be heard, whose individuality is worthy, comes under revision."

3. It's not absolutely clear to me why Steedman "envies" Oakley her easy access to "the outlines of conventional romantic fiction." Like Steedman's, Oakley's account of growing up in postwar England interweaves personal narrative with feminist theory, autobiographical event with social analysis. What's different—Oakely's interleaving of that mix with pages from a love affair that parallels her family life in a poignant counterpoint—emerges, it seems, from Oakley's willingness to offer the reader, in a fictionalized mode, glimpses into the workings of her sexual desire. I don't understand this mode of self-disclosure as a function of class.

4. Eve Kosofsky Sedgwick. *Epistemology of the Closet.* (Berkeley and Los Angeles: University of California Press, 1990). But it is crucial to retain the force of material reality *across which* identifying with occurs. "It also involves identification *as against*" (61).

5. Paul de Man. "Autobiography as De-facement." *MLN* (94) 1979: 919–930.

6. Elizabeth Abel has written a probing and illuminating essay, "Race, Class, and Psychoanalysis?: Opening Questions," in which she reads Steedman's memoir with an essay of Hortense Spillers's "Mama's Baby, Papa's Maybe." (*diacritics* 17, no. 2, Summer 1987). Abel reads in this scene Steedman's subversive revision of psychoanalytic paradigms in which class replaces the symbolic father: "the middle-class woman (rather than the father) who both interrupts and consolidates the mother-daughter bond" (193). And she goes on to conclude, "The daughter's identification with her mother is not produced in a dyadic sphere created by the mother's mirroring gaze but through a common position . . . and a shared perception of a third term.

. . . Identification with the mother is triadic rather than dyadic and triangulated by class instead of patriarchy" (193). In *Conflicts in Feminism*, eds. Marianne Hirsch and Evelyn Fox Keller. (New York and London: Routledge, 1990).

In Regenia Gagnier's review essay, "Feminist Autobiography in the 1980s," *Feminist Studies* 17, 1 (Spring 1991), she comments on the importance of this scene and the symbolics of disempowered fatherhood which characterizes Steedman's childhood world: "In Steedman's childhood, a patriarchal law could disrupt the mother/child dyad in the form of a social worker, policeman, or school inspector, but seldom in the form of a father" (144). Victoria Rosner has written perceptively on Steedman's complex relationship to psychoanalysis, in "Psychoanalysis and Childhood: See Also Myth, Carolyn K. Steedman and The Maternal Return." (ms.)

7. In "War Memories," a moving essay about reading narratives that deal with the Holocaust, Susan Suleiman maps the territory of this style of reading autobiography autobiographically that she calls "autobiographical reading" (what I call "autobiographical criticism" in *Getting Personal*), reading that in some instances—like this one—produces its own text as response *Risking Who One Is: Encounters with Contemporary Art and Literature*. (Cambridge: Harvard University Press, 1994).

8. On the designation and profile of the specifically *professional* middle class, see Barbara Ehrenreich's *Fear of Falling: The Inner Life of the Middle Class*. (New York: HarperCollins, 1990).

9. In an earlier essay, "Prison-houses," published in *Feminist Review* (no. 20, Summer 1985, 7–21), in which she discusses the overlay of ideas about mothering on elementary school teaching, Steedman describes her own experiences in the classroom and their maternally performative effects:

I never left [the children]: they occupied the night-times, all my dreams. I was very tired, bone-achingly tired all the time. I was unknowingly, covertly expected to become a mother, and I unknowingly became one, pausing only in the cracks of the dark night to ask: what is happening to me? Simone de Beauvoir tells you how to avoid servitude: she tells you not to live with men, to work, to attain financial independence; but above all she says, women should not have children, women *should refuse to mother* (Schwartzer, 1984). Children make you retreat behind the glass, lose yourself in the loving mutual gaze. The sensuality of their presence prevents the larger pleasures: the company of children keeps you a child. (19)

10. Steedman seems to have assumed, as did Beauvoir and her sister, and my sister and I, that to have children was necessarily to reproduce one's mother's life in the gender and number of one's children: to wit, that one would have girls (never boys) who would have the identical—negative—feelings about their parents (us).

11. In her review of Steedman's project in *The Women's Review of Books* (June 1988, V, 9), Julie Abraham comments on the silence that surrounds the mother's and the daughter's sexuality. "The mother's advice on the subject of sex remains reproductive: 'Never have children dear, they ruin your life.' " The daughter seems to have no sexuality. Is sex, Abraham wonders, too unimportant, or too difficult, to discuss? (13). I'd ask the same thing about reproduction.

I was startled to read in the brief author bio that accompanied an early and embryonic, so to speak, version of *Landscape*, which Steedman published in Liz Heron's collection of autobiographical writing *Truth, Dare or Promise: Girls Growing Up in the 50s* (London: Virago, 1985; rpt. 1992), that Steedman was married: "I got married in 1971—already an established relationship. No children," she writes, "nor shall have any now, I think . . . " She goes on to quote Hannah Cullick speaking of her baby nephew as she does in *Landscape* at some length (85–86).

12. On Beauvoir and the anti-maternal "choice," see Alice Jardine's "Death Sentences." Jardine's analysis brilliantly opens many of the questions on the maternal body, feminism, and generations that I wrestle with here. In *The Female Body in Western Culture: Contemporary Perspectives*, ed. Susan Suleiman. (Boston: Cambridge University Press, 1986).

13. "Introduction: Fear of a Queer Planet." *Social Text* 29 (9,4), 1991: 3–17. The power

of Warner's insight for autobiographical identity is clear: "Reprosexuality involves more than reproducing, more even than compulsory heterosexuality; it involves a relation to self that finds its proper temporality and fulfillment in generational transmission" (9).

14. In Steedman's construction of her history, she had four years of this good-enough mothering (perhaps directly inspired by her mother's listening to Winnicott on the radio [92]), and then "expulsion from the garden" with the birth of her baby sister, and the concomitant failure of her mother to attach Steedman's father to her and their family by that birth. She associates the cut between Eden and after with her mother's breasts, with the breast-feeding of her little sister, and she comments: "It was with this most familiar part of my mother's body that I came to symbolize her ambivalence towards my existence. What came free could be given freely, like her milk: loving a baby costs very little" (93). Typically, Steedman locates ambivalence in her mother not in herself, but the association, as we will see in a moment, of her mother and knives makes that one-way path of ambivalence fairly suspect.

Abel interprets the casting of the imaginary children to resemble her mother and herself as "a longing to repair insufficient mothering by remothering both her mother and herself" (194).

15. It's curious that Steedman doesn't feel the need to explain why her sister took another path, since she seems to have had even less compassion for her mother than Steedman. "My sister," Steedman writes, "with children of her own and perhaps thereby with a clearer measure of what we lacked, tells me to recall a mother who never played with us, whose eruptions from irritation into violence were the most terrifying of experiences; and she is there, the figure of nightmares, though I do find it difficult to think about in this way" (46). Again, the author bio in *Truth, Dare or Promise* tells us more than the autobiography: "My sister had her first baby at seventeen, her second nine years later. She's done it all by herself on social security. We're both daughters of the state, but she's poor and I'm not" (125).

16. She invokes another working-class account of a mother's body, which reveals a revulsion she claims not to be hers, as support nonetheless of her own ambivalent view, since she recognizes in it "the distance and distaste of the girl child from what has produced her, and what she might become" (94). This contrasts vividly with Ernaux's positive desire for identification, recorded here in a childhood memory of an outing during the war: "When she put on lipstick, she always started with the heart-shaped bit in the middle. She turned to face the wall when she fastened her corset. Her flesh bulged through the criss-cross of laces, joined together at her waist by a knot and a small rosette. I knew every detail of her body. I thought that I would grow up to become her. . . . I am sitting on the crossbar of my father's bike, while she rides down the slope ahead of us, her back straight, the seat firmly wedged between her buttocks. . . . I believe we were both in love with my mother" (35).

But Steedman's disidentifications are even more complex since she frames her discussion by this provocative remark: "A little girl's body, its neat containment, seems much more like that of a man, especially if she does not really know what lies between his legs. His [her father's] body was in some way mine, and I was removed from my own as well as his" (94).

In *Of Woman Born: Motherhood as Experience and Institution*, Adrienne Rich describes the power the sight of her mother's and father's bodies had on her sense of her future identity as a woman:

As a young child I thought how beautiful she was. . . . In early adolescence I still glanced slyly at my mother's body, vaguely imagining: I too shall have breasts, full hips, hair between my thighs—whatever that meant to me then, and with all the ambivalence of such a thought. And there were other thoughts: I too shall marry, have children—but *not like her*. I shall find a way of doing it all differently.

My father's tense, narrow body did not seize my imagination, though authority and control ran through it like electric filaments. I used to glimpse his penis dangling behind a loosely tied bathrobe. But I had understood very early that he and my mother were different. (New York: Norton, 1976, 219)

Rich's reminiscence, which opens the famous chapter "Motherhood and Daughterhood," allows her to explore the ambivalence of these morphological effects, an ambivalence that Steedman almost systematically represses.

17. "Culture, Cultural Studies, and Historians." In *Cultural Studies*, eds. Lawrence Grossberg, Cary Nelson, Paula Treichler (New York: Routledge, 1992), 615.

18. Here Steedman footnotes Chodorow's afterword, in which she takes up objections to (suggestions for) her book. Steedman probably refers to Chodorow's remarks about "the effects of class differences and of whether a mother works in the paid labor force or not" (215). I'm interested in remarks on the same page: "Some friends and colleagues have said that my account is too unqualified. In fact all women do not mother or want to mother, and all women are not "maternal" or nurturant." Chodorow answers the complaint by saying, "I agree that all claims about gender differences [the point of her book] gloss over important differences within genders and similarities between genders."

"Indeed," Steedman writes, "Nancy Chodorow is well aware of the limitations of her account, and knows that it is class and culture bound. Were it not so bound, then the darker social side of the primary relationship between mothers and daughters . . . would have to emerge" (87). Yes, darker, but why locate the breakdown of maternal care, "the removal of the looking-glass," exclusively in the specific scene of material deprivation? What about other styles of maternal ressentiment?

On the question of maternal rage and its universal and particular locations see Susan Suleiman's pioneering "Writing and Motherhood," in *The (M)other Tongue*: *Essays in Feminist Psychoanalytic Interpretation,* eds. Shirley Nelson Garner, Claire Kahane, Madelon Sprengnether. (Ithaca and London: Cornell University Press, 1985). See also Marianne Hirsch's *The Mother/Daughter Plot*: *Narrative, Psychoanalysis, Feminism.* (Bloomington: Indiana University Press, 1989), especially the powerful chapter, "Feminist Discourse/Maternal Discourse."

19. Steedman seems to locate the work of the Good Mother in the years of early childhood before the birth of her baby sister. In that chronology, the Good Mother looks a lot like the preoedipal mother dear to feminist theorists. But Diana Fuss warns against a desymbolized view of that mother. "Preoedipality," she writes, "is firmly entrenched in the social order and cannot be read as before, outside, or even after the Symbolic; the mother-daughter relation, no less than the father-daughter relation, is a Symbolic association completely inscribed in the field of representation, sociality, and culture." "Freud's Fallen Women: Identification, Desire, and 'A Case of Homosexuality in a Woman.' " *Yale Journal of Criticism* 6:1 (Spring 1993); rpt. in *Fear of a Queer Planet*, ed. Michael Warner. (Minneapolis: University of Minnesota Press, 1993).

20. The metaphor of penetration returns at the end of the chapter dedicated to her father: "But daddy, you never knew me like this. . . . You shouldn't have left us there, you should have taken me with you. You left me alone; you never laid a hand on me: the iron didn't enter the soul. You never gave me anything: the lineaments of an unused freedom" (61). If a woman holds the knife, then does she also, by metonymy, rape?

21. Elizabeth Abel discusses Steedman's absolute refusal to theorize either her ambivalent (to say the least!) feelings toward her mother, or the division of feeling between her father and mother in which her father's failures are poignantly lamented (194): "But daddy, you never knew me like this; you didn't really care, or weren't allowed to care, it comes to the same thing in the end" (61). This complaint chiastically echoes Germaine Greer's autobiography: *Daddy, We Hardly Knew You.*

22. See, for instance, several of the autobiographical pieces collected in *Family Snaps: The Meaning of Domestic Photography*, eds. Jo Spence and Patricia Holland (London: Virago, 1991), especially Rosy Martin's, "Unwind the Ties That Bind."

23. Steedman's text is placed under the sign of her mother's death—it begins and ends under its event—but there is no clear indication of when it occurred in relation to the time of writing.

24. Thus Steedman, in the course of her critique of Nancy Chodorow's on the whole cheerful

account of "gendered identification" between baby girls and their mothers in the (white, American) middle classes, remarks: "For it is women who socialize little girls into acceptance of a restricted future, women who used to bind the feet, women who hold down the daughter for clitoridectomy, and who, in more familiar and genteel ways, fit their daughters for self-abasement" (87).

25. This phrase in French—"elle a cessé d'être mon modèle"—recalls Colette's famous celebratory self-identification with her mother: "Imaginez-vous, à me lire, que je fais mon portrait? Patience: c'est seulement mon modèle." This is the epigraph to *La Naissance du jour* [*Break of Day*] and provides us with the euphoric countertext of the daughter's identification with the mother. She describes the cost of separation in her late memoir, *Mes apprentissages*.

26. These become the subject of Ernaux's novels; *Les Armoires vides* (1974) opens on the scene of an abortion.

27. The daughter's pleasure becomes the mother's anxiety about reproduction, which codes an anxiety about class identity. Ernaux takes up this expression in *La Place* as well (London: Methuen, 1987, 100). And the importance for her parents' sense of controlling their future by controlling reproduction: "He had learned the essential condition for not reproducing the misery of the previous generation: not to forget oneself in a woman" (65; my translation). Ernaux's parents determine not to reproduce their parents' poverty by having only one child; when their first child dies, they replace her with Annie.

28. The editor of *La Place* for the Methuen text, P. M. Wetherill, connects Ernaux's project here to that of Pierre Bourdieu (24–25). I think there's a parallel to be worked out here between Ernaux's relation to Bourdieu's thought and Steedman's to that of Raymond Williams: gendering the class analyses through their literary experiments.

29. Steedman seems here to think that she has succeeded in keeping a continuity with her working-class childhood alive, in the sense that Williams means. It's that desire, she explains, that led her to choose the case study as her form. She rehearses all the difficulties the choice of that, indeed, any form of story, entails in her opening chapter, "Stories." What I'm talking about is another kind of silence: that of authorship. We are given no sense of what else that childhood anger has given onto for her as an adult or of what went on between her and her mother as adult women in the aftermath of her fifties childhood.

As Stephen Yeo remarks in his review of the book, "Such childhoods are hidden from history, including the childhood of Carolyn Steedman, even after this book. *Landscape* is her hiding as well as her telling" (37). "Difference, Autobiography and History." *Literature and History* 4 (1) (Spring 1988).

30. In his review of *Landscape*, Raymond Williams comments: "There are ways of telling and reflecting on a story, but also it seems of avoiding it: the quick transitions between uncertain object and analytic subject become elements of a deeper hesitation. . . . [The nine-year lapse] is a situation, a moment, which produces, in this reader at least, a longing, even an envy for a fully developing narrative" (34). "Desire." *What I Came to Say.* (London: Radius, 1989).

In *Truth, Dare or Promise*, Steedman offers a partial explanation—her working as an elementary school teacher—for the space she puts between them: "I think one reason I didn't see my mother during that time is that I knew what she thought: was it all for this? A teacher—like being a nurse or a policeman; something I could have done anyway, without her sacrifice. For the first time, I'd let her down" (124). These remarks are tantalizingly incomplete, but they give us a glimpse of the productive aspect of the bond: the mother and daughter's shared complicity in the daughter's change of class through education and profession.

31. I am indebted to my conversation with Ruth Perry for this reading.

In the earlier version, Steedman includes an explanatory remark about this moment that she subsequently deletes: "Talking to my sister on the phone about the visit she insisted that the feeling of being absent in my mother's presence was nothing to do with the illness, was the emotional underpinning of our childhood." And the sentence above ends differently: "We were truly *illegitimate*, our selves *not there*" (121). If to be in the mother's presence is to not exist, or to exist in intolerable loneliness, installing absence at the center of the relation would indeed seem the key to survival.

It has taken me over a year, during which I read this paper to various audiences, taught *Landscape for a Good Woman* in seminars, and revised the essay for publication, to notice the peculiar lie that grounds this testimony. "She died alone." But Steedman's niece can describe the detail of her dying gaze. Who saw this look of "extraordinary surprise"? The niece? A caregiver? So, the loneliness of this text is perhaps this: *I* wasn't there.

32. This style of separation is described interestingly in Wini Breines's *Young, White, and Miserable: Growing Up Female in the Fifties* (Boston: Beacon, 1992) as a form of cultural dissidence.

33. Oakley writes: "Voice rise and fall but mostly rise. Everyone is tired, everyone has needs. Robin has a look of harassed discontent about him, as though he did not really choose this when he chose to 'have' a family. Neither did I—or they, for that matter. We all would like peace and an army of slaves. What we get is noise and fragmented attention" (86). And in this sense she echoes Adrienne Rich's analyses. But this is not quite where she lands: "I am a member of this second nuclear family as I was a member of my first for powerful historical reasons. Coming from one, I felt impelled to create another. I cannot wipe out that particular historical pattern: all we can do is make this second family different from the first" (90).

What's at stake more broadly, I think, is understanding, at the end of the twentieth century, the nature of that compulsion as a production and a construction. As Judith Butler writes (rereading *The Second Sex*): "If motherhood becomes a choice, then what else is possible?" (42). But despite her seductive arguing, it's clear that the "optional character of motherhood" is far from a transparent option. "Sex and Gender in Simone de Beauvoir's *Second Sex*." *Yale French Studies* 72 (1986), edited by Elaine Marks.

34. She also "reproduces." Ernaux has two sons who appear in the narrative primarily in relation to Ernaux's mother: they allow her to assume the identity of a middle-class grand-mother, and they accompany their mother to the funeral. Like her husband, her children function primarily as placeholders in Ernaux's delineation of class displacements.

35. The term is developed by Adrienne Rich in *Of Woman Born*, but in fact it was coined by Lynn Sukenick, another poet (235). Rich defines it this way: "Matrophobia can be seen as a womanly splitting of the self, in the desire to become purged once and for all of our mothers' bondage, to become individuated and free. The mother stands for the victim in ourselves, the unfree woman, the martyr. Our personalities seem dangerously to blur and overlap with our mothers'; and, in a desperate attempt to know where mother ends and daughter begins, we perform radical surgery" (236). In the *Mother/Daughter Plot*, Marianne Hirsch reads matrophobia as "the underside of the feminist family romance" (136).

36. In describing the writing she elaborated for *La Place* Ernaux talks about a flat style ("écriture plate"), the style of observation ("constat") she used in answering her parents' letters: "They would have have experienced any stylistic effects as a way of keeping them at a distance" (*La Place*, 91). In some way, the writing of *A Woman's Story* is about refusing that distance; it functions like a letter meant to be opened and read.

37. *A Very Easy Death*. Trans. Patrick O'Brian. (New York: Pantheon, 1965; rpt. 1985).

38. Is it necessary to say that I'm not arguing that bodies transcend class? Rather that insistence on their class origins is not the only path to take in the emotional disarray produced by the urgency of death work.

39. Abel makes the point clearly: "What the class configuration consistently inhibits is the direct articulation of anger and the endorsement of psychoanalytic accounts of childhood ambivalence that might seem . . . to blame the victim" (194). The ambivalence Steedman refuses herself—and her mother—traverses her texts by its silence. Ernaux names the ambivalence and incorporates it. Steedman seems to remain a prisoner of past rage.

Stephen Yeo comments: "She uses a second life, that of her mother, as a screen for projecting on to and for hiding behind" (39).

40. Yeo, p. 44. He criticizes Steedman for not connecting with other working-class writers of autobiography, notably those affiliated with the Federation of Worker Writers and Community Publishers (45ff.).

41. "My Monster, My Self." In *A World of Difference*. (Baltimore and London: Johns Hopkins University Press, 1987).

42. Clearly, the record of black women's autobiographical writing in the United States presents another picture of the mother/daughter plot, the most vivid example being Alice Walker's essays in *In Search of Our Mothers' Gardens*. Patricia Williams's *Alchemy of Race and Rights* also inflects the question of maternal legacy in substantially different ways. I'm not prepared at this point to map out the implications of the asymmetries. In "Black Women and Motherhood," Patricia Hill Collins writes: "The absence of a fully articulated Afrocentric feminist standpoint on motherhood is striking but not particularly surprising. . . . In the case of Black motherhood, the problems have been a stifling of dialogue among African–American women and the perpetuation of troublesome, controlling images, both negative and positive. . . . African–American women need an Afrocentric feminist analysis of motherhood that debunks the image of 'happy slave,' whether the white-male-created 'matriarch' or the Black-male-perpetuated 'superstrong Black mother'"(217). In *Rethinking the Family: Some Feminist Questions*, ed. Barrie Thorne, with Marilyn Yalom. (Boston: Northeastern University Press, 1982; revised edition, 1992).

43. The perfect object does both. This is the case of Steedman's mother's New Look coat, which she remembers from a childhood dream, and which becomes the emblem of Steedman's argument: the expensive item craved for by her mother (27–29) and that comes to summarize maternal longings; femininity hostage to class limits. I have in my possession a blue felt circle skirt with a grey appliqué poodle made by my mother in the fifties. She saved it, along with a bone and silver teething ring, a velvet muff, and two other items she made for me, a knitted vest and a baby blanket. I found these items together in a box as though she were constituting a maternal legacy *of her making*. These become the objects of a narrative of middle-class motherhood as her construction.

Peter Stallybrass has written movingly on clothes as memory in "Worn Worlds: Clothes, Mourning, and the Life of Things," a piece in which he also discusses the importance of clothing in Steedman's memoir (ms.).

44. To what extent can we read this confusion as the expression of the mother of a writer who both confesses to her own writerly ambitions and for whom the daughter no longer plays the role of a son (68), no longer the breadwinner but the nurturer? Or perhaps this is also the deathbed confession of a mother's ambition?

45. Susan Suleiman addresses the question of the maternal metaphor and the embodiment of coming to writing autobiographically in "Simone de Beauvoir and the Writing Self." *L'Esprit Créateur* XXIX, 4 (Winter 1989): 42–51.

46. In a recent talk at the CUNY Graduate Center (May 1992), Christie McDonald remarked on the persistence of the maternal/filial metaphorics: "Beauvoir would set the example of a woman whose achievements depended upon and were articulated around the refusal of biological motherhood, yet she became the symbolic mother of the feminist movement. . . ." And she goes on to observe: "Although she could probably not have predicted how complex and paradoxical the question of the mother was going to become, Beauvoir's own private discourse on the mother, as demonstrated in *A Very Easy Death*, shows to what extent she depended on that very person (her mother) whose status . . . she was to reject" (ms.).

In a recent (1992) public British television program called "Beauvoir's Daughters" Ann Oakley, a feminist sociologist, remarks that for women of her generation (she was born in 1944), Beauvoir was like a mother: "In that way, she's been the Mother, the mother we wished we'd had." Despite the fact that as a teacher of feminist theory I certainly think of Beauvoir (like Woolf) as a precursor or "foremother" of modern feminism, even a Symbolic Mother, I was actually quite surprised by that view of Beauvoir as a "real" mother, coming in to cheer one on and say the sorts of things you wished your mother would say. I took her refusal of motherhood seriously enough not to "matromorphize" her into my own. Or perhaps I've always taken her as a dead mother, which is to say an authorizing word, or as some have put it recently, the "Law of the Mother." See Julia Creet's "Daughter of the Movement: The Psychodynamics of Lesbian S/M Fantasy." *Differences* 3 (2) (Summer 1991): 135–159.

47. In "Culture, Cultural Studies,and the Historians," 616. Steedman also speaks here interestingly about her relationship to Raymond Williams, her stint as a member of her invented "all-girl backing group of the very early sixties: the Rayettes, who accompany Raymond's now disembodied voice. . . .)" (615). In *Cultural Studies*, ed. Lawrence Grossberg, Cary Nelson, Paula Treichler. (New York and London: Routledge, 1992).

Other recent memoirs that do this work through the violence of mother/daughter bond are Jill Conway's *The Road from Coorain*, Vivian Gornick's *Fierce Attachments*, and Maxine Hong Kingston's *The Woman Warrior*.

48. I'd like to thank Elizabeth Abel, John Brenkman, Rachel Brownstein, Mary Childers, Elizabeth Houlding, Alice Kaplan, and Sally O'Driscoll, for their helpful comments on earlier versions of this essay.

I'd also like to express my gratitude to the audiences at the English Institute, the University of Wisconsin-Madison, SUNY Buffalo, the Center for Twentieth-Century Studies at Milwaukee, the Center for Literary Studies, Harvard University, the Feminism and Legal Theory Project, and the University of Rochester for their questions and responses to the work in progress. This is a text that needed to be heard.

6.

Criticism and Its Alterity

SARA SULERI

The somewhat skeletal quality of my title bespeaks a necessary theoretical embarrassment toward the project at hand. To my mind, "Autobiography as Criticism" is a graceful rubric: it sets up neither category as an integrity opposed to all other integrities, but it simultaneously implies that whatever the interconnectedness between autobiography and criticism, only the vitality of difference could permit them to serve as surrogates for the other. The topic, in other words, draws a quickened attention to the very status of genre as a complicity of strategies, and disallows dull engagements in how established forms of discourse resist or accommodate alternative and equally impervious "forms." As a consequence, I felt obliged to use that loaded Arnoldian term, "criticism," without resorting to such intellectual coyness that would demand a title like "Criticism(s) and Its/Their Alterity" or "Critic/ Ism and Its Altar-ity." Those days of uncomfortable hieroglyphics with which the academy sought in futility to declare its unease with generic categories now appear to be over. At least, it was something of a shock for me to glance over this year's program for the English Institute and realize that in all the twelve titles for the current talks there was nary a parenthesis, nor a pun, nor a hyphenated term, nor any inverted or disinverted commas: no, there was no point of punctuation more complicated than a colon.

I must be on the right track, I thought. Some critical moment that was neither evolutionary nor retrograde was insisting upon some new attentiveness to generic mirrorings as well as to their differences, and I may as well agree to go through the looking glass. With all facetiousness aside, however, the subject proposed to us is large enough, and serious enough, to license further reconsideration of both the category of genres and—more specifically—of the fake autonomy assumed by that trickster discipline called literary criticism. Its territorial assumption of all things critical tends to obscure the fact that much of the discipline's activity could be far more accurately described under the Paterian title of "appreciations," although those hard gem-like flames seem to appear more flabby and less bejewelled than could be desired. If so much of postmodernist discourse can be recast as a pitiless repetition of what the fin de siècle represented to the previous century, then it is surely time to reexamine what criticism—in believing that it is its own—seeks to define as its other.

To invoke alterity in the context of criticism is by no means to take refuge in an easy dichotomy between a discourse and its relationship to otherness. Instead it is to suggest that critical writing locates its vitality at a discursive border that insists on the congruence between critical language and the idiom of its putative other. Here, it may be necessary to repeat the obvious and to define autobiography as an analytic mode that cannot help but take shape as a criticism of biography. While the narrative of biography seeks a generic third person security to the chronology it constructs, autobiography must play first and third person consciousness at the same time, and must be continually aware that—unlike the confessional form—its voice can only strip into secrecy. In being perpetually critical of what constitutes the genre's parameters, the autobiographical mode is most frequently other unto itself, thereby serving as a tangential illustration of how alterity is always a secret sharer of the critical project. The inherent irony of autobiography points to its affiliation with all idioms critical, and is perhaps most readily emblematized by that episode in the *Quixote* in which the Knight as interpreter meets a galley slave as autobiographer. Have you finished writing your life, asks Quixote. The galley slave's response is indeed apposite to the current topic: "How can it be finished," he inquires, "when my life isn't finished yet?" The theoretical problem of autobiography, and that of criticism, most frequently resides in the embarrassment posed by the deceptively simple gesture of "The End."

Given that the end appears to be an acutely awkward epistemological position for either criticism or autobiography to occupy, an alternative approach would be to identify such a possible border upon which the needs of both discursive practices would appear to coalesce. If autobiographical writing can be posited as a critique of the biographical genre, and if biography can be summoned in as a convenient scapegoat for the idiom, then it remains to be determined whether literary or intellectual histories function as borders or as witnesses to the odd liaison between critical and autobiographical discourses. In such a union, finally, what histories are being told? Here, I must beg my own question by turning—for the purposes of brief illustration—to an exemplary text of borderlines, Coleridge's own *Biographia Literaria*. The *Biographia*, of course, was originally conceived as a treatise on aesthetics and metaphysics, and it was only in 1803 that Coleridge recorded in his notebook the radical decision to collapse treatise into autobiography: "Seem to have made up my mind," he notes, "to write my metaphysical work as *my* Life, & *in* my Life—intermixed with all the other events or history of the mind & fortunes of S. T. Coleridge."[1] In other words, the recast project was from its inception an attempt to sully the putative integrity of the critical mode, and render the latter coterminous with open-ended temporality—or the necessary dischronology—that attends the question of autobiography.

That the text moved from being titled the *Autobiographia Literaria* to the *Biographia Literaria* suggests in itself Coleridge's interest in representing a history of aesthetics as an idiosyncratic narrative that is inevitably situated on the cusp between the idioms of history and of culture. The so-called intermixture of metaphysics with what occurs "as *my* Life, & *in* my Life" produces a narrative in which any potential antagonism that could exist among aesthetic, metaphysic, and historical categories is ameliorated by the production of an alternative narrative that proleptically establishes borders for what could be called today cultural criticism. If the negation of definition and the discrediting of description informs contemporary interdisciplinary studies of culture, then the *Biographia* clearly maps out its prior investment in similar projects. Autobiography, it establishes, is a discourse upon which intrusion is always possible, upon which historical and cultural exigencies can always usurp the plot. In a narrative so seductively plagiaristic on the level of its philosophy and so modest in the context of its generic ingenuity, the *Biographia* works to subvert all singularities of authority. Its celebrated claim remains, "Until you understand a writer's ignorance, presume your self ignorant of his understanding" (*BL*, XII, 134), but its operative manipulation of cultural and aesthetic ignorance reaches far beyond the realm of mere aphorism. The magnificent Chapter XIII of the text, one that has long been heralded as the ultimate definition of the imagination, turns out to be interrupted by a letter from a "very judicious friend." This apocryphal friend advises Coleridge against making public any conclusive philosophical claims, because "I see clearly that you have done too much, and yet not enough" (*BL*, XIII, 166).

The trope of ignorance lends itself to the culture of superlatives, or a narrative in which definition signifies either too much, or too little effort. In either case, Coleridge's crucial self-interruption of a possible seamlessness in aesthetic discourse indicates his recognition that autobiography supplies nothing as a figure of possible evasion. The deferral of Chapter XIII is a deliberate mockery of the fictive nature of definition, which somewhat nakedly establishes the vital publicity of an autobiographic voice. Such an imbrication does not merely complicate any attempt to segregate the ignorance of one genre from the ignorance of the other, but further muddies any easy distinctions between public and private discourses. Here, there is no harm in linking Coleridge's idiolect with the perspicacity of a Bakhtinian model of rhetorical autobiography, in which the latter cannot but assume the status of a public language. The "history" that emerges from such a discourse is doubtlessly idiosyncratic, but it is predicated on an adamant segregation of the autobiographic from the private. In a Coleridge, or in a "biographized" individual, Bakhtin claims, "There was not, nor could there be, anything intimate or private, secret or personal, anything relating to the individual himself, or anything that was, in principle, solitary. Here, the individual is open on all sides, he is all surface."[2] It is the surface, of necessity, that calls for a reformulation of the precariousness with which autobiography constitutes a criticism of culture.

The surface of cultural reality, in other words, is too much of an embarrassment to be contained within the safety of biography. If both Coleridge and Bakhtin posit an autobiographical other that is resolutely opposed to the fiction of privacy, they suggest a form of writing that is indifferent to myths of either self-fashioning or of self-discovery. Instead, such writing positions itself between the discourses of history and culture as though—in John Ashbery's resonant phrase—"to protect what it advertises." The poem "Self-Portrait in a Convex Mirror," of course, obsessively focuses upon the productive superficiality of the autobiographical moment, in which the eye of the painter and the eye of the poet meet to displace any potential interiority of the soul. Much of Coleridge's play with abstract definitions leads to a gay deferral of such pronouncements, the self-portraiture of the mannerist image leads Ashbery to contemplate the emptiness of all sequestering gestures. Both the image and the onlooker become, in a Bakhtinian sense, "all surface," for their locus of cultural identity is refracted only in the mirror of appearance. Further, the question of identity becomes translated into the more vertiginous problem of positionality, which allows Ashbery to reformulate a fundamental difficulty of cultural criticism: his obsession with surface is predicated on the tensions between first and third person narratives, with both serving as secret sharers of the other. Finally, the self-portrait can only evoke the publicity of looking, just as Coleridge's definitive chapter could only evoke the publicity of reprimand. It is this public gaze that constitutes the self-scrutiny of autobiography, and forces the poet to articulate his generic—and indeed cultural—disavowal of secrecy:

> The pity of it smarts,
> Makes hot tears spurt: that the soul is not a soul,
> Has no secret, is small, and it fits
> Its hollow perfectly.[3]

The connection between criticism and autobiography to which I am most drawn is precisely such an unsequestered idiom that has no secret and that fits its hollow perfectly. In order to look more closely at what characterizes the congruence and the divergence possible in this language, I would like to turn to three compelling contemporary examples of the mode, all of which explicitly or implicitly partake in the project of writing cultural criticism. I refer to recent essays by Wayne Koestenbaum, D. A. Miller, and Kwame Anthony Appiah, each of which turns the critical moment into an engagement with the autobiographical surface of cultural reality.

Before engaging in these three exemplary texts, it is important to make a marked distinction between what I call unsequestered critical writing and a more pervasive contemporary intellectual discourse that seeks to interpolate its theoretical practices with reference to lived experience. I have elsewhere expressed some concern over the theoretical efficacy of the latter style, in which radical subjectivity is raised to the power of inanity or functions as an excuse for intellectual shoddiness. This style has less to do with autobiography than it has with a confessional mode, one that is predicated on a belief that there are indeed secrets to be told or to be withheld. As a consequence, it can only reify traditional notions of writing as the production of a private individual engaged in dialogue with a public and a depressingly professionalized world. The unsequestered writing that I pose as a counterpoint takes autobiography as a strategy of dismantlement that dispenses with such dichotomies as public and private or inside and outside in order to position itself at the border of outsidedness. Such a stance could be described as a productive use of a Fanonian third person consciousness, which, rather than functioning as a cultural tyranny, becomes instead a conduit to cultural open-endedness.

The open-endedness to which I refer has everything to do with precision and nothing with some vague experimentality that chooses to concentrate on the category of surface as an ingenious trick through which surface can exist in autonomy of its obvious shadow, depth. Wayne Koestenbaum's essay, titled "Opera and Homosexuality: Seven Arias," is exactly an attempt to figure surface in the service of a meticulous reading of formal structure. Neither the high stylization of the opera nor the so-called subculture of gayness is the impelling subject of this essay, so that the question of depth appears to be strangely anachronistic to its brilliant juxtaposition of varying social surfaces. While it hardly needs to be reiterated that—from Oscar Wilde to Foucault—an obsession with the abstraction of surface has dominated gay modalities of philosophical categories, Koestenbaum's deft manipulation of the superficial establishes a discourse that exceeds neat orders of an underlying deep play. There is no depth to which the surface serves as a referent: instead, the essay in the classical sense superimposes reactive qualities of surface in contact with other immediacies of superficial representation. As a consequence, Koestenbaum's piece singularly lacks a referential depth that could amount to significant conclusions about either aesthetics or homosexuality, with the former serving as the stasis for the temporality of the latter. On the contrary, "Opera and Homosexuality" muddies with affection all categorical lines between aesthetic and erotic realities, becoming in the process the most incisive and arresting vision of gender that has seen published light for many a contemporary critical month.

Koestenbaum's equation with a revisionary autobiographical impulsion is amply illustrated by his opening sentence: "I devoted my twenty-first winter to Mozart's *Don Giovanni* and to the search of a boyfriend."[4] Neither opera nor amorous quest serves as a surrogate for a hidden depth, but both are equally public modalities of stylized interpretation. It comes as no surprise, therefore, that the first aria upon which Koestenbaum turns his exquisitely glancing attention is Donna Elvira's on vengeance. The voice as body is the concern at hand, or the relocation of appreciation within the structure of autobiography. "Sing 'vengeance,'" the essay reminds us, "and you will be doomed to find it in your own larynx" (*OH*, 236). Here, the authority of an outsided autobiographical persona cuts through the dreary agony attendant on all too many disquisitions on the essentialism or the constructivism of sexual identity. Instead, the essay sings its way through the stolid ways of painstaking analysis, and locates its pain in the structure of a passing thought, which translates analysis into a deft revelation of the conundrum of pleasure. As opposed to reaffirming any depth to a monolithic gay category, Koestenbaum's first meditation on opera and homosexuality leads him to speculate on the impact of the aesthetic upon the erotic, and its curious segregation from the discourse of depth. "During my days of [the Donna Elvira vengeance aria]," writes Koestenbaum, "I was certain that my love affair with the boy next door would end any moment. I placed my erotic eccentricity within the fantasy-discourse of *the woman about to be jilted* . . . I hid the discourse I wanted to occupy, *boy meets boy*, like a nestled box inside a larger, more authoritative discourse: *the wronged woman*. In order to speak to myself about *boy meets boy*, I entered the vocal consciousness of a woman who can sing boldly about her erotic life only because she's been deserted" (*OH*, 236–237).

This anecdote achieves what many far more lugubrious readings of gender constructions signally fail in accomplishing. The philosophical category of the surface yields to a dismissal of depth that only an assumption of an autobiographical idiom can hope to effect. Wayne listens to these arias, as it were, from within his own body, but neither the reality of externality or of sensation can serve to cancel out the possibility of a new relativism, in which experience cannot function as an awkward attendant to the culture of philosophy. In fact, the redefinition of such an idiom is intimately engaged in questioning the nostalgia for uniform philosophic categories, or the certainty that cultural discourse pitilessly disallows. Here is where sentimentality quickens as a language of interrogation that is significantly weak enough to withstand the necessity of depth in relation to its commitment to surface. The autobiographical impulse in Koestenbaum's writing is strongly allied to the creative dismissal of any "deep" engagement in what may constitute a vocal, a listening, or an erotic body. His interest in the skin of things is largely translated into an epistemological wonderment at the possibilities of bodily incongruity. Thus, when meditating on the erotic nostalgia of *Carmen*, the shape of the essay allows the claim "I feel Jose's nostalgia for heterosexual monogamy that Micaela represents—a system that has its share of uncanniness, too, because it excavates a lost world from the listener's interior" (*OH*, 248).

Here, lines between the object of analysis and the analyst himself are deliberately and delicately blurred. Heterosexuality is invoked neither as a phantasmatic other nor as an entity against which gay identity defines itself, but as one aspect of collusion through which the aesthetic of sexualities can be addressed. The high art of opera transmogrifies into a cultural conduit through which Koestenbaum poses the most vexingly simple questions of all: "I am driven to ask why operatic female serenity appeals to a body (mine) culturally marked as queer" (*OH*, 237). While the "queerness" in this context may be a homophobic surface that is imposed upon the thinking body, it never remains as an entity or an inflexible stereotype alone, but is made to lend its superficiality to a study of the process of cultural oddities, and the concomitant curiosities of desire.

In its tracing of the very frivolities of desire, "Opera and Homosexuality" achieves an equation to the autobiographical mode that exceeds any standard expectations of symbol and signification in relation to first and third person voices. When Koestenbaum reads the death of Mimi in *La Bohème*, for example, the self-referentiality of his discourse is as tangential as the staged quality of the death itself. "Even before AIDS I listened to death scenes," he writes, "so that I may identify with the dying woman and the bereft man, so that I might locate 'sentimentality' in my body, so that, watching Mimi die of TB, I might stage a departure in myself and experience, by surviving Mimi's death, the revival of certain extravagant and queer emotions I would later dismiss and keep secret, never explaining the power of coherence of these subjective states evoked by melodrama" (*OH*, 251). Neither melodrama nor sentimentality can be dismissed as peripheral to the significance of the death scene, which becomes an occasion for a meditation on the communality of loss. There are, in other words, no property rights that Koestenbaum claims for either the otherness of gay identity or the otherness of operatic sentimentality: both are subsumed into an alternative "queerness" that constitutes a reading of culture.

If Coleridge sought to reconfigure metaphysical discourse into a narrative that pertained most crucially to his life and in his life, Koestenbaum's essay into the work of mourning has equal consequences for a contemporary revision of the act of critical appreciation. That which is appreciated is granted no autonomy or inviolability: on the contrary, its intimacy relies precisely on the onlooker's ability to absorb its aesthetic into the touching mundanity of everyday existence. The work of art, however, is never the depth to which daily life remains the surface: nor is the contrary true. Instead, the circuit of their exchange illustrates that which is vitally unsequestered when autobiographical discourse takes the terrain of criticism as its own. The biographical perspective of a "life"—or a chronology that can trace the birth and death of an individual, a nation, an ideology—is suspended in order to produce an analytic language more interested in mapping the haphazards that define the extreme publicity of intimacy. As *La Bohème* ends, the beholder is even more intricately involved in reading the accidents that allow cultural surfaces to form and disform the necessity of interpretation: "The music, at the conclusion, narrates and justifies our own tears, and hides this otherwise embarrassing expenditure in a social context— operagoing. Protocol determines that the performance will end and that, unable to find exact words to describe or pass on the strange experience, we will dismiss it, underestimating melodrama's power to graft the solitary listener to a collectivity of mourners" (*OH,* 254).

The aesthetic dignity of this claim suggests that the autobiographical imperative cannot be contained in an impulse to confession. Its delicacy is more concerned with a surface protocol of a reading that is ultimately less engaged with the cultural dilemmas posed by sexual preference than with a cultural compassion, or a desire to read through—and along with—a community of loss. Balancing the power of communality against the more easy retreat into identity politics, "Opera and Homosexuality" is a text that manipulates autobiography into a piercing narrative of superficial impression, thereby establishing a new resonance to the manner in which criticism conceives of its chronology. In so doing, the voice of the essay further declares that it is not a voice, is small, has no secrets, and fits its hollow perfectly.

To move from "Opera and Homosexuality" into D. A. Miller's "Bringing Out Roland Barthes" may imply a crude chronology that from the outset I want to disavow. I do not wish to trivialize either piece by suggesting that the alignment of gay writing with autobiographical impulses produces an out-of-the-closet revision of any traditional critical perspectives. Indeed, the great differences between the Koestenbaum and the Miller essays are only remotely resolved by reference to the liberally mordant uses both writers put to the standard expectation of autobiography. On the level of truisms alone, the autobiographical vein can license two highly energizing cultural realities, for the first person critical voice can be racialized and gendered at the same time. Rather than simply writing as a neutral observer of the aesthetics of *La Bohème* or the theory of Roland Barthes, autobiography enables me to present myself as a Pakistani, or a female, or a deviant commentator on any form of cultural production. The texts at hand, however, do not allow such easy lapses into "authenticity," for both are invested in twisting the immediacy of the autobiographical into the high ironies presented by sexual difference to a binary culture.

Where Wayne Koestenbaum studies the aesthetic surface of an informing psychosexual curiosity, D. A. Miller takes up the idea of the structural neuter in order to fill gender into its conveniently empty aporia. Miller attempts to bring out Roland Barthes on several disparate levels: first, he engages in the cultural cliché of the "gayness of great authors." Second, he theorizes the potential prurience of the former revelation by a meticulous demonstration of how readily the structural blank upon which Barthes' writing so frequently depends can be gendered, and more specifically, homosexualized. On both levels, Miller's reading of Barthes' assumption of neutrality entirely resists a biographical complacency that seeks for interestingly dirty linen in order to declare, "I told you so." "Bringing Out Roland Barthes" circumnavigates such dangers of confession by turning instead to the perforating ability of autobiography, which displays neither persons nor home truths, but domesticates theories of gender and the genders of theory.

Miller's essay—now, of course, a book—would be completely predictable if it combed the Barthesian collected works for moments where theory seemed to tremble on the precipice of homosexual desire, moments that in Barthes are most frequently translated into the category of the neuter, or, on a level of more charming facticity, the headache. The issue of confirmation, exposure, and adulation are significantly missing from Miller's work, which takes on these interpretive possibilities through the oblique route of cultural self-exposure. By no means has the essay any secrets to confess, but it has more to say about the category of inbetweenness than about any rock-bottoms of gay identity. "However intimately Barthes's writing proved its connection with gay sexuality," Miller muses, "the link was so discreet that it seemed only to emerge in the coy or hapless intermittences of what under the circumstances I could hardly pretend to reduce to just his repression."[5] What, as a consequence, will the autobiographical critic choose as his trajectory of analysis? In Miller's terms, the analytic process is inevitably positional: "Any knowledge I was able to produce of a 'gay' Roland Barthes couldn't help being a knowledge *between us* and *of us both,* fashioned within the practices and relations, real and fantasmatic, of gay community, and across the various inflections given to such community by, for example, nation and generation" (*BRB,* 40–41). The writer never met—and the body never touched—a writing in which the absence of connection signifies an acutely interesting study of how productive a lack of contact may be. Autobiography is a genre, after all, that welcomes the greatest regret—expressed in a most rarefied eloquence—over events that never occurred.

"Bringing Out Roland Barthes" is a piece of writing in which mourning is skillfully recast as a gesture of proleptic regret. While Barthes is nowhere criticized for his excessive sexual discretion, Miller's reading of Balzac's *Sarrasine* and of *S/Z* carefully raises the issue both of criticism's relation to sexual anonymity and its simultaneous declaration of independent publicity. The category of the neuter—much as that of the surface in Koestenbaum—becomes a wry space upon which Miller can autobiographize Barthes' anxieties and his own. The issue is merely one of what Miller describes as an analytic "anthology of moments," or an essay that attempts to achieve by juxtaposition the significance not to be uttered by traditional criticism. Through the use of vital parentheses, the essay arrives at a dignity that is frequently lacking in more conventional modes of analytic discourse. In discussing the notion of impact, for example, Miller breaks away from typically Hegelian versions of reason to query in brackets: "At Joe's house, after his burial, I looked for the copy of *A Lover's Discourse* that I had given him; it wasn't on his shelf—had Joe, of all things most unlikely, started to read it? had he loaned, or outright given it to someone? to whom?" (*BRB*, 41). Here, the text aches with the weight of its own question marks, and each point of punctuation queries the necessary ignorance that accompanies but does not alleviate ideas of an unsequestered discourse.

"Bringing Out Roland Barthes" is at its most moving here precisely because it does not bring out either the author or his erotic subject. Instead, its point of illustration engages with contemporary culture, demonstrating the inevitable aporias that accompany readings in cultural criticism. Miller refuses to overlook the secret that is no secret, but one that cannot but preside upon the difficulty of what it means to be autobiographical. The critical enterprise in which Miller engages is delicately predicated on the irresolvables raised by his concluding paragraph: "To refuse to bring Barthes out consents to a homophobic reception of his work. But to accept the task? to agree to evincing the traces of a gay genealogy in a text whose even partial success would almost guarantee . . . the faintness of those traces" (*BRB*, 49). The task that Miller rejects in order to take on bespeaks a bravery unaccommodated by a criticism based upon who may, or may not, be gay. If the Miller essay leaves an obligatory ache, then it claims a peculiar combination of honesty and independence that establishes—for critical inquiry—new examinations of the fidelity of loss.

Such an apprehension of loss is nowhere more clearly demarcated than in Anthony Appiah's concluding chapter to a work quite intricately titled *In My Father's House: Africa and the Philosophy of Culture.*[6] Appiah suggests a different relation to the anthology of moments, and in a chapter that remains hard for me to read, the account of his father's death, he makes the link between autobiography and elegy all too available. In a work that unobtrusively but elegantly connects philosophical categories with the particular exigencies of culture, Appiah's final chapter opens with a singular invocation of autobiography: "My father died, as they say, while I was trying to finish this book" (*FH*, 181). Such a sentence performs—in true Coleridgean fashion—both too much and not enough, in that its very facticity belies the promise of confession attendant on a perception of autobiography as a digression from criticism. Instead, Appiah uses the occasion of his father's funeral to examine nuances of cultural ignorance, telling a compelling story of how alterity constitutes itself within the construct of identity. If the cultural and political battle over how the father's funeral was to be conducted impels the understatement of Appiah's narrative, he from the outset is able to articulate critically the autobiographical imperative: "It seemed that every attempt to understand what was happening took me further back into family history and the history of Asante; further away from abstractions . . . further into what would probably seem to a European or an American an almost fairytale world of witchcraft and wicked aunts and wise old women and men" (*FH*, 181).

In this case, the fidelity of loss involves a quiet account of the publicity that can attach to the functions of mourning and the particular rituals they may demand. Appiah's chapter neither sequesters itself from his preceding work, nor does it imply that autobiography is a recourse of those deracinated or disaffiliated. The ignorance inevitable in cultural affiliation is precisely the subject of *In My Father's House*, a work in which a moment of intense privacy is translated into the quietude of analysis. While the clash between secular and ritual burial remains the structure within which Appiah conducts his narrative, he is meticulously conscientious on the score of blurring between fable and moral. Rather than indulging in a somewhat predictable psychologizing of the death of the father, Appiah twists autobiography into a cultural history that is inevitably engaged in mapping the outsidedness of insideness: his concluding proverb reminds the reader that "the matriclan is like the forest; if you are outside it is dense, if you are inside you see that each tree has its own position" (*FH*, 192). This piece of folk wisdom allows Appiah to understand and to communicate—through the conduit of autobiography—the imbrication of the public and the private, or how one quite simply distinguishes the forest from the trees. Where Ashbery would claim that the soul is not a soul, Appiah can conclude his chapter with an analogous recognition: "Perhaps I have not yet disgraced my families and their names. But as long as I live I know that I will not be out of these woods" (*FH*, 192).

If I knew how surface relates to anthology, and the latter to cultural elegy, then I would feel morally obligated to instruct you further. The

anti-chronological impulse of autobiography, however, protects me from
establishing such a critical pattern. Certainly the writing of mourning with
a difference has governed my scattered readings: In which case, call me
Ishmael, and rename this deliberation as the "devious-cruising Rachel, that in
her retracing search after her missing children, only found another orphan."

NOTES

1. S. T. Coleridge, *Biographia Literaria: Or Biographical Sketches of My Literary Life and Opinions*, George Watson, ed. (London: Dent, 1975), xi.

2. M. M. Bakhtin, *The Dialogic Imagination*, Michael Holquist ed., Michael Hoquist and Caryl Emerson trans. (Austin: University of Texas Press, 1981), 133.

3. John Ashbery, *Self-Portrait in a Convex Mirror* (New York: Penguin, 1972), 69.

4. Wayne Koestenbaum, "Opera and Homosexuality," *Yale Journal of Criticism*, Fall 1991, Volume 5, Number 1: 235.

5. D. A. Miller, "Bringing Out Roland Barthes," *Raritan*, XI: 4, Spring 1992: 40.

6. Kwame Anthony Appiah, *In My Father's House: Africa and the Philosophy of Culture* (London and New York: Oxford University Press, 1992).

PART III
BREAKING FRAME(WORK)S: POPULAR
CULTURE AND CULTURAL STUDIES

7.

Don't Talk with Your Eyes Closed: Caught in the Hollywood Gun Sights

WAHNEEMA LUBIANO

Well, some of this is messed up, *yet and still* he *is* a good father and I do like the way he walks across the graveyard."

Towanda Williams, Trenton, N.J.; April 22, 1992

I watched the movie—*Deep Cover*—at the same time Towanda Williams did.[1] I didn't know her; I simply sat behind her in the theater. But I agreed. Mostly. Yes, I thought. Laurence Fishburne certainly is a father. And those last frames are fascinating to watch. Only I placed within quotation marks the "good" before "father" because I find patriarchy problematic even when it comes covered in chocolate.

I first saw *Deep Cover* and wrote some of this work not long after finishing—back in December 1991—an essay on the U.S. political economy and its relation to family narratives in the Anita Hill/Clarence Thomas discourse.[2] I presented a part of it at the CUNY Graduate Center shortly after the Los Angeles uprising in the wake of the LAPD officers' trial for the beating of Rodney King and following President Bush and his attack dogs' assault on the "lack of family values" among urban black single mothers. I wrote most of the longer version that I'm presenting here following on the heels of the Republican Party national convention (and the subsequent damage to my television screen as a result of its encounter with a high-velocity airborne projectile). My own autobiography notwithstanding, I guess you could say that I'm feeling a tad anti-family. Or, to be more precise, a bit anti-family discourse, or that aspect of it which manifests the economy of what Michael Warner refers to as repro-narratives.[3]

On the other hand, my pleasure in watching Laurence Fishburne walk was, well, that was "real." And it is the complications of that pleasure that form the starting point for this discussion. Further, this paper is a continuation, under altered circumstances and vocabulary, of an on-a-city-bus talk that I had with the woman whose language I've just quoted.[4] This essay also intervenes in the almost century-long debate over "positive" and "negative" images in representations of blacks in Hollywood cinema.[5] While the debate itself has often been conducted in simplistic terms, I don't see a way out of such considerations given the politics of the production of popular culture, the political context in which it is consumed, and the psycho-socio complexities of audience engagement with film. What I attempt here is foregrounding some of those complexities to try to escape the too easy dichotomy implied by evaluating representations as either "good" or "bad."

Deep Cover was directed by Bill Duke and written by Michael Tolkin (*The Player*) and Henry Bean (*Internal Affairs*). The major stars are Laurence Fishburne and Jeff Goldblum. The plot is easily summarized. A small boy, Russell Stevens (Laurence Fishburne), who sees his drug addict father killed in the course of a convenience store holdup (and is left with blood-stained money in his hand) grows up to be a cop recruited as a "deep" undercover drug courier by a white DEA agent named Carver. This agent tells Stevens that his psychological profile almost perfectly matches that of a criminal. Stevens is given a new identity—John Q. Hull, drug dealer wannabee—and is told to go undercover in order to get to three Latino drug dealers who inhabit three levels in the drug world hierarchy: Felix Barbossa (whom I see as the lieutenant), Gallegos (the prince—in charge of West Coast distribution), and Guzman (the king—in charge of drug supply from an unnamed South American country, possibly the next president/premier of his country). Carver, the DEA agent, tells Hull to stop after infiltrating level two (Gallegos) before proceeding onto level three. The drug dealer for whom Hull goes to work and with whom he later becomes a partner is a white Jewish lawyer, David Jason (Jeff Goldblum), a man with a beautiful black mistress, Betty McCutheon (Victoria Dillard), who owns an African cultural artifact shop. He is married, with a child and a house in a wealthy suburb.

There are two subplots that are tied together in the primary plot by the end of the movie: (1) Clarence Williams, Jr., plays a good, Christian, and generally black nationalist cop known as Taft; Taft, unaware of John Hull's *real* identity as a cop, runs a consistent black nationalist series of anti-drug lectures directed at John; (2) A small Latino boy, who lives with his crack-addicted mother, is present in the transient apartment building where Hull takes up residence and becomes important in Hull's new existence.

By the movie's end, John has redeemed himself and his mission; he blows the whistle on DEA and federal government political double dealing when the DEA shuts down the undercover operation because the drug king (Guzman) is the U.S. client politico in the region.

Beginning point: while "it may not always be evident, research is always autobiographical,"[6] Andrew Ross tells us. And because I agree with him (and the others who have made the same argument in many, many more words), I want to begin with my own investment. I am a critic and a consumer; what I like or dislike informs the object of my inquiry. Second, Manthia Diawara has mapped the debates around gendered spectatorship that have remained color-blind;[7] hence my interest here builds from his work. I am talking here about looking. And, finally, I'm offering a possible "reading" of the film from a particular black leftist and feminist spectator's position with an eye to the difficulty of accounting for the work of ideology in aesthetic practice and the dynamics of black spectator accommodation and resistance. I'm trying to talk about *seeing* on screen more than what critics (academic and media alike) of black film often hold certain black images to "mean." So, while I'm not trying to talk about what everybody or anybody sees, many critics writing about films that represent black people or some variation of black life don't talk about *seeing* at all even as they speak of "images" or what the sight of something *means*. The hypervisibility, the very publicness of black people as a social fact, works to undermine the possibility of actually seeing black specificity.

Black[8] specificity is literally "disappeared," or replaced by or merged with older, conventional narratives of maleness, family, and racialized "reality"— often regardless of the ethnicity or race of the director and the producer of the project. The racialized other (in this case, the Laurence Fishburne undercover cop character, John Hull) and the drug trade are simply the cover story. *Deep Cover*, the story of that police officer and his quest to "uncover" the deep structure of the West Coast drug trade, is the nexus of a conventional master narrative of identity, family, and the making of a good patriarch, and a *black nationalist* narrative of identity, family, and the making of a good *black* patriarch, set within what is presented as a realistic urban terrain. What I want to begin here is an examination of how those things both come together and separate.

Race representation (in this film, and, arguably in most Hollywood film production), in the aesthetic sense of a selection, or re-presentation, is a rewrite, or a newer picture, of older narratives about race, about masculinity, and about patriarchy. It is, in fact, a generalizing of a specific racial subject into a spectacle written across the public's imagination. Often when race enters the field of representation, the result is a containment of the politically cathected narrative, while the very spectacle of race sometimes blinds us to its emptying out of cultural specificity. In other words, under the cover of the presentation of racialized subjects and racialized circumstances, the fiction that results is often another reinscription of older master narratives that elide any specific imaginative play with the materials of storytelling by replacing them with the already-understood materials tied to race.

If "race" as it is understood in the political imagination of the U.S. public (of any race/ethnicity) is both theoretically useless (because of its inherent instability) but socially and politically inescapable, how might one talk about it, in this instance, to say something specific about a film? I am almost paralyzed by the difficulty concomitant with assuming the burden of criticizing the problem of representation, of the re-presenting of people and circumstances generally marginal to the cultural production of the dominant U.S. cultural industry. As the incredibly convoluted syntax and overabundance of prepositions in the preceding sentence suggests, unpacking the way people "do otherness" is hard and complicated work. And it is Valerie Smith's phrase "doing otherness" that animates my discussion here. "Doing otherness" foregrounds what is at stake in considering the representation of race—regardless of who is doing the representing. Bill Duke, the director of *Deep Cover*, is black, and while that makes some differences that I could talk about, I don't think that, finally, it makes much of a difference in this project. What is "otherness" on the ground of master narratives of family, masculinity, and patriarchy even with a black director, even in a story with black nationalist elements? But before I move on to the gist of this paper I want to define black nationalism.

Black nationalism, in its broadest sense, is a sign, an analytic, that describes a range of historically manifested ideas about black American possibilities that include any or all of the following: racial solidarity; cultural specificity; religious, economic, and political power and/or separatism—this last has been articulated as a possibility both within and outside of U.S. territorial boundaries. Black nationalism in the realm of black cultural common sense is a name for a range of cultural and material activities and behaviors from vague feelings of black racial solidarity in the face of a white supremacist worldview and white dominance, to various cultural and behavioral manifestations of that solidarity (including but not limited to religious practices, musical and art production, educational projects, etc.), to programs designed to intervene materially along black racial lines in order to achieve some economic and political advances. Within the terms of black nationalism, blackness and the black dreamed-of, autonomous subject is inevitably male, heterosexual, and in training to be a powerful patriarch—only in and on "black" terms, terms that are both separate from and continuous with those of the hegemonic culture. Having said that, I want to make clear that how I "feel" about any form of black nationalism depends on what is at stake. In an essay on Anita Hill and Clarence Thomas I was very critical. But when I consider what some deployments of it have allowed those of us engaged in black cultural studies to consider as a corrective to other and racist concepts, I am appreciative.

Notwithstanding my appreciation of black nationalism's strategic possibilities, black nationalist anxiety over racial virility,[9] or its historical lack, plays itself out continually in black cultural production. My interest here is in examining that anxiety as it plays itself out in a Hollywood film that is about a black undercover cop, but is also—in fascinating ways—a hysterical black nationalist revision of a patriarchal family romance.[10] I say hysterical because the film's obsession with patriarchy is also the terrain for its anxiety over a "sufficient and necessary" heterosexuality. That is to say, its cakewalk to straight black masculine "realness" not only remakes a master narrative, but trips all over its own attempts to discipline its homo-eroticism. This hysteria is further complicated in the film's representation of the relations among various ethnicities: the black Americans, the Jewish lawyer, and the Latino drug lords.

My focus on this film, then, includes what I found pleasurable, dismaying, and interesting about it, as well as the problems of that dismay, pleasure, and interest. My discussion is intended as a corrective to some of the shortcomings of black film criticism; as such it joins the work of Jacqueline Bobo, Manthia Diawara, Valerie Smith, and Coco Fusco—among others.

Image-centered critics of black film often think of a black audience as a monolithic aggregate completely at the mercy of a film.[11] Such an audience is educated in the "right" way by a "good" movie and duped by a "bad" one; it is misled by the lack of "reality" and edified by accurately represented social "reality." In other words, image-centered criticism often rests on arguments that suggest that images literally "make" the audience or viewer; that absent the "work" of a particular cultural production, the viewer is a blank slate.

As a counter to the notion of an always "duped" or "dupeable" black film audience, Lisa Jones argues that black audiences refuse to completely suspend disbelief as an opposition to being manipulated by Hollywood imaginings of their reactions:

The industry [Hollywood] often overlooked the statement that black actors made in their *performances* and focused on the *roles* themselves. This goes back to "Gone with the Wind." The industry [simply] saw Mammy standing by Scarlett, not Hattie McDaniel, the powerful actress.[12]

Black audiences not only saw Hattie McDaniel the actress, I might add, but could see her making a monetary killing in a role that they could "see" as a parody of labor and racial inequality, and a send-up of white employers' attempts to extract the surplus value—emotional attachment—from the labor of black maids.

A black spectator could know that the "subjects" in the film are actors.

What such a spectator "sees" is both the fiction and knowledge of social "facts": a "real" actor, for example, who is part of other "real" films (which are also fictions), and who is discussed in *Jet*, *Ebony*, and *Emerge* magazines. These are some of the building blocks of film reception, then, especially among a marginalized group such as black Americans.

An illustration: in *Deep Cover*, Fishburne/Stevens/Hull, our hero, is first seen as clean-shaven with irregular, bumpy skin and strange complexion color. He is, therefore, alienated from the bearded Fishburne "we" all know from earlier films (like *Boyz N the Hood*) and from media interviews. That "other" Fishburne might be simply another fiction, but against the *Deep Cover* Fishburne, the earlier one is part of a complicated apparatus for re-creating a more critical "reality" for the "knowledgeable" black spectator. Fishburne returns, before long into the film, as hairy-faced. This is his "real" self—which in the film is also a false "self" because the beard is part of being a "fake" drug dealer.

I am not arguing here that black film spectators, myself among them, are never duped. Spectators—fragmented and differential—are duped *and* unduped (as Towanda Williams and I were)—often at the same time. Those critics, myself among them, interested in ideology and aesthetics, in the politics of pleasure, thus have our work cut out for us. The effect of ideology is that the world is re-created in such a way that the stitches are hidden. I am not talking necessarily about deliberate *mis*representations but the various ways that constituted realities are perceived as natural, as inevitable. Inability on the part of critics and audiences to "see" the artificial nature of constructed blackness seems to be one problem, but so is the inability of particular cultural productions to do much with black cultural specificity outside of representing it as legal transgressiveness. I've indicated that white and black critics saw the cop/drug nexus; I did not read one critic who saw this as a heavily patriarchal family romance. I did. Towanda Williams did.[13]

In this film, John Hull/Larry Fishburne is the subject of a white gaze; he becomes the "spectacle" and the working out of others' desires. He and his circumstances are the visual markers of urban blackness, which are somehow emptied of any specific within-the-group meanings, while a family romance, a quest for the trappings of patriarchal power, is played out as the film follows his movement deep undercover to trap what the media tells us is one of the most dangerous and persistent enemies of the contemporary U.S. social order—a Latino drug lord.

What are the manifestations of consistent U.S. fascination with that blackness as spectacle? The film evokes what is presented as realism with its baggage of essential blackness manifested in the drug trade. And what is missing from the drug world "realism" of this movie? Missing are the many whites engaged in it and the economic impact of that participation. I'm not necessarily interested in a more social realist text, but given this film's mode

I am criticizing its skewed realism. This movie's narrative logic turns on the amassing of multi-millions in drug trade. That kind of money is amassed in the higher, white American-dominated end of the trade, cocaine—not the black American-dominated lower end, crack. But that is the problem with the use of some forms of "essential blackness" (like the "black drug trade")—they beat out the more complicated (and racially integrated) "real" everytime.

On the other hand, particular narratives of "the black" as irretrievably "other" are both presented and criticized in this film. Criticized after a fashion: after all, the criticism comes from David Jason, the Jewish lawyer who is responsible both for *using* jungle beast metaphors and similes in describing John Hull *and* for *being critical* about those metaphors. I'm not sure, however, how one weighs either his use or his criticism of those metaphors and similes, because he is, by the film's logic, a thoroughly discredited character.

Jason, and his Jewishness, however, function in a number of ways as the mediator between blackness and whiteness. Through the vehicle of his character, blackness is evoked by its opposite: whiteness is a manifestation of a world of order—clean, well-lit rooms, the bright suburbs, clean white shirts and well-made suits, a daughter in a breakfast nook doing her home-work, tidy shelves of law books, all in all a seeming lack of chaos. Whiteness, however, also flirts with black chaos—in a hotel room with a black hooker, in the disco, and in the crack house. All of these flirtations involve some kind of white "slumming" or are attributed to a specific white man, who the film reminds us several times is a Jew and who also refers to himself as a Jew outsider in kinship with his black "brother."

The film not only sets up Jason as the Jew who is the "outsider," its narrative represents (and by extension sometimes criticizes) the anti-Semit-ism of the judicial system and media who would love to have a black and a *Jewish* lawyer as drug dealer villains. That critique, however, is both complicated and undermined by the film's climatic resolution of the threads of black nationalism, its drive to reclaim "blackness," and its disciplining of black and Jewish male homoerotic possibilities. As I point out below, David Jason represents the graying boundary between whiteness and black-ness, between Jewish ethnicity and black racialism, between "real" and "false" masculinity and patriarchy.

Given the film's re-creation of and critique of a disturbing black essence, what is the black nationalist presence in this film and where can we note its comings and goings? Its presence is the core of the family romance written to accommodate it. I have argued in my own early work that black nationalism's cultural arm—the black aesthetic—in its opposition to white dominance produces a narrative, an aesthetic project, that is fully as monolithic (even if not as politically powerful) as that of the dominant group. Caution: fully as monolithic in linguistic structure does not necessarily mean consistently so or unquestionably consensually articulated, nor is a monolithic black aesthetic in any way as active in our social formation as that of the dominant group. And while it is important to mark the moments of patriarchal formation in black American cultural discourse, it is not sufficient. We have to explain how the formation takes shape and what it does when it coheres. Patriarchy might be damn near universal, but we have to account for, or at least trace the representation of, its specifics nonetheless.

Much of the discourse of black cultural nationalism is given over to masculine-centered, homophobic, and heterosexist rhetoric and political physicality; it has insisted that black integration with whites represents an "unnatural" relationship just as it has also insisted on the positioning of good black women as mothers and inspirers of black men and/or teachers of their (or others') children. The extravagantly displayed homophobia and sexist language and behavior of "blackness" is not necessarily always aimed at gay men, lesbians, or straight women, but is instead a form of "drag" assumed to construct masculinity for a straight, politically and economically powerful white male gaze. The anxiety against which this masculinity is performed is the (historically specific but consistent) de-masculinizing of black men—first as chattels and then as universal and de-powered "others" to white males.

Black nationalism in this film is articulated in the family narratives and in certain metaphors: David Jason tells John Hull that Hull reminds him of a black panther, for example, but not, Jason hastens to add, in a racist way but in a way that understands the panther as a dangerous but powerful beast. The moment of this "naming" in the film is loaded with supercharged significance: Jason is staring at Hull, subjecting Hull to the extended scrutiny that generally marks film representation of sexual or romantic attraction. For historically savvy viewers, however, the image of "panther" also resonates with images of the Black Panthers, another kind of "dangerous but powerful" beast and one of the sure markers of black political nationalism. And, importantly, a marker for "manly" opposition to white men. The most explicit manifestation of black nationalism, however, is articulated in John Hull's voice-overs, in language like "I shot a man who looked like me, whose parents looked like my parents," or in the language of the good cop, Taft, who calls John a "Judas" for selling drugs. The way in which black nationalism most thoroughly coalesces into a conventional master narrative, however, is by means of its centering of the family romance.

While *Deep Cover* is ostensibly about the drug trade and is even critical about white political complicity in that trade, it is framed on both ends by family narratives. The film's beginning, and structurally essential, point is the father/son scene (a late-twentieth-century "blackened" version of the primal scene) with a conventional enough U.S. black movie scenario of a black junky robbing a convenience store. The film's ending—structurally anticipated—is the constitution of a new, improved, and multicultural family for the little Latino boy whose "bad" mother, a drug addict named Belinda Chacon, dies.[14] She's "bad" largely because she is so destroyed that she doesn't even provide proper nutrition for her child; the audience sees John doing so instead—albeit in extremely rudimentary fashion: he gives the child money for milk and a chicken burrito instead of the "junk" that Belinda is offering him. And John's paternal sensibility so overwhelms her maternal sensibility that she offers to sell her son to him. John, according to the film logic, is a better "mother" than she is.

Throughout the film family functions as the moral ground evoked again and again in the rehabilitation of John Hull. The family narrative on display, however, is a departure from the historical black nationalist family narrative in regard to the importance of the mother—who according to black nationalist convention is omnipresent as the nurturer of black children, the cultural carrier of the anti-racist black essence, and the teacher of the community. In contrast, there are no "fit" black mothers (or any mothers of color) left alive or visible in this film until Betty McCutheon, David Jason's mistress, is rehabilitated at the end (and left offscreen) to be the "mother" along with John Hull, the father, of the Latino boy.

McCutheon is the marker for black male reclamation of "his" history. Hull's wooing of McCutheon away from Jason, and his ability to overpower her original resistance to and suspicion of him (because she first met him while he was fully under Jason's tutelage), is not only the black nationalist filmic reclamation *from the Jewish middleman* of black history/territory, it is also Hull's way of claiming his right to male ownership. That ownership represents Hull's bid for Jason's attention and respect in a new and sexual way. Now they have something in common: Hull's sexual intercourse with McCutheon is a totem exchange between the two males[15]—a homoerotic nuance almost completely covered over by the change in ownership of the female body, a totem exchange with even greater resonance given Jason's assertion earlier that he was crazy about "black black" women. McCutheon is not only a dark-skinned black woman, but she is cultural gatekeeper for African artifacts. Because she represents the commodification of African art, her reclamation is doubly important to a black nationalist project. And McCutheon doesn't just switch boyfriends and return to the black homeland via Hull, she also makes the first step along the film's path to her remaking into a "fit" mother.

So, we have dead bad families at the movie's beginning and at the end: a dead bad black father at the beginning, and a dead bad white father (Jason) at the end. In the beginning we get a look at a good but invisible black mother—of whose existence we only learn retrospectively when Hull looks at her photograph after killing a bad black drug dealer while mouthing the black nationalist apology for within-the-group killing. Family—dead or alive, dying or being resurrected—is everywhere in this film. Hull's pedigree is established at the beginning of the film by his own father—a junky, but one gamely (the film insists), however ineptly, trying to be a good father. The good black cop's family also comes into the family structure of the narrative when Taft talks about his children and shows their pictures to Hull during an interrogation. (Again, the mother is absent; she doesn't even rate a picture.) That cop articulates, along with Jerry Carver, the corrupt DEA agent, the tie between the drug trade and killing children/babies. Such articulations are the coming together of family narrative and black national-ist common sense: "Don't destroy your own people." This admonition gains resonance in the dramatic high point of the moment when the good cop dies in Hull's arms, dies, in fact, for Hull's "sins" against his people. The death of that *good* father brings Hull back into the black family as well as back into the law-and-order family: Taft, the good, black nationalist cop, dies saying "You and me are one. Don't forget who you are."

But the same film that represents the constitution of a black nationalist patriarchy also "shows" us a homosocial/homoerotic romantic triangle: Goldblum's character, Fishburne's character, and Williams' character.[16] Goldblum/Jason kills his rival for love/fathering—Williams/Taft; but the "right" love wins in the end. Fishburne/Hull reemerges as the "good" cop, the ideal cop; he kills Goldblum/Jason, the bad father/bad lover/drug dealer, and "arrests" the fruits of the drug trade—the $11 million—and the "bad" government. One could say that Williams/ Taft and his "love"—the "dead" part of the triangle—is resurrected in rather spectacularly changed circum-stances for Fishburne/Hull's character.

Despite the existence of that triangle, the patriarchy is never in danger. Once McCutheon is remade (beginning with her desire to get out of the drug trade), then the future John Q. Hull (a play on "John Q. Public"—only the substitution of "Hull" for "Public" indicates that this is only the frame of the vessel?) family takes shape. The contrast to Hull (who emerges by the end of the movie as a good father) is provided by Jason, who has a family and who *seems* to be a good father—he provides materially for his family and even helps his daughter with her homework—but is definitely not a good father. Jason, in fact, is a walking critique of the straight, white, bourgeois male: surburban provider extraordinaire. But he and the suburbs—shot in blinding sunlight—are corrupt underneath (despite his daughter's innocence). And his blonde wife knows his "real" occupation and urges him out of the business—but not because it's corrupt. Rather, she's concerned that the drug lord, Barbossa, doesn't appreciate her hus-band's abilities and, worse, hurts him. Jason is not only a drug dealer—and a real one (unlike Hull, who is faking it)—but his family isn't enough for him; he wants to have his cake and eat it too: the blond suburbs and the "black black" hookers, too. And, I might add, his black male buddy also.

Via the film's narrative logic, Hull's heterosexuality is established most explicitly (and its potency underscored) while the black nationalist germs of his family are brought together in his seduction of McCutheon—whom he steals away from the corrupt white patriarch/drug dealer. The two black lovers bond together, against Jason's increasing psychological anarchy. The proof of Hull's heterosexuality is enhanced by Felix Barbossa's recognition of Hull as a "real" man, unlike Jason, whom Felix goads with homophobic insults.

And Hull goes up the aesthetic ladder as he climbs the drug distribution and patriarchy ladder: he dresses better and buys a nice apartment. Jason is his style "father," although interestingly enough Hull, the "real" drug dealer in Barbossa's eyes, wears suits that are American cut, while Jason (the "outsider" Jew and insufficiently manly drug dealer—again, according to Barbossa, the Latino "real" drug dealer) wears suits that are European cut—emphasizing the Jewish lawyer as the European outsider in the American (albeit illegal drug) mise-en-scène. As Hull climbs the corporate ladder, he moves away from B-Boy style toward *EM* (*Ebony Male*) style. Ironically, while the middle-class style makes him look more like the lawyer Jason (notwithstanding the difference in cut of suits), it also makes him look more like the drug lord Jason, who both is and is not (depending on whether one believes one's eyes or Barbossa's rhetoric) a "real" drug dealer. The Fishburne/Hull fashion makeover is not only an instance of guidance on the part of Goldblum/Jason, it remakes Hull into a suitable aestheticized companion for Jason.

John Hull's patriarchal fitness, nonetheless, has to rest on something other than fashion style (however fine) and intentions (however noble). And the means by which he is able to consolidate his position as future patriarch arrives via a rather heavy piece of symbolism: a truck full of money—more than $11 million in smallish bills—that hangs in the air dangling from a large shipping crane, a fairly literal god from the machine. His patriarchal status is secured by the means of that money from above, visibly severed from its means of production. No longer "owned" by the U.S. drug trade or the Latino originators, it is transformed into Hull's "own" money. Not only is money an absolute (and fetishistically overdetermined) value in the film, but it is contingent and exchange value also—it is found money, reward money, for Hull's unveiling of the drug lord, destruction of his drug partnership with Jason, his killing of Jason, and, most dramatically, his "uncovering" of U.S. political complicity in the international drug trade. And like all good and wealthy patriarchs, his relationship to the source of his new power is ambiguous, as the rather heavy-footed voice-over makes clear.

Within a black nationalistic symbolic economy, Hull's individual triumph also narratively represents the triumph, as I noted earlier, of black nationalism over the symbolic management of black people by the Jew-as-ethnic-middleman. This ability to interrupt another's manipulation is of small significance within a system where masculinity is predicated on the ability to dominate, not be dominated, to manage, not be managed. Jason as the almost white controller of the female gatekeeper of Africanness is pushed aside as the black male becomes the discipliner of the other ethnic "interlopers" on U.S. terrain—the Latinos.

Despite the film's display of black nationalist sensibility, from the beginning Hull's identity as cop is both emptied of specific cultural meaning—being a good cop is a raceless absolute—and, at the same time, filled with race meanings—a good black cop can always be further mobilized by being reminded of his work, theoretically at least, on behalf of his people.

Deep Cover is, finally, a story that reproduces the depth logic of identity. Deep inside, he is a *true* cop; he has a *true* relationship to a racial group; he is a *true* father (as opposed to a bad or absent father and as opposed to an absent or bad mother); and he *truly* cares about black people. His black sentiments, contrasted to the facile declarations of the inept (and murdered dealer Eddie who glibly called out "stay black" in passing) are "real" and run deeply.

We are taught by the film to appreciate Hull's depth from the beginning. He signs on for "deep" heavy-duty undercover work, unlike, I suppose, the undercover "shallow" cops who go home every night. His depth is in contrast to Jason, who is not a "real" drug lord because he too goes home at night to the suburbs. Hull is so deep and true a cop that he remains one even when he thinks that he isn't: in a low moment of self-disgust and loathing for DEA hypocrisy he says, "I've been a cop pretending to be a drug dealer, but I'm really a drug dealer pretending to be a cop." Hull emerges as a real cop precisely because he undergoes the (romantic) dark night of the soul that such self-criticism frames: he is what he is.

To return to my earlier argument, some representations actually empty out race specifics—at the same time they inscribe racialized generalities—leaving narrative vessels that could be anything, could revolve around anyone. Still, I want to account for the pleasure of those of us who constitute the group against which this film in some meaningful way transgresses, however complicated and attenuated that pleasure might be. The political and historical conditions of racism add both exoticism and poignancy to the representation of a racialized other. Against the racist discourse of bad or absent "black" fathers, this film represents a "good" and present-on-the-scene father within the terms of a repro-narrative about which most black people are not inclined to be critical—especially given the salience of the family and the idea of generational succession and progression as a bulwark against a racist world.

In short, we cannot attribute any purity of political expression to popular culture although we can locate its power to identify ideas and desires that are relatively oppositional alongside those that are clearly complicit to the official culture.

Andrew Ross, *No Respect*

In black nationalist terms, Hull "wins" over Jason: a white male is dead. A bad, white patriarch is dissolved. But a black male doesn't just win, a black masculinist version of virile history wins and it does so because the triangle (which I described earlier) formed by Williams/Taft, Goldblum/ Jason, and Fishburne/Hull—the ambiguous black cop/drug dealer trembling on the brink of the historical void—is shattered. Taft, the Christian and black nationalist rival—literally—for Hull is shot by Jason (the finishing touch of the film's establishment of his super-villainy) because he wants to end both Hull's "flirtation" with his earlier cop history and black male bonding. But Taft (and black history) prove stronger than the attraction that Hull's character has admitted he feels for Jason's world: the money, the clothes, the interior design.

Ironically, Taft, embodying black brotherhood, black patriarchy, and selfless devotion to the (white) law wins back (just about from the grave) Hull, not only to black history but also to the master narrative, the "master's" narrative. Freed by that murder, Hull rejects Jason's corrupt whiteness, the seduction of his drug world, and the "not real" patriarchy for the "real" things: blackness, black solidarity, legality, and not so incidentally, the white judicial system. The film's logic that makes it necessary for Hull to kill Jason is also "killing" the homoerotic temptation he represented, leaving Hull fit for the new, black, grand family narrative.

A new black patriarchy is enframed not only by a black (American hero) killing the Jewish outsider, but also at the expense of the dead, finally femininely quiet Latina: Hull's voice-over tells us that until Belinda was dead Hull never knew how pretty she was. (Complete and final silence is more effective than any kind of cosmetic makeover could possibly be.) But she is dead and so are all the black mothers in this film, including a black mother with no existence outside of a wallet photograph. Fishburne/Hull is quite a family man but leaves a trail of corpses in his wake: dead, missing, or absent black and Latina mothers, other dead black fathers, a dead white father, a missing or absent Latino father. Quite a body count and those are only the dead *parents*.

We watch the creation of a black patriarch. And while we know that not all patriarchs are created politically or economically equal, this one plays a complicated game with the master hero narrative. By being true to "himself" and his identifications—remember the psychological profile of his character—he is a perfect drug dealer *and* a perfect cop. By not giving up his mission he makes the bust, gets the woman, the family, and $11 million dollars that "doesn't know where it came from." By being "true" to one, two, or three of his "real" selves he is able also to embarrass the U.S. government and expose a corrupt DEA. Of course. Patriarchy with a difference. But within-the-group manhood is tied nonetheless to fatherhood (and, in this film, respect for the law); it is the political imaginary for many members of the group, male and female, across the political spectrum. There is dissent, of course, or I wouldn't be writing this.

Caught up in the importance of the manhood = fatherhood equation, the movie *needs* certain killings and certain resurrections in order to generate the "proper"—and in this film ethnically mixed—black family. The very same drug trade destroys, or weeds out, some families (the "bad" or pathological ones) and creates the means for the sustenance of the other "good" ones. Isn't this the regulation patriarchal myth revised and replayed? Yet, the logic and overpoweringly attractive aesthetic of this movie to an audience constantly confronted with reiterations of their familial pathology is the cover story that fades everything to black.

However, the film provides one last marker of black American specificity. At the end of the movie—after laying his talisman, the blood-stained money from his junky father, on Belinda Chacon's grave—John Hull "straightens up" from his crouch over the grave. I watched him walk (on his way to claim "cleaner" money?) in a particular and instantly recognizable way across the graveyard, and saw what Towanda Williams saw, what other black Americans could see: a manifestation of the subcultural style that *is* one of the markers of black American specificity.

The walk across the graveyard: not quite a swagger, not quite the gait of a model on a fashion runway (male or female), but yes, it *was* quite like that. Each leg swinging loosely as it crossed over and in front of the other. Not quite lower limb "vogueing" but not quite not either. And again what are the words that kept coming to me while I tried to make sense of that movement? Runway, model, showcase, style. The ending is a display of patriarchal "drag" *and* subcultural style. The new, stylish black father. The tension between the newly aestheticized via subcultural style object of our visual delight and his newly won patriarchal status on display. Walking across the dead Latina's graveyard.

This film is about men making themselves men for other men as much as for themselves. By now, following the work of Hortense Spillers, the contributors to Toni Cade Bambara's *The Black Woman*, Alice Walker, Judith Butler, and, of course, Eve Sedgwick, we've learned how to recognize this dynamic as a trade that goes on over and through women's bodies, a site for gender performance and performativity.

The voice-over and the film frequently articulate the black nationalist sentiments of group unity and black family sanctity. And herein the knot of pleasure and dismay. The film creates and almost parodies the cathected nexus of patriarchy and homoerotic sublimation—a parody that I found pleasurable. But recognizing the black nationalist aesthetic, I looked for the black women who, according to that discourse, are required to nurture and teach their children. However, there were no mothers on that screen. Horrifically confining as that black nationalist narrative is, by the end of this movie I would have been relieved to at least *see* them alive.

But why? What would "seeing" them there, having them represented, mean? Where would it mean and to whom? These questions are irritants that push me back to my beginning; the positive/negative image representation discourse is as cathected as it is precisely because films and audience remaking of and remarking on films is part of world making. At some point this film stopped being a black nationalist family narrative—with all of the possibilities and limitations of that narrative—and became something else. It became more simply a film of masculine display against a larger white master narrative. And it became a film that produced a father completely self-sufficient because he could nurture better than any woman.

"Yet and still," the last thing I saw was Fishburne walking that walk. Again: the ending is a display of patriarchal "drag" and subcultural style. I "see" the two together. Towanda Williams did also; although she didn't say so, her syntax—including the conjunction—gave her away: " . . . he *is* a good father and I do like the way he walks across the graveyard." In other words, we "saw" some things together, after a fashion, things like his "fashion." What the difference is or means is the work that remains.

Recognition of some aspect of its treatment of black specificity is no reason to "forgive" this film all of its trespasses. On the other hand, it reminded me of a concern of those of us—critics and cultural producers alike—who want to help bring about politically interventionary projects: what we need to map is a way not to de-aestheticize our cultural specificity, but to aestheticize a different political agenda for cultural production.

NOTES

1. This essay is the revised version of a presentation made at the English Institute, Harvard University, August 1992, and part of a longer work-in-progress that uses the film under discussion here—*Deep Cover*—to explore the phallocentric depth logic of certain deployments of black nationalism, including the positive-versus-negative image discourse around black film. The original program listing at the English Institute was "Criticism and Black Film." Special thanks are due to Raphael Allen, and to the members of the Wesleyan Center for Humanities seminar, where I presented a draft of this essay—especially to Ellen Rooney, Ann duCille, Indira Karamcheti, Elizabeth Weed, Joel Pfister, Dick Ohmann, and Karen Bock—for their comments and suggestions.

2. This essay takes for granted what have come to be commonplaces of a number of overlapping discourses: nineteenth- and twentieth-century black feminism, twentieth-century black aesthetic theory, poststructuralism, Marxism, critical race studies, and queer theory; however, space does not permit even a brutally reduced genealogy of the intersections and interstices of those various discourses.

3. "Fear of a Queer Planet," *Social Text* 29 (vol. 9, no. 4): 3–17.

4. Despite what Towanda Williams and I agree about, I am not suggesting that she and I are "sisters" in some racially transcendent way—that would be romanticism by yet another means—or that our areas of agreement are transparent. Yet, I'm willing to engage in amateur (and partial) ethnographic research in order to think out loud about the possible significance and usefulness for "reading" the film of the congruence of our responses. And my interest in black cultural studies and Jacqueline Bobo's work on the necessity of addressing black spectator response convinces me that negotiating the differences and similarities *within* racialized, gendered, classed, and sexualized groups is important albeit incredibly difficult work for politically and theoretically engaged intellectuals. That the questions raised in doing such work won't be answered "once and for all" is all the more reason to do it. If by theory we mean "trying to account for" instead of producing a finished account or trajectory, then the slipperiness of something like "identity" or "black nationalism"—for example—is fecund ground for reconsidering our assumptions about representation, spectatorship, and reception.

5. While I am not persuaded by the particularities of Clyde Taylor's argument about positive and negative image discourse in the recent (volume 7, number 2) issue of *Black Film Review*, I agree with his sense that the debate itself is both central to and problematic within black film criticism.

6. *No Respect* (New York: Routledge, 1989): 14.

7. "Black Spectatorship," *Screen* 29.4 (Autumn 1988): 66.

8. I'm using the word "black" instead of "African-American" because I want to keep before us an ongoing tension of race relations in the United States between people of African descent and all others here on this ground regardless of those others' cultural, natal, or political positions. While people of various races and ethnicities have been constituted in various ways by the formidable plasticity and fecundity of racism in the United States and elsewhere, for much of the history that the production of Afro- or African-American Studies maps, racism has found its most virulent expres sion in the division of the U.S. public into black and white.

9. Articulated most succinctly in Robert Park's assertion that "the Negro is the lady of the races" (*Race and Culture: Essays in the Sociology of Contemporary Man* [Glencoe, Ill.: Free Press, 1950]: 280). Indira Karamcheti has reminded me that in so doing Park was himself following Leo Frobenius's lead (private conversation, Wesleyan Center for the Humanities, December 4, 1992).

10. This film's screenplay was written by two white Americans. Given, however, the ubiquity of black nationalist cultural common sense, such authorship does not preclude either the representation of that common sense, or representation of its hysteria. And while I don't want to elide the complications inherent in the writers' relation to their material by falling back on theories of auteurship that would center the black director as the source of the film's cultural logic, it would be foolish to "write off" his input into the film.

11. Re my willingness to refer to a "black audience": In order to refer to any group constituted as a social fact, one risks reducing and simplifying the complexities of that group. On the other hand, what could any of us say if we were denied the rhetorical indulgence of referring to social collectivities? Much cultural production theory and commentary is predicated on speculation about possible audiences. It is on that ground and with the assistance of my chat with Towanda Williams, then, that I am willing to speculate about or attempt to account for such a group's response to this film. And by that means join the hordes who try to resist the heady pleasure of spinning a self-originating only close reading.

12. *The Village Voice (Film Special)*, June 1991; interview with Donald Bogle.

13. As I asserted earlier: I do recognize the obvious difference(s) between us. And could write an essay about those differences as well as the correspondences between our respective "readings" of the film—and the possible epistemological statuses of the respective positions. (Sigh: all things in time.)

14. By one-third of the way through the movie we see the familial structures established that will be dissolved and reformed: family one, small Latino boy and mother; family two, John Hull (later orphaned) and his father; and family three, drug lord prince level—nephew, and drug lord king level—uncle. Any repro-narrativity possibilities of a Latino/Latina family combination are disrupted by John Hull's takeover of the Latino boy after his mother dies. Given the contingent nature of ethnic relations and identity politics in the current U.S. political mise-en-scène, this colonizing of the Latino/Latina family combination by a black American is complicated to say the very least.

15. I am indebted here to Eve Sedgwick's arguments, particularly those articulated in *Between Men: English Literature and Male Homosocial Desire* (New York: Columbia University Press, 1985).

16. I sometimes interchange the characters' names with the actors' names because I want to underscore the point that Lisa Jones (quoted earlier) makes: that black audiences refuse to accept that the "real" actors "disappear" into their roles. Whether or not dominant-race audiences make the same refusal under all or some circumstances is not my concern here. My concern—within the terms of the positive/negative debate around black film—is to foreground the ways in which a black audience fights off or can fight off racist and caricatured representations of "blackness," as well as the points at which the caricature (racist or not) can become overwhelmingly attractive.

8.

Cultural Studies/Black Studies

MANTHIA DIAWARA

One of the appealing aspects of cultural studies is its critical, or even polemical, attitude toward every form of theoretical orthodoxy. The term *elabore,* used by Gramsci to stretch and test the limits of Marxism, captures better the sense of critical attitude I have in mind here. Elaboration has become for cultural studies a means to be critical of poststructuralism while working within the discipline. Cultural studies, in its attempts to draw attention to the material implications of the worldviews we assume, often delineates a literal and candid picture of ways of life that embarrass and baffle our previous theoretical understanding of those forms of life. This elaboration, candid and ethnographic in its approach to ways of life, has helped cultural studies to ground some of its key concepts in material conditions: for example, levels of abstraction, uneven development, articulation, positionality, and cultural specificity. On the other hand, the manner in which cultural studies posits identity politics as moments of difference and rupture in the discourses of Marxism or psychoanalysis has led its detractors to dismiss the "literal reading of events" as examples of nothing more than journalism among its practitioners.

I am specifically interested here in the concept of elaboration in cultural studies because I want to follow its development from the Birmingham school to the London-based black filmmakers to departments of black studies and feminist studies in the United States. If we look at some model texts which helped to ground this critical theme as a constitutive element of cultural studies, Gramsci's southern Italy comes to mind as a thorn in the foot of orthodox Marxism. Here, the elaboration of positionality, uneven development, and the articulation of Marxism with specifically southern Italian ways of life stand as a major embarrassment to global theorizations.

It might be useful to describe how the tools developed in the elaboration of the southern question were rethematized in the British context by Raymond Williams and Stuart Hall. But that is not my focus here. I am interested in elaboration as an enabling tool for the constitution of black British cultural studies in London, and later in black studies and feminist studies in the United States. Even though the figure of Hall is central to the development of this critical school, I am distinguishing what I call the black British cultural studies in London from the Birmingham school of cultural studies. For example, while in the 1960s and 1970s the Birmingham school was mainly interested in the British working class, and an attempt to constitute a unique and an alternative British Marxist theory around that subject, in the 1980s black filmmakers, artists, photographers, and writers in London were decomposing and reconstructing the terms of Britishness. They were using race as the modality through which to read class. While the Birmingham school was concerned with the elaboration of a British Marxism which could challenge Althusser and Lévi-Strauss in France and the Frankfurt School, the black British cultural studies took as its main subject the elaboration of black Britishness over and against ethnic absolutism in Britain, the hegemonic construction of blackness by black Americans, and other manifestations of diasporan aesthetics.

I realize that this distinction is difficult to maintain in light of the fact that figures such as Hall, Paul Gilroy, and Dick Hebdige played and continue to play key roles in our understanding of both schools. But it is a useful distinction if we want to understand why in the United States today we have two types of cultural studies made in Britain. One posits race at the center and uses metaphors of racial constructions to bring to light the ways of life of oppressed groups. It is concerned with issues of black appropriation of modernity, black performance as construction of identity, crossover texts, ambivalence, and the critique of sexism and homophobia in black communities. Thus, it is both "victim studies" and "performance studies" at the same time. In Britain, the works of Paul Gilroy, Kobena Mercer, Sonia Boyce, David Bailey, Sankofa, Ceddo, and Black Audio film/video collectives center around these issues. In the United States, bell hooks, Michele Wallace, Marlon Riggs, Wahneema Lubiano, Tommy Lott, Henry Louis Gates, Jr., Houston Baker, Jr., Cornel West, Jane Gaines, Cora Kaplan, Hazel Carby, and Herman Gray, to name only a few, have entered into dialogue with this strand of black British cultural studies. The December 1991 conference on black popular culture organized by the Dia Foundation in New York brought together most of these critics and reasserted the centrality of the discourse of blackness to cultural studies.

The other cultural studies in the United States links itself directly to the Birmingham school of cultural studies, and continues the description of people's ways of life in the areas of rock music production, postmodern films, the so-called new ethnicities, and anti-essentialism. Games, the notion of reflexivity, and a penchant for what Gianni Vattimo calls "weak thought" are at the center of this school. The practitioners describe the forms of life of new ethnicities, or ethnicities in the process of becoming, or ethnicities projected in the future by computers. They also describe for us cultures produced by the development of the medical profession, the leisure industries, and the internationalization of the electronic media. In their abstractions they have more in common with the Frankfurt School, Walter Benjamin, and a certain poststructuralism a la Foucault than they do with the recent development in feminism and Black Studies, and the black strand of cultural studies. The cultural studies conference organized in Champaign–Urbana represented not only the best and highest levels of abstraction in the discourse of this brand of cultural studies, but also a decision to evacuate race and gender as important issues.

It is obvious that the two forms of cultural studies are not as oppositional as I seem to imply here. The same cultural workers cross the boundaries of each field. The purpose of my binary opposition is to use the one to criticize the other, to elaborate the one in order to show the limitations of the other. Black cultural studies, for example, has been criticized for essentializing blackness, for fixing black ways of life even as it debunks the ethnic absolutism it associates with Englishness and black nationalism. In particular, Kobena Mercer's critique of Paul Gilroy as a strong thinker and populist nationalist is now famous in cultural studies. Black cultural studies as a paradigm for "victim studies" may also lead to the production of equally essentialized feminist, gay, and Chicano "victim discourses." Along with the anti-essentialist critique of black cultural studies we can also see its emphasis on identity politics as a limitation of revolutionary struggles.

Similarly, the import of the Birmingham school of cultural studies to the United States must take into account an elaboration which will enable it to ground itself in United States material conditions. In other words, how can the tools of the Birmingham school, no matter how sophisticated they are, and no matter who the enunciator is, speak to the material conditions of this country? The ways of family, nation, and spectatorship in the United States are not the same as those in Britain. As with the import of poststructuralism in the United States, this form of cultural studies disengages theory from its spaces of application. In its attempt to replace deconstruction as the new academic discipline, cultural studies, too, has made anti-essentialism its strongest critical tool, and turned its back on the cultures of resistance linked to Marxists, feminists, and Black Studies. The anti-essentialism of cultural studies may now be described as the essentialism of the second kind, that is, the reification of discourse.

Clearly, if cultural studies can learn anything from Gramsci, it must include his notions of uneven development and different levels of abstraction. For the practitioners of the Birmingham school and for the black British cultural studies group, this involves the ground already covered by black studies and feminist studies in the United States. For example, the studies of postmodern films and theories of global systems might do well by looking at such area studies as African studies, Asian studies, and Latin-American studies before declaring that we are beyond history, development, and recovery. The perspective of British specialists of cultural studies on such issues as essentialism and binarism may also be nuanced in the United States by case studies by American feminists and African-American scholars on racism, oppression, and exclusion. One of the complaints against the cultural studies conference at Champaign–Urbana was that it excluded Third-World and ethnic studies scholars. These people felt that they were being silenced while other people were brought in from Britain and Australia to speak for them. The most celebrated protest was launched by bell hooks, who traveled to the conference, disrupted one of the panels, and forced the participants to hear her voice. Trinh T. Minh-ha too registered her dissatisfaction by turning down an invitation to show one of her films.

Having raised these questions about cultural studies, I will now return to the term *elabore* to consider how its application to the black cultural studies might help to ground American cultural studies in material conditions. First, it is important to understand that the London-based black cultural workers found a language specific to their condition of black Britishness by submitting to a critical reading not only the texts of the white left, which often ignored race, but also the texts from the black diaspora. Some of the fascinating moments in Paul Gilroy's *There Ain't No Black in the Union Jack* (University of Chicago Press, 1991) include a critique of George Orwell and Raymond Williams for their English ethnocentrism. To carve a space for blackness in Britain, Gilroy had to denounce Williams and Orwell in the same way that he denounced the British right-wingers such as Enoch Powell for their celebration of a homogeneous and nostalgic way of life of the English working class. Isaac Julien found a film language specific to him through recourse to a critical reading of the white avant-garde cinema: Julien states, "On the left of avant-gardism is pleasure, which the avant-garde self denies, clinging to the purism of its constructed ethics, measuring itself against a refusal to indulge in narrative or emotions and indeed, in some cases, refusing representation itself, because all these systems of signs are fixed, entrenched in the 'sin or evil' of representation. The high moral tone of this discourse is based on a kind of masochistic self-censorship which relies on the indulgence of a colonial history and a post-colonial history of cinema of white representations based on our black absence. The problematic that surfaces when black film makers experiment with the idea of black film text and the subjective camera, is that subjectivity implies contradiction. But this is not, in itself, fixed" (From "Aesthetics and Politics" in *Undercut*, No. 17, Spring 1988, 31–39).

The texts from the diaspora are also submitted to critical readings. The biggest diaspora influence was linked to the works of black Americans such as June Jordan (whose *Civil Wars* helped the young black British to theorize policing in their own context) Manning Marable, Cedric Robinson, James Baldwin, and the black women writers; the Caribbeans included C. L. R. James, George Lamming, Wilson Harris, Fanon, Cesaire, Braithwaite, and Walcott; the African influences included Ngugi Wa Thiongo and Sembene Ousmane. But these diasporic texts had to be articulated with black Britishness in such a way that they take on new forms which are attentive to the fluidity of identities, class, and sexual politics.

The black British took the black American culture of the 1960s and 1970s and elaborated it into something specifically British and energetic. Now it is the turn of black Americans to take the British cultural studies and turn it into a cultural work that is capable of addressing challenging issues such as the plight of inner-city youth, and what Cornel West calls the institutions of caring in the black community. We cannot wait for Isaac Julien, Sonia Boyce, Stuart Hall, and Paul Gilroy to tell us how to do it. On the contrary, we must read them in such a way that they do not recognize themselves. We have to look for elaborations of Hall's and Gilroy's works in the American context, not blank approvals of their works. Cultural studies in our hands should give new meanings to terms such as hybridity, essentialism, identity politics, the black community, and ambivalence.

BLACK CULTURAL STUDIES MADE IN THE USA

If the Dia conference is any indication, black cultural studies made in the USA will help Black Studies to make a move from "victim studies" to performance. Greg Tate and A. J. Filter led the way by couching their styles in the jazz tradition of Lester Young, and the rock and roll of Jimi Hendrix. For the young performers like Trish Rose, Lisa Kennedy, Jacquie Jones, and Greg Tate, the emphasis is less on what legal scholar Regina Austin calls crossover dreams and the narratives of the dream deferred, than it is on the communicability of a black public sphere that is envied by both blacks and whites. They are heirs of the civil rights movement and the black nationalist movements of the 1960s. They are different from the civil rights intellectuals and activists in that they are less concerned with integration and "oppression studies," which dominated black studies, women studies, and Chicano studies in the 1970s. They are also different from the 1960s style black nationalism which was as sexist, racist, and homophobic as the white supremacism it was set to fight.

Their most important discovery is, on the one hand, that the civil rights movement occasioned an unprecedented mass literacy and a cultural consciousness among blacks, who were before limited to the church and the music media as their only arenas for cultural and political debate. For this literate mass of African-Americans, who are starved for books, films, the visual arts, and music, integration and belonging are no longer the principal issues. Seeing one's life reflected at the *center* of the books, the films, the visual arts, and the music takes precedence. On the other hand, it is here that black nationalism enters with its theme of what Cornel West calls the politics of caring about black people. The old exclusionary themes of black nationalism are reversed in the works of writers such as Terry McMillan and filmmakers like Reginald Hudlin, Spike Lee, Julie Dash, and Charles Burnett into themes of the good life society for black people. As black nationalism becomes materially and culturally grounded as another version of the American dream, to be envied by Americans of different origins and races, what is good for black Americans becomes good for *capital*, that is, America. The integrationist thrust of the civil rights movement, by shying away from advocating the theme of a black bourgeoisie side by side with other ethnic bourgeoisies in America, underestimated the economic and cultural realities of social integration. Today, black artists, from rap musicians to filmmakers and new writers, are deriving fame and success from exploiting the themes of a black public sphere, or, as Public Enemy puts it, a "Black Planet." The consumers of the art about the black good life society are black, white, and international. Contrary to the fear of civil rights activists that nationalism will lead to ghettoization, white youth and the international audience are more and more fascinated by black art that calls itself authentic. They use it for exotic reasons as well as a means of liberation from their own ethnic cultures that position themselves as universal. In fact most white youth have crossed over to black culture through hip-hop, leaving some to join the afficionados of the Grateful Dead, and causing the revival of country music among those who resist hip-hop music. Two recent white films, *Wayne's World* and *Stay Tuned*, emanate from the same resistance to hip-hop through recourse to a cultural nostalgia for the white youth 1960s and 1970s as narrated by TV sitcoms and commercials. Rap has moved from the underground to the center, making it the object of parody by Deadheads and country musicians.

As the work of younger scholars shows, black cultural studies can make an important intervention in the analysis of the new arts produced about the black good life society. Even though cultural studies made in Britain, with its emphasis on hybridity, crossover, and the critique of homophobia, yields some tools with which to check the regressive consequences of any nationalism, it is not sufficient to analyze the art of the black good life society and the consumers of that product. British cultural workers have a love and hate relationship with black American culture which enables the former simultaneously to use the latter as raw material for its own artistic and critical endeavors, and to criticize it for not being reflexive enough. With the exception of the work of Paul Gilroy, many black British cultural workers assume a high moral ground with which they dismiss black American culture as regressive, obsessed with the discourse of race and slavery, and nationalistic in the worse sense. They cannot therefore identify with the notion of a black good-life society, let alone with the consumers of a Spike Lee film.

I submit that a measure of identification with the black public sphere, its cultural consumers and reproducers, is necessary for the production of engaging texts on the black good life society and its art. In other words, the cultural worker too is not totally immune to regression. First one must understand the forms of life of blacks and whites in America in order to appreciate the reversible techniques that black artists impose on well-established white meanings, and vice versa. The unique form of black life in America has endowed black Americans with a reflexive attitude toward modernity that is both innovative and anti-modern. Black Americans live in the most modern country; yet, until recently, they have been excluded from the center of the inventions, the discourses, and the emancipatory effects of modernity. While the paradigm of "oppression studies" has said much about this situation, and much still needs to be said, it need not overshadow black people's dramaturgical actions at the margins which helped to refine the tools of modernity and advance its democratic ideals. By being situated at the margins, black people were able to observe the advancement of the most efficient modernity in the world from upside down. W. E. B. Du Bois, the grand theorist of modern social thought, feared a link between modernity and fascism in the way racism was reproduced in the modernization of Atlanta. The performative acts of black leaders such as Ida B. Wells, Frederick Douglass, and Martin Luther King, Jr. served as the background to rewrite democratic laws which had been written to protect the rights of whites only. In music, black people redirected classical instruments, horns, and drums from army bands to create jazz, the music of modernity. While such reversibilities appear literal and anti-modern from the outside, they take on rich textures for insiders. Clearly, blacks have constantly rede-fined the meanings imposed on the tools and products of modern life by Eurocentrism, which often moves modernity in a linear and destructive manner.

Today, even a partial identification with the consumers of the black art produced by rappers, writers like McMillan, and filmmakers like Julie Dash will lead the cultural critic to appreciate the reversibility technique as an authentic art form. An important fact of uneven development is that while Americans as a whole are said to be reading fewer and fewer books, blacks are starved for books, films, and artworks about the black experience. The emergence of cultural identity among blacks—with such Afrokitsch symbols as kinte cloth ornaments, Nubian signs, rap music with "authentic" Jamaican patois, the exhortations to "buy black and stay black," the T-shirts with "It's a Black Thing, You Wouldn't Understand," and the celebrations of black heroes—does not have an equivalent in white youth culture.

To return to the two paradigms of Black Studies, oppression and performance, it is clear that, as a consequence of the civil rights movement, which forced many doors open, oppression narratives are no longer felt by all the blacks in the same way. Nowadays, first-person narratives about discrimination and oppression are more and more aimed at subgroups of the black public sphere organized along class, sexuality, and gender lines. The uprising generated by the Rodney King incident, and the Willie Horton case, which united black people across class, gender, and sexual orientation lines, are exceptions among self-reflexive narratives which emphasize the specificity of being woman and black, young endangered male and black, gay and black, middle-class and black. The Mike Tyson trial and the Clarence Thomas and Anita Hill dispute illustrate the modes of existence of these fragmented narratives of oppression.

Performance, on the other hand, records the way in which black people, through a communicative action, engender themselves within the American experience. Black agency here involves the redefinition of the tools of Americanness. To put it in other words, performance presumes an existing tradition and an individual or group of people who interpret that tradition in front of an audience in such a way that the individual or group of people invent themselves for that audience. At the Dia conference, for example, Greg Tate used his intimate knowledge of jazz, funk, and science fiction to propose to his audience a new realism of black life in the city. The essential elements of performance involve the audience and tradition. In other words, a performance must be based on a tradition that the audience can verify, and rate the performer against. It is interesting that black musicians and sometimes preachers are the preeminent models for performance in black studies. In literature, film, and the other arts, the artists either simply play the records of great musicians, and preach to the audience, or use their own artistic medium to rethematize great moments of performance by a Coltrane or a Bird in order to redefine the historical condition of black life, and the mode of existence of the art form used. Thus we can speak of a jazz novel, a jazz painting, a hip-hop film, or a preacherly essay. It is through performance that we move away from stereotypes and fixed images of black people, toward great men and women, ordinary people, bad guys and good guys. It is also through performance that black people provide the most important critique of modernity, which continues to reify black lives. Performance is a political representation that enables the actor to occupy a different position in American society, and to interpellate the audience's approval of the new and emerging images of black people.

Let's now return to the notion of a black good-life society and imagine how black cultural studies made in the United States might use performance as a mode of interpellating the people in the black public sphere. I suggested earlier that the civil rights movement has created a mass literacy among black people, but its politics of integration has left this mass starved for black-centered books, films, paintings, music, and so on. There is also a legacy of identity, survival, and self-determination aesthetics created by black nationalism during the dreadful years of oppression and discrimination. Clearly, any attempt to dupe the new black public sphere by repressing or putting under the shadow these nationalistic black structures of feelings is doomed to a rigorous critical scrutiny and suspicion by the members of the good-life society. In fact the limited success of poststructuralism and postmodernism among blacks is due in part to the suspicion that they decenter and undermine the black subject for political reasons. It is equally remarkable that the people in the black good-life society are no longer as attentive as before to the very leaders of the civil rights movement and the nationalist groups who gave them literacy, cultural awareness, dreams of economic stability, and a multiplicity of desires. There are discontinuities between the new members of the black good-life society and their predecessors in the civil rights movement and black nationalism which need to be addressed urgently for the black public sphere to reproduce itself.

The black good-life society which is now an audience in search of books, films, and philosophies about itself will, obviously, not be satisfied with texts produced about it which interpellate primarily white audiences. To reproduce itself, the new black public sphere does not only need an economic base which provides jobs for the young people, but also definitions of the culture it is producing daily. These definitions, as we see them in rap music, the literature by McMillan, and the films of Spike Lee, may seem regressive to an audience in another level of abstraction, but this does not justify contempt for them. Every identification with a work of art, no matter how reflexive it calls itself, is a regressive slip.

It seems that performance, with its emphasis on audiences, catches better the spirit of the new black public sphere. As a tool of black cultural studies, it positions the people of the black good-life society as its "ideal readers" as it narrates the break with the first tenets of the civil rights movement and black nationalism, and moves on to higher levels of abstraction along the lines of sexual politics, class, and labor relations. Some of the major difficulties the school of Afrocentrism encounters emanate from its neglect of these levels of abstraction. However, Afrocentricity shall remain king of the hill for the black good-life society until that time when black artists, economists, philosophers, and politicians intend their texts primarily for black audiences.

Contributors

Anita Goldman is Assistant Professor of American Literature at the University of Illinois at Chicago.

Mae G. Henderson is Associate Professor of English and African-American Studies at the University of Illinois at Chicago. Her collection, *Speaking In Tongues And Other Essays*, is forthcoming.

Kathryn Hellerstein is a Lecturer of Yiddish at the University of Pennsylvania.

Mantia Diawara is Director of Africana Studies and Professor of Comparative Literature at New York University. His latest book, *Black American Cinema*, is published by Routledge.

Wahneema Lubiano is Assistant Professor of English at Princeton University.

Scott L. Malcolmson is a Senior Editor at the *Village Voice Literary Supplement*. He is the author of *Borderlands: Nation and Empire* (1994).

Jane Marcus is Distinguished Professor of English at the City University of New York and the C.U.N.Y. Graduate Center.

Nancy Miller is Professor of English at the Graduate School and University Center, City University of New York. Her most recent book, *French Dressing*, is published by Routledge.

Sara Suleri is Professor of English at Yale University.